A SHADOW OF MAGNITUDE
The Acquisition of the Elgin Marbles

A SHADOW

THE ACQUISITION

FOUNDED 1838

GPPS

OF MAGNITUDE

OF THE ELGIN MARBLES

by Theodore Vrettos

G. P. Putnam's Sons, New York

To
the memory of my mother and father,
Zacharoúla and Leonídas

Acknowledgments

I OWE MUCH THANKS to Mr. D. E. L. Haynes, Keeper of Greek and Roman Antiquities at the British Museum, for his generous assistance and to the Trustees of the British Museum for permission to reproduce their photographs. I am equally indebted to the Trustees and the Librarians of the National Library in Scotland for their patient help in tracking down elusive papers and manuscripts concerning the family records of Lord and Lady Elgin, particularly the several hundred pages of court records on the trial against Robert Fergusson.

I am grateful to Mr. A. Anderson, Deputy Keeper of the Scottish Records Office in Edinburgh; also to Mr. G. R. Barbour, Assistant to the Curator of Historical Records, and to Miss D. M. Hunter of that same office.

I wish to thank John Murray (Publishers), Ltd., London, for permission to quote from *The Letters of Mary Nisbet, Countess of Elgin,* and Oxford University Press for permission to quote from *Lord Elgin and the Marbles* by William St. Clair.

The Gennadios Library in Athens, the Library of Lambeth Palace in London, and Widener Library of Harvard University offered much aid. Mr. James Damaskos and Mr. Stratis Haviaras were specially cooperative, as were Dr. David Mitten of the Fine Arts Department at Harvard's Fogg Museum, and the staff of the Classical Arts Department at the Museum of Fine Arts in Boston. Additional

7

advice was provided by the staffs at Victoria and Albert Museum in London, the Greater London Council, the national museums at Athens and Olympia, and by Mr. P. Chrissicopoulos and Miss Niki Alissandrakis of the Royal Greek Embassy.

I am deeply grateful to Herbert Selenkow, M.D., of Harvard University for medical advice on plagues and diseases of the East, to Mr. Stanley M. Epstein, Esq., for a clearer look into the laws of nineteenth-century England, to Marcia Magill of Putnam's for her editorial counsel, to Mary McClean of Putnam's for her many helpful suggestions, to my wife, Vas, for her invaluable assistance throughout.

THEODORE VRETTOS

Contents

Illustrations follow page 128

Under the penalty of death, no interruption shall be given His Excellency, Lord Elgin, nor to his painters who are engaged in fixing scaffolds around the ancient Temple of the Idols. And in modelling the said ornaments, or in measuring the ruins of fallen temples, no obstacle shall be thrown in their way by the Voivode, the Cadi, or any other officer of the Turkish army. No one shall meddle with the scaffolding or implements, and if the said painters wish to take away any pieces of stone with inscriptions or sculptures therein, no opposition shall be made.

In the above-mentioned manner, see that ye demean and comport yourselves.

Signed with a signet,
—SEGED ABDULLAH KAIMMACAM

"Had not these lovely things been preserved in England, they would have been destroyed during the Greek War of Independence!"

Now that is the very argument which has been used, and repeatedly used, whenever the British have had qualms of conscience about the Elgin Marbles. It is a rotten argument. In the first place, those statues and sculptures which escaped Lord Elgin's depredations survived undamaged the battles of the Greek War of Independence. In the second place, if they were restored now to Greece they would certainly be as safe as in the British Museum. And in the third place, it is not for a receiver of stolen goods to claim that the goods are safer in his care than if restored to their original owners.

—SIR HAROLD NICOLSON

Prologue

ON A COLD December morning in 1816 the British historical painter Benjamin Robert Haydon wrote in his diary: "This year the Elgin Marbles were bought and produced an Aera in public feeling."

The bitter controversy over the acquisition of the Elgin Marbles continues unabated for more than a century and a half. Among the millions of travelers who yearly visit the British Museum in London and the Acropolis at Athens,. increasing numbers join hands with Lord Byron in denouncing "Lord Elgin's robberies." In 1961 England's Prime Minister Harold Macmillan addressed the House of Commons and urged it "to consider returning the Elgin Marbles to Greece," but he was soundly criticized the following day in the *Times*: "Mr. Macmillan is advised to dismiss the idea from his mind, and the sooner the better. The Elgin Marbles are *bought and paid for,* and are the legitimate property of the British Government!"

Lord Elgin is not without his many supporters who insist that "Elgin's aims from the beginning were entirely honourable," and that he had obtained proper legal authority for his actions. But Lord Elgin's foes refuse to accept that he had legal sanction to despoil the Parthenon. His so-called authority did not come from the Greeks, the rightful owners, but from the Turks, who had no regard for works of antiquity.

And so the battle rages on.

13

Chapter One

Sicily

THE SICILIAN SKY was on fire when HMS *Phaeton* dropped anchor off Palermo at noon. Inside the stifling bowels of the frigate's only stateroom the young bride trickled more vinegar into her silk handkerchief and dabbed it weakly over her face and wrists. A glass of Portuguese brandy lay untouched on the small oak table beside the bunk where her husband had placed it before leaving the cabin earlier that morning. She had been stricken by the sea from the moment she stepped on board the *Phaeton* at Portsmouth. "A fortnight in Lisbon offered no relief"; nor the vinegar now. Its obnoxious odor augmented her misery, and in desperation she fled once again to Archerfield; forced her tortured brain to conjure a picture of peaceful Scottish woods protecting her father's house from the western winds as fields of autumn grass frolicked along the golden sands of Aberlady Bay. She still found it hard to believe that she was the wife of Thomas Bruce, Seventh Earl of Elgin and Eleventh of Kincardine.

Lord Elgin was born on 20 July 1766 of noble and ancient ancestry. The Bruce name of Broomhall and Culross in the Kingdom of Fife was traced directly from Robert de Brus, a Knight of Normandy who accompanied William the Conqueror into England. From this same lineage was born the famous Robert the Bruce, King of Scotland (1306-1329), whose heart is buried in Melrose Abbey, and whose sword still hangs at Broomhall. Lord Elgin's mother was in particular favor at Court as the Countess of Elgin. She was governess at one time to the young Princess Charlotte of Wales, the only daughter of George IV.

Elgin inherited the earldom in his boyhood. After an education at Harrow, Westminster, St. Andrews, and Paris, he was commissioned an ensign in the Foot Guards, passed swiftly through the lower ranks, and eventually took command of his own regiment, the Elgin Highland Fencibles. He was elected to the House of Lords in 1790 and the next year, at the age of twenty-five, was given his first diplomatic assignment by Britain's Prime Minister William Pitt. It came at short notice, and within twenty-four hours Elgin had set off for Vienna as Envoy Extraordinary to the newly-crowned Emperor Leopold II.

For almost one year Lord Elgin accompanied Leopold on long trips to the Austrian territories in Italy and tried to persuade him to bring Austria into alliance with England. His long months of hard work and dedication proved unsuccessful, but within that year Elgin had established a diplomatic reputation. He was quickly rewarded by Lord Grenville, the Foreign Secretary, with a second appointment: Envoy at Brussels, remaining at this post for two years, mostly as a liaison officer between the Belgian and Austrian armies.

Lord Grenville's next assignment to Elgin was the Court of Prussia at Berlin. As British plenipotentiary Elgin became involved for the first time in his life with the many intrigues of diplomacy and was unhappy to learn that intelligence work was to be an important function of his embassy. As a gentleman nurtured in the old school he was solidly entrenched in outdated principles and old-fashioned conceptions of honor and tradition. But Elgin was far from naïve. Although he remained in Berlin until his thirty-second year and still had not married, he was by no means unacceptable to women. A steady visitor to the Embassy House at Berlin was a certain "fair favourite, Madame Ferchenbeck." However nothing came of the relationship, and Elgin returned to

England in 1798, stopping first at the office of the Foreign Secretary and then continuing to Brighton for a well-earned holiday.

A short time later, while dancing with the Princess Augusta at a ball given by the fleet at Weymouth, Elgin was drawn aside by King George III who suggested that Elgin should apply at once for the post of Ambassador to Turkey. It was further intimated to Elgin that he find himself a wife. His prolonged bachelorhood was considered a distinct disadvantage for an ambassador, especially in the Levant.

Although there were countless young ladies on both sides of the Firth, attractive and of sound family fortune, Lord Elgin chose Mary Nisbet who lived in Dirleton, a small town less than ten miles east of Edinburgh. William Nisbet's estates brought in eighteen thousand pounds annually, and Elgin was well aware of this when he made his heralded appearance at Archerfield, the Nisbet home, on the raw morning of 11 March 1799 and took Mary's hand in marriage. It was not an easy victory for Lord Elgin. William Nisbet did not favor the discrepancy in age; his daughter was only nineteen and Elgin thirty-three. Aside from this, some of Edinburgh's wealthiest young men had already expressed the desire to marry his only child. The Nisbets knew that Lord Elgin had incurred heavy debts restoring Broomhall, his palatial residence on the Fife side of the Firth; and Elgin had never been a rich man. But William Nisbet was delighted to marry his daughter into nobility and he gave his consent.

While the *Phaeton* strained at her anchor, the ship's courier Charles Duff was sent into Palermo to secure lodgings. He returned with the discouraging news that it was "impossible to get on shore tonight. Never were such places seen; no chairs, nor beds. So we must take our own with us!" Duff added however that Sir William Hamilton had learned of their arrival and was offering the use of his house.

The Elgins balked at the thought of living under the same roof with the notorious Emma Hamilton. They had been one whole month on the high seas, confined in a damp cabin which was divided into six insufferable compartments by a hideous green curtain. Not one day passed without the same complaint from the embassy's chaplain, Reverend Philip Hunt: "My Lord and Lady, how can I be expected to share this molecular compartment with four other gentlemen? Measure it closely, my Lord and Lady: twelve feet long, six broad and six high. Now count the five beds, the thirteen trunks, six basins, hats, dressing gowns, boat cloaks ... a cabin-boy brushing our shoes, servants preparing our shaving apparatus, five foul clothes bags, four portmanteaux, brooms, blankets, quilts, an Eighteen-Pounder with carriage tackles, iron crow, balls, grapeshot!"

Despite these annoyances Hunt managed to perform his ministerial duties on board the *Phaeton* and also conducted services on deck every Sunday morning, even in bad weather.

Lord Elgin selected a sizable staff for his embassy. The men were youthful and well qualified. Foremost among these was Professor Joseph Dacre Carlyle, who previously had held the chair in Arabic at Cambridge. He had just turned thirty-nine and already had several important books published. He also had a weakness for poetry and "beleaguered everyone in the party with his poor verses." His main purpose in joining the embassy was to fulfill a sincere desire to convert the natives of Asia and Africa by distributing an Arabic version of the Bible over which he had labored for several years. Lord Elgin saw no objection to this as long as Carlyle was able to fortify the embassy with his knowledge and scholarly achievement.

Reverend Hunt was twenty-eight and had been for a short period of time a clergyman under the patronage of Lord Upper Ossory. The opportunity to join Lord Elgin's Embassy excited him, and he wrote to his father:

> As the Turks have now made a common cause with us to stop the progress of the French desolation, it has been thought expedient by our court to send a *splendid* Embassy

to Constantinople in order to enter into certain treaties for the mutual advantage of both countries. The Earl of Elgin is appointed Embassador Extraordinary etc. to the Porte, and by the interest of my worthy and excellent friend the Reverend Mr. Brand, Rector of Maulden, the situation of chaplain and private secretary to the Embassador will most probably be filled by me.

I have consulted Lord Ossory and my other friends here who all concur in describing it as a most brilliant opportunity of improving my mind and laying the foundation of a splendid fortune. I need only add that it is a situation by which the younger son of a Nobleman might aspire; that it will be certainly attended with great *present* advantages and most probably lead to an independent fortune.

A meticulous scholar, Hunt could dissect the history of many archeological sites in Europe and Asia, and had a sound knowledge of Greek.

Elgin's secretaries were both twenty-two. John Morier knew about the East, having been born in Smyrna where his father was consul. This was his first diplomatic assignment, and he religiously supplied his diary with many details of the voyage, particularly Lord Elgin's coldness of manner and frugality. Even during their first day at sea Morier noticed "a great indifference on the part of Lord Elgin towards those most immediately dependent upon him." But part of this could be attributed to Elgin's chronic indisposition. He suffered constantly from rheumatism and was susceptible to catching cold which was a deep source of vexation for his young and lively wife. Everyone else in the embassy soon discovered that Lord Elgin did not intend to pay one penny of the salary agreed upon until the embassy was closed by order of the government. He even "stood by and allowed all in his party to pay their expenses and studiously avoided any mention of money."

William Richard Hamilton (no relation to Sir William) was also on his first assignment. He had studied at Oxford and Cambridge, and when his sponsor wrote to Lord Elgin the letter brimmed with hyperbole: "He has much good sense and great activity of mind. He is industrious and in the highest degree anxious to render himself useful. His manners are most pleasing and his principles perfectly good, so you may use him at once as your campanion, your confidant, and your fag."*

Doctor Hector McLean was the embassy physician. "An esteemed medical authority," he was at his wit's end in effecting a cure for Lady Elgin's mal de mer, and with exasperation finally decided that the *Phaeton* should stop briefly at selected ports of call to afford her some measure of relief. McLean had a weakness for alcohol and confined himself in his compartment throughout most of the voyage.

Lady Elgin saw her husband's desire for this post in Turkey as vain and senseless. The world was already spinning into the nineteenth century, yet Turkey still remained a barbarous country, her plague-infested towns swelling with harems and dens of hashish. To seek such an embassy at a time when England was at war with Bonaparte seemed even more absurd but Lord Elgin refused to be dissuaded and continually reminded her of Constantinople's ancient beauty, the matchless splendor of Aghia Sophia,† the Gardens of Pera, the Bosphorus, the Seraglio,** and the intriguing moods of the Black Sea.

However, Lord Elgin had a deeper reason for seeking the post at Constantinople: From the time he was a young student at Westminster he had a fond affection for art, and especially sculpture. Largely through the influence of Thomas Harrison whom he had engaged to restore Broomhall, Elgin learned that the best models of classical art were to be found in Greece, not Rome. Harrison further suggested that while Elgin was at Constantinople he could

* Not to be confused with the modern definition. In Elgin's day a fag was a public school boy who was required to perform menial tasks for a student in a higher class.

† The Church of St. Sophia was Justinian's greatest work. It was begun A.D. 532 and it marks the highest development of the Byzantine style of architecture.

** The Palace of the Sultan.

make periodic visits to Athens where excellent opportunities for improving his knowledge of Greek sculpture and architecture were agelessly present. Although many books had been recently written by English and German scholars, Harrison insisted that books could not truly inspire. Far more important were plaster casts of the actual objects as well as paintings and drawings done on sight under the brilliance of the Grecian sky.

Harrison's words stirred Lord Elgin. This was the opportunity he had been seeking from the time he was at Westminster. Here was the chance to restore the entire position of the fine arts in Great Britain and to improve British architecture, painting, and sculpture. Classical designs could be used everywhere, even on furniture and household goods. His embassy would thus benefit the whole advancement of the arts and literature in England. It was a grandiose scheme, and soon after Lord Elgin had learned that he had been accepted for the post he put these ideas to Lord Grenville, the Foreign Secretary. Requesting sufficient money to support such an important undertaking, Elgin furthermore asked for painters, artists, architects, draftsmen, and formatori, but these demands exceeded Grenville's authority, and he suggested that Elgin present them in person to the Prime Minister. Pitt's response was disheartening: "His Majesty's Government cannot equip your Embassy with such grand ideas. If you choose to embark upon this venture you must do so at your own expense."

Elgin's salary had already been fixed at only six thousand five hundred pounds per year. Nevertheless he was determined to carry his scheme forward and soon the best painters of England offered themselves at Broomhall. First to arrive was Thomas Girtin. He waited two hours in the great hall before being interviewed, only to learn that Elgin could offer him thirty pounds annually, which was half the salary of an English valet.* In addition to his main task as artist of

---

* Lord Elgin's frugality was the subject of considerable gossip, even in parsimonious Edinburgh.

the Embassy, Girtin was also expected to assist Lady Elgin in the decoration of fire screens, work tables, and other household duties "requiring artistic knowledge."

Next came Richard and Robert Smirke* and William Daniell.† With each of them Elgin was forced to adjust his price, but the basic terms remained unacceptable and further negotiations broke down. Elgin had the same results with the rest of the artists whom he interviewed during the following weeks. Shortly before embarking on the *Phaeton,* he called upon Benjamin West** for further advice, and the venerable painter suggested the name of J. M. W. Turner, who was only twenty-four, but had already gained stature in the art circles of London. Turner seemed willing at first, but when Elgin demanded sole possession of all paintings, and that Turner's leisure hours were to be devoted to drawing lessons for Lady Elgin, "the young artist retaliated with a salary demand of four hundred pounds at which point the interview was brought to a sharp halt by Elgin."

---

*Of the two Smirke brothers, Robert was the more famous. At the age of thirteen, he was apprenticed in London with an heraldic painter. Seven years later, he studied in the schools of the Royal Academy. His works were usually small in size, humorous, graceful, and accomplished in draftsmanship. He also executed many clever and popular book illustrations. In 1814, Smirke was nominated Keeper to the Royal Academy, but King George III refused to sanction the appointment because of Smirke's revolutionary opinions. Smirke died in 1845, at the age of ninety-three.

†William Daniell (1769-1837) was the nephew of the great English painter Thomas Daniell. William accompanied his uncle on a voyage to India when he was only fourteen. Shortly after this, his many sketches engraved in aquatint were published: *Voyage to India, Zoography,* and *Animated Nature.* Later in his life, Daniell turned to panorama painting and in 1822 was elected to the Royal Academy. His most famous painting is a panorama of the "Battle of Trafalgar," for which the British Institute awarded him one hundred pounds.

**Benjamin West (1738-1820), was born in Springfield, Pennsylvania. He executed his first painting at the age of seven while sitting by the cradle of his sister's child. The infant happened to smile in its sleep and young Benjamin drew its portrait. West settled in Philadelphia as a portrait painter at the age of eighteen. Two years later he moved to New York. In 1760 he traveled to Europe, visiting Italy for three years and then settling in London. King George III took him under his special patronage from which many commissions resulted. In 1802, after the Treaty of Amiens, West visited Paris and inspected the many masterpieces of art at the Louvre. After the death of Sir Joshua Reynolds, West became President of the Royal Academy and held the office for twenty-eight years. One of his largest and most important paintings, "Christ Healing the Sick," was done when West was sixty-five. He died in London and was buried in St. Paul's Cathedral.

And now the *Phaeton* had covered more than half her destination yet Elgin was still without an artist. A heavy melancholy seized him and he became even more cranky with the members of his staff. Lady Elgin tried to lift him from his despair, but she had her own discomfort to consider. Fortunately the lodging problem was solved the next morning when Duff succeeded in his search for a private palazzo. It was not far from Sir William's house and it overlooked the Bay of Palermo. The drawing room was so enormous Hunt paced it off: "Seventy-six foot long and twenty-five wide!" The ceiling was lavishly decorated with a pastoral scene which painfully reminded Lady Elgin of Archerfield, and a huge window led onto a balcony from which every ship in the harbor was plainly visible. Lady Elgin's mal de mer found instant relief here, and during the noon meal she even exchanged puns with Captain Morris. Later in the afternoon they received an invitation for dinner at Sir William's and quite surprisingly Lady Elgin did not raise one word of objection.

The Elgin party chose to walk to the Hamilton house, climbing leisurely up the narrow cobbled street that coursed through rows of white stucco houses with green tile roofs. Lord Elgin still felt dispirited and refused to converse, but Captain Morris quickly remedied this with a boisterous account of what had happened to him on the previous day when he called upon Lord Nelson* at Sir William's house:

---

* Viscount Horatio Nelson (1758-1805), British admiral and naval hero whose genius reached its greatest height at the Battle of the Nile, one of the most brilliant naval battles in history.

Nelson married Frances Nisbet (no relation to Mary Nisbet), a widow and the daughter of a West Indies doctor, after having gained her favor by romping on all fours with her little boy under the drawing room table.

Soon after his great victory against Napoleon's fleet in Egypt, Nelson arrived at Naples and fell headlong into an affair with Lady Hamilton, whose husband was the British Ambassador at Naples. A strikingly beautiful woman the subject of much gossip throughout Europe and the continent, Lady Hamilton quickly wasted most of Lord Nelson's money, dragged him around "like a bear," and finally forced him into gambling and heavy losses. Nelson had no children by his wife but Lady Hamilton bore him a daughter, Horatia.

Under his leadership the British warships annihilated the French fleet at the Battle of Trafalgar, but Nelson was struck in the chest by a musket shot and died a few hours later.

"I was met at the door by a little old woman in a white bed gown and black petticoat. "What do you want, Sir?' says she. 'Lord Nelson,' I reply. 'And what do you want with his Lordship?' again says she. I rebuked her on the spot and warned that she should look after her own business, at which point a male servant appeared and escorted me into the hall. 'You have inquisitive house-keepers,' says I to him. He coughed behind his hand then replied: 'But she is not a house-keeper, Sir. That is Lady Hamilton's mother!' "

It was unfortunate that the world knew Sir William Hamilton only as the aged husband of the famous Emma. However, Lord Elgin was well aware that Sir William had already achieved a well-deserved reputation as an antiquary. While serving as Ambassador at Naples, Sir William developed a fond passion for collecting many works of art, particularly vases, and was one of the first to appreciate the true origin of Greek vases which up to that time were erroneously called Etruscan simply because they were found in Southern Italy. His treasures were innumerable: hundreds of vases and priceless gems, a splendid thesaurus of valuable coins, and many fine pieces of sculpture. But like most passions, this soon became an obsession and it brought financial ruin to Sir William, forcing him to sell the entire collection at a great loss.

Two male servants escorted the Elgins into the front hall whose walls and floor were constructed of marble. On the wall beyond the foyer was a sweeping mural which Elgin instantly disliked, calling it Italian flamboyancy: pudgy little angels with pouting lips hovering around a youthful figure while high above loomed the awesome presence of God the Father.

They were greeted by Lady Hamilton and Sir William inside the drawing room. A middle-aged Naval officer in full dress stood rigidly by the bow window. His arm was severed at the elbow, and he wore a brown leather patch over one eye.

Lord Elgin was struck by Lady Hamilton's beauty. Extricating himself from the melancholic mood of the past few days, he whispered to his wife: "Now that is a fine woman for you. Good flesh and blood. A whapper!"

Lady Elgin could not understand why a fine gentleman like Sir William allowed this sick goat to roam freely in his house for more than a year. Nelson had no upper teeth, and there was an ugly wound on his forehead. "He seemed to be quite dying!"

Sir William graciously toasted their health, then wished Lord Elgin success in Constantinople. The drink was anisette and it encouraged their appetite for dinner: lamb swimming in thick tomato sauce, summer squash, okra, broccoli, cheese pie, small puffs of fried meats, and a wide variety of wines. Later during tea, they were all amused by Nelson's remarks about "that lean and sallow little man whose boots and hat were much too large for him." Yet in the very same breath Nelson readily admitted to Napoleon's genius.

Lord Elgin had been well-briefed on Napoleon and the French invasion of Egypt. His instructions ran to twenty-six pages and concluded with the stern warning that "not only was he to keep vigilant watch over the interests of His Majesty, promote commerce, maintain British privileges, persuade the Turks to open the Black Sea to English trade, establish a postal station at Suez . . . but above all, he was to assist in every possible way to expel the French from Egypt and thus keep the Ottoman Empire on friendly terms with Great Britain."

Only a few months before Lord Elgin accepted his Embassy, Napoleon had already amassed a powerful force on the channel coast for the purpose of invading Britain. In the final hour, however, he changed his mind and reported to his government that the plan was impossible, suggesting instead that these same forces which numbered over fifty-four thousand men be used in an invasion of Egypt: "Europe is a molehill. Everything here wears out; my glory is already past. This tiny Europe does not offer enough of it. We must go to the Orient; all great glory has always been acquired there."

Bonaparte's armada blanketed the harbor of Toulon. The sea was choppy and almost to the man the army was sea-sick, but Napoleon buoyed their spirits by reminding them that when he took command of the forces on the Ligurian coast they were in the greatest want, lacking everything and having sold even their watches and family possessions to provide for their daily needs. He promised them an end to their privations and then led them successfully into Italy where all was given them in abundance. But he did not stop there. He made a solemn promise if they would now follow him into Egypt: as soon as they returned to France every soldier would be given enough money to purchase six acres of land. And so this great force set sail from Toulon in May of 1799. The Admiralty and Lord Nelson never expected this; and the Egyptians, who had been under control of the Mamelukes* for five centuries, soon realized they were no match for the French, and offered little resistance.

Bonaparte boasted that "the Battle of the Pyramids was a general's dream: decisive victory, few casualties, enormous booty, and hardly a prisoner." But Lord Elgin strongly disagreed. The victory was far from decisive since a large part of the enemy force escaped intact with its leaders. It was to this force that Lord Elgin had to direct his immediate attention as soon as he arrived at Constantinople.

The dinner party at Sir William's had almost drawn to an end when Lady Hamilton walked to the glass doors of the drawing room and loudly clapped her hands. Several musicians appeared with cellos and violins. They seated themselves quietly in the center of the room and waited for Lady Hamilton's nod. She sang a medley of French tunes in a strong and melodic voice as Lady Elgin winced at her pretentious mannerisms.

---

* First introduced into Egypt by the Sultans in the thirteenth century, these fierce soldiers from the Caucasus took control of the country within a few years. They kept replenishing their forces by bringing in a steady flow of young soldiers from the Caucasus. When Napoleon invaded Egypt the Mamelukes had a powerful army of 10,000 men, but they were soundly defeated by the modern weapons of the French.

Precisely at noon of the next day a servant of Lady Hamilton came to the palazzo with an invitation to dine at two o'clock, after which they were to watch a rowing match at four where the King and Queen of Naples would be present, and then finally to a grand ball that evening: a gala fete to celebrate the birthday of the royal son and heir to the throne. Lady Elgin wore her choicest pink gown with white lace cloak. At Sir William's Elgin again became sullen and hardly touched his food. However he perked up after tea when Sir William suggested a short stroll through Palermo. Lady Hamilton hastened to her bedchamber and returned in a dress of white silk with matching gloves and hat. Most of her bosom was exposed, but it bothered only Lady Elgin who was determined by this time not to enter into a degrading competition with such a fickle woman who changed clothes and jewelry at the twinkle of an eye.

As they walked in leisure down the sharp hill leading to the bay, Sir William unveiled much of Palermo's history: how it was built originally on a tongue of land between two inlets which resulted in the creation of two excellent harbors that eventually joined into one and formed a small bay facing entirely to the east where Palermo now lay. A few more meters and they came to rest before the porch of an ancient church that was built by an English archbishop named Walter who was sent to Sicily by Henry II as a tutor to the King. Lord Elgin was unimpressed with all this and even remarked to Sir William that he found Roman architecture appalling. Here Lady Hamilton suddenly complained of fatigue and took leave of them, but assured everyone that she would recover for the rowing match later in the afternoon.

The harbor was deserted. Palermo's museum stood a short distance away, and Lord Elgin's eyes came instantly alive when he beheld the abundant collection of Etruscan sarcophagi, the sepulchral urns, the numerous bas-reliefs, and the large assortment of Greek vases. Along with these were many oil paintings and an extensive array of Sicilian majolica.

Sir William was genuinely pleased to find someone who shared his love for antiquities, and Lord Elgin seized this opportunity to say that Sir William's book of engravings not only had inspired him while at Westminster but in fact had brought about several altercations with a classmate who refused to accept that "Josiah Wedgwood the potter was completely influenced by Sir William's inspiring text." Elgin then proceeded to tell Sir William about his real reason for seeking the post at Constantinople, and how he had to abandon his plans when he could not find a capable artist to supervise the project. Dourfully Sir William replied that Palermo was no substitute for Naples and therefore he could be of little assistance. He also had the unpleasant situation in his house. Lady Hamilton was at that age in life which demanded insatiable attention. "Only an old fool gets married at sixty-one!"

Aside from all this, Sir William's health had begun to deteriorate, and he suffered greatly from bilious fevers. This rapid approach to dotage accounted for his senile devotion to Lady Hamilton, and for his complaisance in her relationship with Nelson.

Lady Elgin was sorely distressed over the whole situation: "I never saw three people make such thorough dupes of themselves as Lady Hamilton, Sir William, and Lord Nelson!"

As they were leaving the museum Sir William remarked that Nelson planned to set sail for Minorca in a few days. Lord Elgin already knew about this and was half-tempted to say "many people were laying bets that Nelson would not go."

In the dusty street Lord Elgin repeated his ardent hopes of sending professional artists, architects, and molders to Athens. Sir William urged him to persist and then suddenly exclaimed that he knew the ideal person for the Athens project: "The first painter in Italy, Giovanni Battista Lusieri," who lived in Messina and was fondly called Don Tita. Sir William first heard of him when Lusieri served as court painter for the King of Naples.

Lord Elgin's interest mounted when he learned that Don Tita was not one to quibble over money. As for his work, Lusieri devoted himself almost entirely to large panoramas. "They are upon a considerable scale in length, not less than seven or eight feet, and generally they embrace the eighth of a circle. He even has one (a view of Constantinople) eighteen feet by three or four feet high which comprehends the fourth of a panorama. These drawings are merely careful outlines done with a hard pencil or crow-pen. No attempt is made at light and shade. He takes an incredible time in doing them; the outline of Constantinople alone was a study of three months. On examining the subjects from which several of his outlines have been made, I confess that I could not perceive the minutiae described in them and I am thus led to suppose that he must have used a telescope."

The rowing match proved to be a dull performance, and when it was finished the Elgins were brought back to the palazzo in Sir William's carriage. Lady Elgin was in a quandary over what she should wear for the ball that evening since Lady Hamilton upon several occasions during the rowing match tried to make light of the matter by calling it a silly little birthday party. After much deliberation Lady Elgin finally chose her blue and silver silk gown to which she added her pearl necklace and diamond bracelet. At quarter past seven they were summoned outside where Sir William's carriage again awaited them. Lady Hamilton sat between her husband and Nelson in the rear seat. She wore a gold silk gown studded with jewels and a tiara of glittering diamonds!

Soon after their arrival at the palace there was a thunderous display of fireworks, and while the air still lay heavy with clouds of smoke a large platform was cleared and the dancing commenced. Servants in Chinese dress moved through the crowd serving wine and small morsels of fried meat. Meanwhile, the men cast lingering looks toward Lady Hamilton as their wives whispered into each other's ears. Only a few couples were dancing. Lady Hamilton took this moment to proclaim that "Her Majesty had spent more than six thousand pounds for this affair," which Lord Elgin under his breath called an extravagant waste.

Their table rested alongside a Japanese bridge that spanned an artificial pond. A covey of ducks swam peacefully at one corner while rows of brightly-lit lamps cast their reflection on the water. In time the food was served. Under the soft hue of the dancing lamps Nelson cleared his throat and asked Lord Elgin if he realized exactly what awaited him at Constantinople. Nelson went on to say that Elgin's predecessor, Sir Sydney Smith, would never live down his sudden removal from the embassy post. Sir Sydney had made captain at sixteen and fought in several battles of the American Revolutionary War, but soon thereafter he found life rather dull and, disobeying Admiralty orders, "he accepted an invitation from the King of Sweden to be his naval advisor in a war against Russia and conducted his naval operations from the King's yacht."

The Admiralty forgave him, however, and eventually sent him on a fact-finding tour of Turkey, but as soon as war broke out with France Sir Sydney purchased a ship at his own expense, collected a crew of unemployed sailors at Smyrna, and set off to join the Mediterranean fleet. His Majesty's Government then saw fit to appoint him Minister Plenipotentiary at Constantinople to serve jointly with his brother John Spencer Smith. Nelson strenuously fought this appointment, claiming it was a hazardous risk assigning political duty to an active service officer—let alone to a man who had attained his reputation through disobedience. And so there he stood, Sir Sydney Smith on the bridge of his *Tigre* laying siege to Acre with drawn sword and puffed chest while the treacherous Turks praised him to Allah. One Smith brother in charge of British affairs in Constantinople, the other a national hero holding both naval and diplomatic rank, Nelson soon to be on his way to Minorca, and Bonaparte firmly anchored in Egypt defying the British to throw him out. This was the complicated situation into which Lord Elgin had so willingly thrust himself.

After dinner Sir William introduced them to the King and Queen of Naples. They conversed in French. Standing beside her obese husband, the Queen looked tiny and fragile. Her purple gown was adorned with jewels, and two fingers of each hand sagged under the weight of huge diamonds. In a charming manner she explained that she was the sister of Marie Antoinette, then tearfully revived each frightful moment of the war, culminating with the sad announcement that half of their kingdom was already lost to Bonaparte.

Lord Elgin had no real aversion toward her, save her inability to converse in better French. As for the King, (Ferdinand I, a Spanish Bourbon) he spoke hardly at all, but his face did light up when Lady Elgin conveyed her polite assurance that this was indeed the most gala day in her life—what with the rowing match, the fireworks, the music and the delicious food. Lord Elgin then picked up his wine glass and drank to Nelson upon which Lady Hamilton "actually GREETED!"*

Three days later the Elgins traveled into Messina for a meeting with Giovanni Battista Lusieri. It was a tedious journey over bad mountain roads, and although their guide claimed to know the way blindfolded, they did not arrive at Messina until noon of the next day. They were directed into the heart of the old city and down a narrow street of cobblestones. Lusieri's house was a two-story structure of white stucco whose walls were cracked at many places, and the inner staircase shook under their weight.

Lusieri was a tall man with deeply-set eyes, a full black moustache, and a short pointed beard. Elgin showed his impatience immediately when he discovered that Lusieri did not speak English. However, Don Tita had a fair comprehension of French, and Elgin carefully explained the purpose of their visit: "Lusieri was to supervise an artistic commission which was to include an architect who would

* Scottish for "wept."

take notes of buildings and temples; also to employ several formatori who would mould such sculptures and works of art that were found to be accessible. All drawings, pictures, sketches, and mouldings were to remain in Lord Elgin's possession and be his sole property."

This was not an uncommon practice in the nineteenth century. Many men of nobility and station were often accompanied in their travels by famous painters: Jacques Carrey was in the suite of the Marquis de Nointel, Lord Charlemont took Richard Dalton on a tour through Egypt, and even Lord Elgin's predecessor at Constantinople, Sir Robert Ainslee, employed Ludwig Mayer for a similar purpose.

Lusieri's salary was set at two hundred pounds sterling per year, and when he asked that it be in writing Lord Elgin drew the contract in French:

It is agreed between Lord Elgin and Signor Luzieri that the latter must accompany his Lordship in his embassy to Turkey as a painter and especially to employ his time and his art under the direction of his Excellency. It is understood that all works which Signor Luzieri shall do during this time will be at the disposal of his Excellency, in consideration of which he will receive two hundred pounds sterling per year, living always at the expense of his Excellency.

In case Signor Luzieri wishes to make copies of some works done during this employment for his own use it is agreed that the choice will be made through the consideration of both parties. Signor Luzieri will also be at liberty to return to his country before the expiration of the term of his employment should unexpected circumstances oblige him.

> Made in Messina in the presence of
> Lord and Lady Elgin.

Elgin misspelled Lusieri's name and it had to be corrected. After both parties signed the document Elgin wasted no time and informed Lusieri that he was to travel at once with

Elgin's secretary William Hamilton into Rome and Naples to engage the rest of the artists:

1. A man for casts.
   A painter of figures to work under Lusieri.
   All work to be entirely Elgin's property and the salaries fixed at the second table. (Fifty pounds per annum.)
2. Also of procuring all necessary materials for the painters; and casts for the moulders.

Here Lady Elgin made a request for herself: "A Caro of Vertioso"* similar to those employed by Lady Hamilton: someone to accompany the pianoforte, a cellist or two, and a violinist. But Lord Elgin hardly felt inclined to burden his embassy with such luxury. He assented however after Lady Elgin hinted that good musicians could be engaged in Italy at the second table of salary, for which they might even be induced to wear livery and act occasionally as servants.

At any other time his wife's extravagance might have bothered Lord Elgin, but on this warm October day he had suddenly found a new happiness; and that night he slept soundly in Messina, knowing that at last he had taken the first real step toward his one goal in life.

Hamilton and Lusieri were in Rome one whole month before Lord Elgin finally received word from them:

My dear Lord:
   Please be advised that many Italian artists have found it necessary to quit Rome because of the French. Those who have remained are generally of a suspicious nature and we have been forced to inquire about their political principles as well as their professional ability. Aside from this, those who have offered to sign on with us have presented various objections as to character, age, line of life, and talent. But

---

* Lady Elgin should have spelled it: Carro of Virtuosi. (A cartload of musicians.)

after many weeks of extensive search, and largely through the influence of Signor Lusieri's acquaintances here, I am able to report to your Lordship that I have completed all arrangements according to your Lordship's instructions.

The first to be engaged was a draughtsman for figures and sculpture. We had been told that he was trained at Carlsruhe. He has great skill and his concise drawings indicate taste and mind. We are led to believe that he is the only man of culture his nation has ever produced, for he is a Tartar and a native of Astracan! We have fixed his salary at one hundred pounds per annum.

Upon Signor Lusieri's insistence we secured the services of two architects, since it is impossible for one man to cope with such a great undertaking as this. The chief architect is an extremely deformed humpback—however your Lordship must remember that only his head and hands were the object of our search. He shall take with him a young man who has been accustomed to study under him as a scholar. We have fixed their total salary at five hundred Roman piastres, or one hundred and twenty-five pounds.

We have also recruited two men for making plaster moulds. Each shall receive one hundred pounds per annum. I need not remind your Lordship that we were indeed fortunate to avail ourselves of their employ, since there are only six moulders in all of Rome, the rest having gone to France.

Her Ladyship will be pleased to hear that I had the good fortune to procure at Naples a Maître de Chapelle with all the qualities her Ladyship desired, except the inclination to appear occasionally as groom of the chamber. As he is a very well-mannered young man, I did not think it proper to press this added burden upon him, particularly as I learned from every quarter that persons of his profession would, with natural vanity, rather starve than stoop to such imaginary degradation.

He is bringing two other musicians with him: one plays the clarionet and the other, the violincello. I believe it will be possible though difficult to prevail upon these to wear livery, or at least a separate uniform, which would answer fully to her Ladyship's request.

Because of the war, we have been completely excluded from communication with the rest of the world, and although we are but a short distance from each other I fear this message will not reach Palermo until after your Lordship's departure for Constantinople, in which event I shall await your Lordship's further instructions.

Believe me to be,
Your most humble servant etc.
William Richard Hamilton

Even Hamilton's lavish distribution of money did not upset Lord Elgin at this time. Early the next morning he was awakened by Reverend Hunt and Professor Carlyle. They wanted him to accompany them "on an exploration of the ruins at Taormina; also to investigate the phenomenon of Scylla and Charybdis,* and perhaps climb Etna too," a feat that Elgin had always yearned to accomplish.

They were gone five days. During their absence Lady Elgin kept busy with afternoon teas and nightly soirées. She attended the opera with the Queen of Naples one evening and was the honored guest at a reception several hours later. She encountered Lady Hamilton there and made two efforts at conversation, but Emma was aloof and disinterested. Nelson indeed had gone to Minorca!

Lord Elgin returned from the excursion looking rested and apparently in good spirits. At dinner that night Captain Morris announced it was imperative that they sail immediately for the Aegean, since wind and sea were at last favorable. Elated, Elgin dispatched a quick message to Hamilton at Rome, ordering him to embark at once for Constantinople with Lusieri and the party of artists. The Elgins then called upon Sir William and Lady Hamilton for the last time. Sir William was sorry to hear they were leaving and assured them he would be at the docks in the morning to see them off. Emma still looked downcast.

They were transported to the docks at dawn in Sir

* A treacherous whirlpool off the southern coast of Italy.

William's carriage. There were sad farewells and endless toasts. Lady Elgin became nauseated the moment she set foot on the *Phaeton's* deck, but she clenched her teeth and waited until Sir William had pulled out of sight before making a frenzied dash to her compartment below where her maid Masterman stood waiting, the brown vinegar jar clutched in her nervous hands.

On the last day of February the wind failed and they had to drop anchor off the Isle of Tenedos at the entrance to the Dardanelles. Within an hour they were met by a Turkish vessel and, after a loud exchange of salutes, invited on board and brought before a young Turkish officer in pompous dress whose raven beard and thick eyebrows consumed most of his face. A red turban rested proudly on his head. He introduced himself as Capitan Pasha then took Lady Elgin's hand and kissed it. Turning to Lord Elgin, he happily declared that Turkey had just entered into a treaty of alliance with England. Elgin was shocked to learn that the treaty was negotiated by Sir Sydney Smith and his brother, Sir John Spencer Smith. "Provisions were also made to open the Black Sea to British shipping which had been Elgin's primary objective."

When they returned to the *Phaeton* Captain Morris feared they could be forced to lay at anchor off Tenedos for an indefinite period since the wind generally remained contrary at that time of year. Elgin insisted they would be in Constantinople by Thursday of that week. Fortunately for Lady Elgin the sea was calm and she caught a few hours of needed sleep. She was awakened by the sound of voices on deck and after climbing up the steps she saw Captain Morris conversing with the Capitan Pasha. Elgin was nowhere in sight. Captain Morris relieved her anxiety by saying that Elgin had gone ashore with Reverend Hunt immediately after the noon meal. Capitan Pasha again kissed Lady Elgin's hand and extended a dinner invitation for that evening on board his ship, the *Selim III*.

Throughout most of that afternoon Lady Elgin and Masterman searched all the trunks in the hold of the *Phaeton*. Gowns and jewelry were retrieved, along with evening slippers and hats. Shortly before dusk Elgin returned to the ship with Hunt. At first he voiced objections about dining with the Turk, but since Lady Elgin was already dressed for the occasion he relented. Putting on his white uniform with sword attached, he explained that Hunt had wanted him to look at something in Yenicher, a small village just off the shore from Tenedos. Lady Elgin did not press the matter any further. They climbed into the Pasha's small boat and boarded the *Selim III* where Capitan Pasha stood at attention alongside his crew in full uniform with red fez and plume. There was a sudden blast of cannons and as they passed along the deck the Turkish crewmen saluted.

It was a lavish dinner.

Elgin was still aggravated over the news concerning the Smith brothers' treaty with the Turks. After the dessert Capitan Pasha invited them to sit on floor cushions while Turkish coffee was served in fragile demi-tasse cups. Eventually the nargileh* was brought out and passed from hand to hand. Elgin guardedly puffed from it when it came his turn. During a moment of silence Capitan Pasha disclosed an unsettling piece of news relating to Elgin's appointment as Minister to the Porte:

When Sir Sydney Smith announced Lord Elgin's appointment to the Grand Vizier he was much grieved on his friend being displaced and asked: 'But why should there be any change? We went on very well together; things went on very well.' Sir Sydney went on to say that the newly-appointed ambassador was a great landed proprietor in Scotland, that he had great influence there, and that the English Government were in the habit of conciliating such people by the appointment to high situations as being the best things they had to bestow. The Vizier then said: 'Ah,

* A Turkish water pipe.

then I understand that your government has also got its mountain chiefs to conciliate.' The Vizier asked what the new ambassador was called; what his name was. Sir Sydney gave the name in Arabic. 'Oh, but Elkin is very bad,' cried the Vizier. 'It is evil genius. It is the Devil! How could the English Government send us such a person!'

At crack of dawn the next day Lord Elgin awoke in good humor and suggested they all go on a picnic to Troy which was just across the channel. The weather was unseasonably mild, and a basket of cold meats, oranges, grapes, bread, cheese and wine was prepared by the servants. Captain Morris and Doctor McLean chose to remain on board, but everyone else went along, including Masterman. After crossing the channel in the captain's barge they encountered a swift current and did not land on the Asia Minor coast until noon. The crewmen were ordered back to the *Phaeton* after Elgin made arrangements with them to be picked up precisely at dusk. Hunt carried the basket of food while Professor Carlyle armed himself only with his worn-out text of Homer so as to prove the exact site of Troy to the doubting Hunt.

They proceeded at a slow pace and came eventually into a village where Elgin bargained for a guide and half a dozen asses. At first Lady Elgin was uncomfortable on her beast, but she soon accustomed herself to its strange gait. Within an hour they arrived at the desolate village of Sigaeum, stopping beneath a large plane tree to eat and rest, then moving on again across a barren plain where herds of camels grazed under the watchful eyes of fierce-looking shepherds in long cloaks of burlap. "Along the way Carlyle frequently consulted Homer much to the dismay of Hunt who had his own theories about the actual site of Troy."

The asses labored up a long slope and at last reached the summit. Below them lay Yenicher, sprawled against the bleached sand like a crumpled white blanket. The guide quickly led his beasts to the well for water while Elgin hastened toward a small white church which stood directly across the dust-filled street. Only a few inhabitants were in sight. At the entrance to the church and on each side of the door rested two marble seats. One was a sculptured relief of mothers with their children; the other bore an ancient Greek inscription which perplexed Hunt momentarily until he discovered that it read from right to left to prevent interpolation.

Lord Elgin had known about these seats for a number of years. "They were first discovered by Lady Montagu in 1718 and she could have had them for the price of a small bribe but the captain of her ship did not have the proper tackle to remove them." When she offered to purchase them from the townspeople they objected vehemently because they regarded the seats as a sure remedy for all forms of sickness.

There was nothing further of interest in Yenicher and the party headed back for Sigaeum, arriving there just before dusk. The crewmen from the *Phaeton* had yet to appear and the travelers were obliged to seek shelter from the night's dampness inside a small cave. Hunt lit a fire and the rest of the food was consumed. Huddled under the same blanket with her husband, Lady Elgin broke the news that she was pregnant. Lord Elgin was overjoyed, hoping for a boy: "Lord Bruce, the Eighth Earl of Elgin and Twelfth of Kincardine!"

When the crewmen finally arrived Elgin did not admonish them for their tardiness. Instead he slapped each of them on the backside and was the first to leap into the captain's barge.

The next morning Lady Elgin awoke from a deep sleep and found a note on the table beside her bunk: Elgin had gone off with Captain Morris and the crew, and would return before nightfall. After a light breakfast she and Masterman again busied themselves with the trunks in the hold of the *Phaeton,* getting everything in readiness for their arrival in Constantinople. Just before the noon meal Hunt went ashore with Carlyle and came back laden with baskets of bread, fruit, and casks of wine. Lady Elgin spent the rest of the afternoon strolling leisurely along the deck and tossing bread chunks to the gulls in the harbor.

Lord Elgin returned to the *Phaeton* about five o'clock. He was alone and had a strange look on his face which frightened his young wife. He explained that he had gone to the Capitan Pasha and asked if he could have the two marble seats from the church at Yenicher. "Permission was granted immediately and Elgin dispatched the full complement of the *Phaeton* to Yenicher. At first the Greek priests wailed and tried to prevent the crewmen from taking away the seats but when they realized that Lord Elgin had a firman* they withdrew in tears."

* An edict or official order issued directly from the Sultan.

Chapter
Two

Turkey

A THOUSAND MINARETS jabbed the cloudless sky while in the bustling harbor vessels of all sizes and description surrounded the *Phaeton* and saluted her with deafening cannon fire. As soon as they arrived at the docks they were accorded official greetings and given flowers, fruits, and sweets by a long line of servants assembled in brilliant costumes along both sides of the quay. Speeches were made; gifts exchanged. Elgin passed out gold watches and chains to the young Turkish officers; also English pistols and rings set in diamonds. Even the servants were included, each receiving some manner of gift or token. At the conclusion of the formal ceremony they were carried in golden chairs to the British Palace, an aged structure of white stone whose facade was pock-marked with holes and ugly cracks. A crowd of Turks in bright-colored robes flocked around them, and they had to seek the assistance of Janissaries* to get inside.

While Elgin was driven to the Seraglio for an audience with the Sultan, Masterman drew a warm bath for Lady Elgin. Later in the afternoon Elgin returned to announce they were invited to the official ceremony of welcome by the Sultan himself, but since Turkish custom forbade the presence of women at such affairs the Sultan reluctantly agreed to let Lady Elgin come, provided that she dress as a man.

---

* The elite troops of the Turks.

The idea fascinated her, and Duff was sent outside to obtain the necessary costume: blouse, vest, pantaloons and fez. The pantoflas* were too large for her feet and she had to stuff the toes with cotton. Meanwhile, Lord Elgin put on his full dress uniform. When they came out of the British Palace they discovered several hundred Janissaries on both sides of the street, lined in parade formation. After climbing into the carriages they were escorted to the Tophana docks, from where they crossed by boat to the Seraglio.

Lady Elgin felt ill-at-ease. The pantaloons were hot and uncomfortable; in addition to this, Elgin fumed everytime the Janissaries stopped, which they did repeatedly and for no apparent reason. The procession lasted two hours. Finally they were met by the Sultan, who personally conducted them into the audience room. It was very dark and they had to walk past rows of eunuchs and guards. Each piece of furniture was decorated with jewels; mosaics adorned the floor and walls. The Sultan's throne looked like "a good honest English bed; the counterpane on which the Monster sat was embroidered all over with immense large pearls. By him was an ink-stand holding even more diamonds. In his turban he wore the famous Aigrette,† his robe was of yellow satin trimmed with black sable, and in a window nearby there were two more turbans covered with diamonds. You can conceive nothing in the Arabian Nights equal to that room."

The Sultan did not cast his eyes even once toward Lady Elgin during his formal address. When he finished, Lord Elgin stepped forward and presented him with a gold chandelier, a bezoar stone, and several hundred yards of satin and damask. Later, during the introductions, the Sultan still kept his eyes glued to the floor, especially while Lady Elgin was presented as "Lord Bruce, a young nobleman." The weight of her pantaloons was now unbearable, and hot perspiration began pouring down her face.

*Satin slippers.
†A jewel from the Sultan's head-dress representing a mark of the highest honor.

Elgin quickly came to her rescue, making hasty apologies to the Sultan then helping her out of the room. The moment they reached their carriage Lady Elgin flung off the vest and fez, and was about to do the same with the pantaloons until Elgin warned her of the Janissaries that had already encircled the carriage and were forming ranks for the march back to the Palace. Moving off at last down the narrow street, Elgin let loose a tirade of epithets against His Majesty's Government for refusing to give him one penny to improve the fine arts of an entire country . . . and yet here was the King, throwing seven thousand pounds away on idiotic gifts for treacherous Turkish hands!

Any preconceived feeling that Lady Elgin had entertained about Constantinople slowly melted away in the happy months that followed. From her bedroom window on the second story of the Palace she could see every corner of the city. The domes and mosques seemed to rise up from the sea like the outstretched fingers of Neptune; multicolored houses clashed under the rays of the winter sun and sent a splash of beauty over the earth. Elgin was a patient teacher and called many things to her attention, even how "the dwellings of the Turks were painted in the brightest colors whereas those of the Greeks, Armenians, and Jews were subjected to morbid shades of black and brown." An enormous garden surrounded the Palace and through it coursed a network of walks, all leading to a high gate overlooking the Bosphorus.

But what impressed Lady Elgin most was the elegant dress of the Turks. Each class had its appropriate costume: The Janissaries wore an upright white felt cap with a broad flap that hung half-way down the back. The officers had a long roll of coarse linen over their heads which was carefully crossed and intertwined until it made their heads appear even wider than their shoulders. The merchants wore thick white turbans with long-flowing red robes; and the Hamals who plied the docks at Tophanah, although bare-chested and destitute, found a great source of pride in their baggy white pantaloons. The Turkish youths were uncommonly handsome, each with a manly air that touched upon insolence, and dressed in the same manner as their fathers. Every corner of the city had its mendicant Dervishes: wild-looking men, half-naked, heads crowned with wreaths of flowers . . . they wound their way through the dense crowds, shoving their tin cups before each strange face and calling frantically for contributions in Allah's name.

The Gardens of Pera were the favorite haunts of the Turkish women and each evening they flocked there in shapeless white cloaks and Mahramáh* which concealed everything but their brilliant black eyes. They all possessed a winsome gait, a delicate shuffling of the feet. Those who preferred to ride came in small tilted wagons drawn by four oxen gaily decorated from head to hoof. Lady Elgin had never witnessed such merriment and light-heartedness among women. This same mood proved quickly contagious, and along with the joyful awareness of new life inside her womb, her days were filled with happiness.

Meanwhile, Lord Elgin complained constantly about the bad weather, blaming it for his persistent attacks of rheumatism, although his wife suspected that his agitation arose from a deeper source: he had not heard from his secretary Hamilton in many months and was on the verge of sending him a blistering letter when at last the spell of silence was broken. Hamilton had posted the message at Palermo:

My dear Lord:
The long anxiety to hear from your Lordship at Constantinople has finally been relieved by the sight of your letter dated 15 January, however the pleasure I received from reading it was lessened by the sad account you gave of your health. The bad weather we have long had here gives me little room to hope that it has been more favourable

---

* A black veil of silk.

with your Lordship. I was greatly astonished at your Lordship's saying that you had received none of my letters from Messina, Naples, and Rome. I trust that the letter I wrote on the first day of January from Messina will have been more fortunate. I am confident however that your Lordship will attribute your not hearing from me rather to a failure of the Post than to my neglect.

From the time I arrived at Messina on 30 December, I have been continually prevented from proceeding on my voyage by the most provoking circumstances of dilatory merchants and captains, contrary winds, and bad weather. At that port the only ship in which I could hope to proceed to Constantinople was a Greek Polacca which was loaded with corn for Malta. To accommodate me, the captain offered to direct his ship, (after leaving her cargo at the Isle of Malta) go thence to Girgenti, and there take in a cargo of sulphur for Constantinople—but this on the condition that I consent to advance money for half the lading, since he would not embark in a new speculation to a higher amount. For the object of dispatch I consented to his offer and have advanced on my own account the necessary sum—but instead of leaving Messina in four days we were detained three weeks by strong winds which continued to persecute us in a voyage to Malta of nine days, and from there to Girgenti of eight days. Here fine weather would have permitted us to load and sail in four days but winds still contrary and violent, and the intervening of three idle holidays on which no Sicilian would work even to procure his bread, again assured us another delay. I therefore determined to come over to Palermo for a few days where I shall procure a collection of antiquities which I hope to present to your Lordship safe at Constantinople.

In the meantime I have left employed among the temples and sarcophagi of Girgenti our architects and painters. I trust that their work will in some degree supply the inconvenience your Lordship cannot but feel in their absence from Constantinople.

I am,
Your Most humble servant,
William Richard Hamilton

The news from Hamilton only partially relieved Elgin's melancholy. There were the Smith brothers also: Sir John Spencer continued to behave as though he were still the Ambassador to the Porte. He refused to keep a file of official papers, dealt directly with Turkish authorities without informing Elgin, and even ordered British representatives in the Levant not to correspond with Elgin. Each irregularity brought a sharp reprimand from Elgin, and although Smith promised never to allow such incidents to occur again, Elgin now felt certain that Sir John Spencer was bent on sabotaging the embassy.

Elgin's relationship with Sir Sydney Smith was equally vexing. Soon after Egypt had capitulated, Bonaparte realized that his position there was untenable, and he was forced to make several overtures toward a term of peace. At this time Sir Sydney was cruising the *Tigre* off the coast of Egypt. Grasping the opportunity to bring about a peace settlement, Sir Sydney invited the French representatives on board his ship without saying a word to Elgin. He even led the French to believe that he was negotiating on behalf of both Turkey and England. Consequently, when the Turkish authorities heard of it they put the full blame on Lord Elgin.

Finally Elgin had General Koehler on his hands. When he first arrived at Constantinople Elgin insisted that Koehler's British Military Mission should be called back from repairing the Dardanelles forts and placed instead on more active service. Koehler suffered from an inflated ego which daily introduced itself as: "General Officer Commanding His Majesty's Land Forces in the Ottoman Empire." These *forces* numbered only seventy-six men, most of whom were already depleted by disease.

Elgin submitted a full account of his difficulties to Lord Grenville, urging him to remove Sir John Spencer and to reprimand Sir Sydney—but the Foreign Secretary answered curtly and reminded Elgin that since England was at war there were more important matters requiring his attention.

Then came El Arish.

In this small town of Syria Sir Sydney Smith, without Elgin's knowledge, concluded the terms of peace under which the French were to leave Egypt neither as victors nor conquerors and be conveyed to France in British warships, provided they never again lift up arms against England or Turkey. This was another humiliation for Elgin; nevertheless, he put it aside for the moment and wrote immediately to Grenville: "I have infinite satisfaction in informing your Lordship that on 24th ult. a capitulation was signed in the Grand Vizier's camp at El Arish, in consequence of which the French are to evacuate Egypt within the space of three months." Determined more than ever that Sir Sydney would not take credit for the treaty, "Elgin then wrote to Nelson and ordered him to provide ships for the evacuation of the French troops." Finally he undertook the long and arduous task of issuing passports for the safe conduct of every French soldier from Egypt into France.

Grenville's reply came quickly, instructing him not to enter into an arrangement with Bonaparte under any condition, except that Bonaparte surrender himself and his troops as prisoners of war! The Treaty of El Arish was thus rendered null and void, and Elgin had the unpleasant task of invalidating the passports. Crushed with mortification, Elgin called upon the Sultan and strongly suggested that the Turks should arrange a graceful withdrawal from the treaty. The Sultan refused: "In the eyes of Turkey, Sir Sydney had acted as Minister Plenipotentiary and the Treaty of El Arish was valid!"

Within a fortnight Elgin received still another message from Grenville: "The British Government has been informed of the Treaty at El Arish, and although it is quite contrary to the policy laid down in our last dispatch to you, we have decided to accept its terms after all."

By this time, however, the Grand Vizier was in Egypt with his sad collection of soldiers and had prepared to take over Cairo in accordance with the treaty. Bonaparte, on the other hand, had been duly informed by Elgin that the English could not assent to any other terms but unconditional surrender. It was a terrible muddle. Countermanding all previous orders for evacuation, Bonaparte now notified the Grand Vizier that the armistice was over. A few days later he attacked the Turks at Heliopolis and soundly defeated them.

Even though the French were once again in full possession of Egypt, Elgin had strangely vindicated himself with the Turks, who now looked upon him as their true champion, whereas the brothers Smith, being solely responsible for the fiasco at El Arish, soon lost all favor and were officially scorned. Elgin's spirits were rejuvenated and again he wrote to Grenville, imploring him to remove Sir John Spencer Smith at once from Constantinople and to terminate Sir Sydney Smith's affiliation with the Levant Company. This time his request was heard and a meeting of the British Cabinet was called. Its decision was unanimous: "Sir John Spencer was dismissed; and Sir Sydney was relieved of all diplomatic rank!"

It was a great victory for Elgin.

Lady Elgin, who had to live with these disturbing events day and night, now settled back into her previous mode of life and began attending afternoon teas and concerts; she also resumed her daily strolls through the Gardens of Pera. Fearing that the Smiths had drained most of Elgin's energy, she felt that another ambassadorial assistant was needed and even volunteered to make the choice herself: "a very pleasant and lively chap named Alexander Stratton . . . and a most capital whist player!"

With the Smiths at last out of his hair, Elgin was able to give full attention to the prime purpose of his mission, especially after Hamilton sent further word from Mykonos Isle and reported that "he had hoped in a few days to present himself and his artist companions to Elgin at Constantinople." Almost overnight Elgin became a changed man. He even enjoyed a brief period of relief from the rheumatism that had bothered him throughout the winter, although Doctor McLean claimed it was his treatment that effected the cure: "Seven leeches on the temples each night for two weeks." However Elgin's euphoria was short-lived. During the late days of spring a dreadful disease swept over Constantinople and in his weakened state Elgin contracted a mysterious fever which produced disastrous results: within a matter of months most of his nose was eaten away! McLean did his utmost to curb the infection, but it was futile. By the end of May nothing remained of Elgin's nose but a raw blotch of skin whose open wounds refused to respond to treatment.*

Lady Elgin tried hard to ignore it even though at times she could not bear to look at him. One morning, in an effort to free him from his dejection, she suggested a tour of the city. Both Carlyle and Hunt thought it an excellent idea and urged Elgin to comply. He agreed, but only after Hunt added that he had struck an acquaintanceship with the Sultan's gardener, a German who had offered upon several occasions to guide Hunt through the deepest secrets of the Seraglio. His was a unique position, and although he was employed in the Sultan's garden, he often joined in the many receptions given by the different foreign ministers through which he eventually came to know a large number of influential people.

They found him in his cottage, taking his midday nap, and although Hunt apologized for the intrusion, it made

---

* Dr. McLean maintained that Lord Elgin's affliction had resulted from an ague, a fever characterized by successive attacks of cold and hot fits, much sweating and shaking chills, and intense pain in the bones and joints. But McLean was unable to explain why an ague of this type should confine itself so catastrophically to the nose. Byron cruelly attributed Elgin's disfigurement to venereal disease:

> Noseless himself he brings here noseless blocks
> To show what time has done and what the pox.

Perhaps Byron was on the right track. In his *Treatise on Venereal Disease*, published in London (1786), the renowned physiologist and surgeon John Hunter discovered conclusive evidence that the most characteristic forms of a particular infection were deposits called gummata, which were of tenacious appearance, ulcerous and oozing with discharge, and attacking one particular organ of the body, the nose. According to Hunter, the disease constituted the tertiary manifestations of syphilis.

little difference. The German was gruff and discourteous. Nevertheless, Hunt persisted and prevailed upon him to have Lady Elgin accompany them, disguised as Lord Bruce again.

They came out of the cottage and climbed into the gardener's carriage. When they reached Pera they were escorted into a gondola for Tophana where another carriage took them to a gate of the Seraglio which faced the southern side of the Bosphorus. A contingent of Janissaries stood guard by the main portal, but at the German's curt nod the Janissaries stepped aside and permitted the party to enter. Inside the courtyard a nest of giant cypresses protected a neglected sarcophagus. Fortunately it was the season of Ramadan* and not one Janissary could be seen within the grounds. Hunt explained that the Turks imposed strict privations upon themselves during this season and even avoided the use of tobacco from sunrise to sunset—but at night they gorged themselves on food and wine which induced heavy sleep throughout the day.

The German seemed to take courage at this point and decided to undergo an even greater risk by showing them the interior of the harem. He pointed to a long, gloomy avenue that led from the gate of the garden and ran parallel to the high double walls of the Seraglio. He explained that the Sultanas passed through there every morning to take their air. A few meters to the right stood a sun lodge where on overcast days the German often hid and watched the women even though it was forbidden under the penalty of death:

> First to appear are the black eunuchs. They examine the entire garden, running before the Sultanas and warning all persons in the vicinity to avoid approaching or beholding them. Three of the four Sultanas are Georgians with dark smooth complexions and very long black hair. The fourth is fair and has flaxen hair. Not one of them

* A Moslem holy period similar to the Lenten season.

dyes her teeth black as do other Turkish women. Their
dress is rich beyond imagination: long spangled robes,
open in front, with silk pantaloons embroidered in gold
and silver, and adorned with large pearls and precious
stones so heavy as to impede their movements. Their hair
hangs loosely and in very thick tresses on both sides of the
face, completely covering their shoulders and reaching
down as far as the waist. The tresses too are studded with
diamonds but in a haphazard manner as though scattered
at random. On top of their heads, and leaning to one side,
they wear a small circular diadem. Their faces and necks,
even their breasts, are quite exposed.

After this vivid description, the German cautiously led
the Elgin party down a long gravel path, past a small grove of
orange trees in full bloom. Sparrows frolicked in the fountains that spouted along both sides of the walk; and there
were countless rows of white trellis-work burdened with jasmine and other flowering vines. They passed a small
greenhouse containing plants as well as tropical birds, then
climbed a sharp staircase and stepped finally into the upper
gardens of the Seraglio. From its heights they were able to
see a long stretch of the Asia Minor coast and the mouth of a
winding canal through which moved a steady flow of ships,
gondolas, caiques,* and merchantmen.

At that moment Lady Elgin felt a stab of pain. Her husband became alarmed. Weakly, she whispered: "Lord
Bruce!" but got no further before dropping into uncon-
sciousness.

Bouyouk Déré†

My very dear Mother
   I must tell you of my sublime joy as I sit here on the sofa
in the parlor while the Greek Paraman** is rocking Bruce

* Small fishing vessels.
† A suburb on the outskirts of Constantinople.
** A nurse or mother's assistant.

to sleep. I still find it difficult to believe that several years have passed since I last held you and my father in loving embrace.

On Tuesday we plan to go to Belgrade. Elgin has been there frequently and has found much relief from his rheumatism. He says it lies in the middle of a wood and consists chiefly of fruit trees watered by a vast number of fountains. The springs are known for their therapeutic value and hundreds of visitors go there. It has many shaded walks and endless gardens of flowers—all this within view of the Black Sea! The richest of Christians inhabit the town. They meet at the fountain each night to sing and dance. Elgin was quite struck by the beauty and dress of the women there and brashly claims they resemble the ancient Greek nymphs. Pshaw!

Mr. Hamilton and his cartload of artists have been hard at work in Athens for many months. Meanwhile the musicians continue to remain with us and I can truly say that I have never heard anything to equal the first violin. You will be pleased to know that he once led the orchestra at the opera in Naples. I did not tell you that the artists in Athens are under the supervision of Signor Lusieri who is a handsome devil but quite taken to moods.

And now for some sad news: Doctor McLean is dead. He was stricken with the palsy and although he never let on to us the gravity of his illness the poor man never recovered. He was an excellent scholar, a skillful physician and a warm friend. We shall all miss him dearly. Only yesterday I learned from Elgin that McLean had received the approval of the Duke of York to embark with us for the East so that he could investigate and make a further study on plagues.

Even after several years the strange illness that has devoured most of Elgin's nose shows no sign of abating. I have the darkest fear that it is leprosy although Doctor McLean repeatedly assured me to the contrary. In fact these were his dying words. Meanwhile we expect his replacement to be here shortly. His name is Doctor Scott and I trust that he will be better prepared to help poor Elgin.

By the bye, you would be entertained if you could see
Elgin at whist. I pique myself amazingly upon having made
him like to play two or three rubbers, and uncommonly
well he does it. I have also given a general invitation to
young Stratton, our new ambassadorial assistant. He comes
every evening so that it is more like a party. Our expenses
here are astronomical. Imagine having sixty people to feed
every day, independent of the company at our own table!
This seems to get worse with each passing year.

   I cannot wait to get to Belgrade and thus be rid of them.

                    Your own Mary,
                    AMBASSADRESS VERY EXTRAORDINARY!

   Immediately after their return from Belgrade Lord Elgin
persuaded the Turks to allow General Koehler to join the
Grand Vizier's army in Syria. Carlyle requested permission
to accompany Koehler, hopeful that this would afford him
the long-awaited opportunity of visiting the monasteries in
the Holy Land. Elgin did not favor the idea but when Carlyle
reminded him of his sincere desire to search for ancient
manuscripts and his goal for their eventual publication from
which he hoped to derive a satisfactory source of income,
Elgin gave his approval and even arranged to have the party
leave Constantinople secretly. Koehler was to take only a few
of his staff and make the journey as far as possible by land,
after which it could be concluded by the much easier sea
route. In addition to Koehler and Carlyle, the party consisted of two officers, a military draughtsman, and thirty
attendants. All were dressed as Turks and were well-armed.
Their plan was to head straight across Asia Minor, something which no other European had done in more than one
hundred years, since the route took them through the territories of many fierce Pashas. A few however were reported
to be friendly, depending on their current status with the
Porte. To preserve the party's safety, Elgin laid down certain
rules, and to make certain they would not be forgotten, he
made Hunt write everything down:

PREPARATIONS FOR A TOUR FROM CONSTANTINOPLE

The best night quarters are in the Greek monasteries which are to be found almost everywhere. On your departure, pay the full value of the provisions which you have consumed and leave a few piastres as a present to the church. In default of a monastery, a peasant's cottage neatly swept out is infinitely preferable to a Turkish Konak, for in the former you will be protected from the night air and will feel no inconvenience from fleas; in the latter you will be exposed to the wind on all sides and devoured by bugs.

Immediately upon your arrival at a new village visit the chief, whether Greek or Turk, and present your firman. He then becomes responsible for your safety and good treatment. A Turkish guard is an encumbrance and attended with much expense, although frequently expedient by way of protection from insult or robbery.

Presents of money are always expected by the attendants of persons whom you visit. These in fact constitute their wages. It is best to distribute this money yourself instead of employing a deputy. At every house you are treated after the fashion of the country, with pipes and coffee. When you retire, the attendants will be at the door expecting their fee.

When you travel through a village suspected of harbouring the plague, make every effort to leave it immediately. You will of course be told there is no plague. Truth and Turks rarely mix. In most cases they will concede there is a feverish complaint in the village but will assure you a thousand times it is not the plague. Needless to say, this makes the place suspect and you should suffer no intercourse whatsoever with such people.

As to dress, the Tartarian or Polish costume will be found the most convenient. In this case a defense for the eyes will be wanted; and the best is made with a piece of paste board cut into the shape of a crescent, covered with green silk and bound round the front of the cap by means of a silk ribbon. The best European dress consists of a white hat with a broad brim, a light-coloured broadcloth greatcoat, silk and cotton mixed waistcoat, trousers or loose pan-

taloons of Manchester or Nanking, and strong roomy half
boots. A large Venetian mantle or German cloak would
prove a useful and salutary companion at night. A portable
bed frame would conduce much to comfort in a country so
full of vermin, particularly if furnished with a mosquito
curtain.

On the mode of conveyance by land, horses are to be
hired in most places but if the country is very rocky and
mountainous it would be advisable to choose mules. In the
Isles of the Archipelago you must be contented with asses.
The usual rate of going is about three geographical miles
per hour. The horse hire varies from two to three piastres a
day for each beast, including all expenses. There is usually
a man to every two horses who accompanies them on foot
and receives a backshish or gratuity of twenty paras a day.

Finally, if you should be questioned about the motives
of your tour, you may reply that it is the custom of your
country and that you have read much of Greece in ancient
books, as well as of Egypt. The most current notion is that
you are in search of hidden treasure, since it is impossible
for Turks and Egyptians to conceive that you merely travel
to examine the mouldering ruins of ancient towns and
temples.

The party was gone a little over a week when Elgin received the first news from Carlyle. Several times during the
journey General Koehler had become annoyed with Carlyle's
many diversions at ancient ruins, but Carlyle was not dis-
mayed and kept to his numerous notes. He had the
draughtsman draw any interesting ruin or fallen temple and
also made a rough map of the entire route, noting points of
geographical interest and identifying modern villages with
ancient names. Within another two weeks Carlyle followed
this dispatch with many others, supplying Elgin with much
information about the modes and customs, and even the
political thoughts of each village along the way. From the
monastery of St. Saba in Jerusalem, he wrote: "The library
here contains nothing valuable except twenty-nine copies of
the Gospels and one of the Epistles. I was permitted by the

Superior to bring along with me six of what I judged the oldest manuscripts. These include two copies of the Gospels, one of the Epistles, two books of Homilies and Apostolic letters, and a copy of the sophist Libanius. I expect the Patriarch will allow me to convey them to England."

Carlyle also found the time to aggravate General Koehler with his poor verses:

Nicaea hail! renown'd for fierce debate,
  For synods bustling o'er yon silent spot.
For zealous ardour—for polemic hate—
  For truth preserv'd, and charity forgot . . . .
Those scenes are fled—those domes are swept away—
  Succeeding domes now totter to their fall,
And mouldering mosques on moulder'd fanes decay
  While desolation bends to grasp them all.

Elgin's patience was eventually rewarded by Carlyle's detailed report from the Grand Vizier's headquarters at Jaffa:

Bonaparte is not idle. He has turned his full attention on the French forces in Egypt and has decided to send an army from Toulon to reinforce them. Meanwhile his commander in Egypt* is more interested in the colonization of the country rather than the military aspects of his assignment. He was warned repeatedly by Bonaparte that an invasion was imminent yet he did nothing to strengthen his units stationed near the coast.

The relief forces from Toulon under the command of Admiral Gauteaume behaved equally as bad. No sooner did they sail for Egypt when they swung abruptly around and returned to port, without making any contact with Nelson. Enraged, Bonaparte ordered Gauteaume to sea again but the admiral, more afraid of Nelson than of Bonaparte, hastened once more to Toulon. And fortunately for us. The British Expeditionary Force under your trusted friend

---

* General Menou, who had succeeded General Kléber.

General Abercrombie, landed at Aboukir Bay and although they were vigorously opposed by shore artillery and musket fire, their fine training at Marmoris, which they owe largely to your Lordship's labours, enabled them to make a good account of themselves. Those in the Expeditionary Force constantly tell me how your Lordship exerted yourself, and at your own expense, securing vast quantities of stores for this Force, scouring the whole of Asia Minor for horses, building special shipyards, sending grain ships to every port in the Mediterranean . . . and much more. When our beachhead was finally established it was here that the French commander proved himself inept in military affairs. He procrastinated while we consolidated our forces on shore, and when he at last chose to attack the results were disastrous. He was soundly defeated and had to escape to Alexandria.

General Abercrombie was then able to bring in more reinforcements by sea; also to consolidate plans with the Grand Vizier's army which was drawn up outside Cairo. At this point the ancient dykes around Alexandria were breeched and as the sea poured in around the outside of the city our forces were able to put it under siege. Thus we had the French blocked in two places. On the side of the Turks surprisingly stood fifteen hundred Marmelukes which so shocked the French commander in Cairo he submitted to an immediate surrender—but when the French forces at Alexandria heard of this they declared they would fight to the last man for the honour of the Republic. Not so however. Seven days later they too surrendered.

It therefore is my most pleasant duty to inform your Lordship that the last French resistance in Egypt has come to an end, and the British Expedition under your supervision shall be recorded by history as a great military victory. Unfortunately I must add one note of sadness: General Abercrombie has died of wounds inflicted upon him during the assault at Aboukir Bay. Koehler too was lost but not in battle. He died of a severe contagion which is spreading rapidly over Egypt.

I expect to reach Constantinople within two fortnights,

depending of course on favourable sea passage. If I am
forced to travel by land it may require longer.

> Believe me to be,
> Your obliged servant,
> Joseph Dacre Carlyle

For seven days and nights Constantinople was insane
with joy. There were firework displays, music, dancing in the
streets, and endless cannon volleys. In the harbor, Turkish
warships reenacted scenes from the triumph at Aboukir Bay
and Elgin joined in by hiring a special ship over which a
gigantic star and crescent were to be hung, but the celebra-
tions had brought about a complete sale of all lamps in the
city and he was forced to cancel his plans. Lady Elgin accompanied him to Seraglio Point on the first night of the celebra-
tions. It was raining, but this did not deter the Turks from
proceeding with the festivities. The fireworks did not go off
well. The man in charge was immediately replaced by
another whose luck was more fortunate, since by this time
the storm clouds had vanished and the Turkish sky gave
birth to a new full moon and millions of stars which of course
the Turks took as a good omen from Allah. Young girls in
masquerade danced before Elgin in long lines, shouting
gleefully: *"Elkin! Elkin!"* while both sides of the Bosphorus
reverberated from the steady blast of rockets, guns, and cannons. Lady Elgin had to suppress a laugh: "Indeed, the
Turks might have conquered Egypt without Elgin's help had
they but fired half the number of cannons in earnest that
they were now firing in joke!"

The next morning the Elgins were taken by the Sultan's
carriage and conveyed into the gardens of the Seraglio
where Elgin was accorded the highest honors of the Porte.
The Sultan personally presented him with an Aigrette from
his turban; also with the Order of the Crescent which was set
in diamonds, a full-length pelisse* and a superbly caparisoned horse. Lady Elgin too was granted an unprecedented

---

* A fur cloak bestowed by the Turks as a special mark of favor.

honor: "She was carried in a gold chair by an escort of black eunuchs and brought to the Valida, the Sultan's mother." From there they all went to the Greek Kiosk of the Seraglio where the Sultan showed his face to the people. The Moslem priests immediately touched off the cry: *"Selim the Conqueror!"* and every Turkish woman in the throng responded by loudly wishing him a son.

Later in the afternoon while Elgin conferred with the Turkish Ministers Lady Elgin was rowed about Seraglio Point as the Sultan watched from under his canopy on shore. When the gondola pulled up alongside the Sultan, he made no acknowledgment, but as soon as it glided away Lady Elgin glanced back and caught him peering at her through his telescope. She also noticed the Sultanas waving from the window of the harem under the vigilant eyes of the black eunuchs in the garden below.

At dinner that night Elgin reported that they were not the only ones to benefit from the sudden love of the Turks. "All British warships were to be granted free provisions and immediate refitting privileges in any Turkish port; and each English officer who took part in the Egyptian campaign (eighteen hundred in all) was to be given a gold medal and a pelisse." Finding the Turks in this benevolent mood, Elgin persuaded them to release all French subjects imprisoned in any part of the Ottoman Empire, impressing upon them that it was contrary to the customs of civilized nations to imprison civilians. He also made another request. From the time of his arrival at Constantinople he and his embassy were obliged to use a deplorable building. A new structure was necessary and the Turks surprisingly agreed, bestowing upon him a site of land not too distant from the Seraglio. Wasting no time, Elgin commissioned an architect to begin work on a design for a house that would closely resemble his beloved Broomhall in Scotland.

The final concession from the Turks was totally unexpected: the release of all Maltese slaves who for centuries had been subjugated and maltreated by the Porte while confined in chains at the prison of Bagnio. These expressions of gratitude from the Turks vaulted Elgin to a high pinnacle of diplomatic stature which was crowned a month later by an official letter of commendation from the Government: "His Majesty is well pleased. All aims of your embassy have been achieved and Britain is once again the dominant power in the Eastern Mediterranean." The message bore the signature of a new Foreign Secretary: *Lord Hawksbury.*

Before retiring that night Elgin sat down and wrote a lengthy response, titling it: "Memorial to the King," and recording a complete account of his career to date in which he listed his many successes and the enormous personal expenses he had already incurred in order to finance the Egyptian campaign. He closed with a straightforward request for a mark of Royal favor, a knighthood perhaps or a United Kingdom peerage which would save him the trouble of being elected to the House of Lords as a Scottish peer.

It was denied.

Meanwhile Lady Elgin was nostalgic for Scotland and kept begging her husband to quit the embassy. Throughout these hectic two years she had grown tired of diplomatic life, its stiff demands, the endless receptions, being nice to those whom she detested, listening to foolish Turkish gossip, feeding an army of people day after day. But Elgin would not hear of it. He had no desire to see Scotland until his real work at Athens was completed, and "thus he remained at his desk that same night and wrote a second letter—this one to Lusieri, commanding him to press the artists into more diligent efforts and to show concrete results immediately."

Shortly after Carlyle returned to Constantinople he requested permission to leave the embassy and go back to England. He had in his possession several dozen manuscripts which he borrowed from the monastery of St. Saba near Jerusalem and also from the library of the Jerusalem Patriarch at Constantinople. In addition to these he had purchased several hundred Arabic manuscripts from private sources and from open bazaars in various parts of Egypt and Palestine. He was a bitterly disappointed man. His only reason for joining the embassy had never been realized. Far worse, he had ruined his health and spent most of his money. At times Elgin's frugality was too much to bear, but Carlyle was not one to make trouble. On the day of his departure he asked Elgin for firmans and letters of introduction which would at least authorize him to visit more monasteries in Greece before journeying back to England. The Elgins were sorry to see him leave. He had lent an air of cheerfulness to the embassy, and Lady Elgin in particular would miss his poetry.

The household was mired in gloom for days and although Dr. Scott tried his best to perk things up, he was a poor substitute for Carlyle. In the thickest moment of their dejection good news came from Lusieri:

My dear Lord:

From the day of our arrival in Athens which was a long time ago we have been under the continuous protection of Mr. Logothetis (the British Consul in Athens) with whose assistance we daily pay our respects, along with the usual gifts, to the Turkish authorities.

As your Lordship requested, it will be of interest to know that Athens remains a shabby and miserable town. It is inhabited by a mixed population from every part of the world and its dwellings are confined to the northeast slopes of the Acropolis Hill. At least half of the residents here are Greeks, a quarter Turks . . . and the rest Albanians, Jews, and Negroes. Mr. Logothetis tells us that there are no more than thirteen hundred dwellings in all. Around the city stands a wall ten feet high which was built about ten years ago for two reasons: to keep roving bands of pirates away, and to make the taxes of the enclosed inhabitants easier to collect. Not one of the houses is well-built or commodious and the streets here are all narrow and irregular.

We have found the Turkish inhabitants in Athens of a more amiable disposition than those of Constantinople. No doubt they feel the happy influence of a more acceptable climate which causes them to lose their ferocity. Of the Greeks, I give a far less favourable report. Their character does not rank high amongst the rest of their countrymen in the mainland; nor in the Isles of the Aegean. A proverb circulates daily around the city: *As bad as the Turks of Negroponte, the Jews of Salonica, and the Greeks of Athens!*

As your Lordship requested, I now submit a report on the government of Athens: since the middle of the 17th century the most powerful man here has been the chief officer of the Sultan's black eunuchs who is called the Voivode. His top military aide is the Disdar who commands from his citadel on top of the Acropolis Hill, along with his garrison of soldiers. He alone has the authority to regulate the access of strangers to the Acropolis. Despite Mr. Logothetis' unceasing efforts we have each been forced to pay the Disdar the monstrous sum of five guineas per day. In addition to this we are subjected to constant insult, interruption, and extortion from his soldiers—and even from his young son. However through the intervention of Mr. Logothetis, the Voivode was summoned and the Consul demanded that all Englishmen be allowed to visit the Acropolis Hill at any time without interference, then forthwith Mr. Logothetis substantiated our complaints to the Voivode who turned to the Disdar's son and ordered him at once to be sent into exile. He had compassion for the old Disdar, since the man is ill and at the point of death. Here Rev. Hunt* interceded and obtained a pardon for the Disdar's son but only on the condition that if another such complaint occurred the young Turk would be sent immediately to the galleys as a slave.

The meeting ended with promises from the Voivode that the Acropolis Hill would be open to all Englishmen from sunrise to dusk and that your Lordship's artists should have access to all facilities without payment of any fee or bribe. Rev. Hunt then presented the Voivode with brilliant cut-glass lustres and firearms, after which he asked the Voivode for an official firman, whose complete context I now submit to your Lordship:

---

* Hunt had accompanied Carlyle on a tour of the monasteries at Mt. Athos, and as a result was in Greece at this time.

FIRMAN

It is hereby signified to you that our sincere friend, his Excellency Lord Elgin, Ambassador Extraordinary from the Court of England to the Porte of Happiness, has represented to us that he is anxious to read and investigate the books, sculptures, and other works of ancient Greek science and philosophy—and has therefore engaged five painters now dwelling in Athens to examine, view, and also to copy the above works remaining here; also to freely go in and out of the citadel of the said city and fix scaffolding around the ancient Temple of the Idols, to model the said ornaments and visible figures in plaster or gypsum, to measure the remains of other ruined buildings, and to excavate where necessary in order to discover inscriptions which may have been hidden in the ruins. Under penalty of death, no interruption shall be given them; nor obstacles put in their way by the Disdar or any other person.

Signed with a signet,
Seged Abdullah Kaimmacam

It was a stroke of luck to have Hunt present in Athens. Normally Elgin would have dispatched one of his secretaries to assist Carlyle in his search for ancient manuscripts, but Hamilton was in Egypt* and Morier in England. From the day of Egypt's capitulation, the French fleet lay at Toulon and was a constant reminder of Bonaparte's intention to invade Greece. On advice of his government, Elgin was forewarned to send someone into Greece for the purpose "of visiting all the Pashas in the country and impressing upon

---

* Hamilton was a busy man in Egypt. He acted as Lord Elgin's correspondent and representative with the Expeditionary Force and gained distinction by the part he took in the negotiations for the capitulation of Alexandria. His efforts were crowned by the acquisition of the Rosetta stone. Tradition has it that Hamilton rowed out with a small escort to recover the stone from a fever-stricken French ship where it was concealed. Hamilton was accompanied by Edward Daniel Clarke and his pupil, John Marten Cripps. Hidden with the Rosetta stone, in the hold of the ship, half filled with filth, and covered with the rags of the sick people on board, was also a large sarcophagus which Clarke mistakenly called the Tomb of Alexander. It turned out to be the sarcophagus of Nekht-Hezu-Hebt, the first King of the Thirtieth Dynasty. (A. H. Smith, *Lord Elgin and his Collection*, p. 221.)

them the mistake of entering into any negotiations with the French." Whoever was sent also had to file a complete report on their military strength and make adequate preparations for the reception of a garrison of British troops. Hunt was just the man.

To protect the project at Athens from further Turkish intrigue, Hunt armed himself with a sufficient number of documents from the Porte. Along with these, he also brought a full supply of gifts for the Voivode and his staff of officers: chandeliers, firearms, telescopes, jewelry, and endless rolls of fine silk and damask. He did not remain long in Athens. It was urgent that he continue on his diplomatic tour of the country in the hope of strengthening British ties with the local Pashas. At Ionnina in northern Greece he carved a strong friendship with Ali Pasha and got the Turk's promise to send Elgin whatever antiquities he found in all the provinces under his jurisdiction. Ali Pasha had observed certain statues which "only seemed to want breath" to make them real. At Thebes Hunt paid an exhorbitant price to a peasant for an exceptional cameo of a female centaur suckling her infant. Writing from Olympia, he recommended that Elgin should think seriously about embarking upon a definite program of excavations and even suggested the removal of the Lion Gate from Mycenae. He rescinded after realizing that Mycenae presented transportation problems since it was too far from the sea.

During Hunt's absence from Athens Elgin made arrangements with one of the survivors of Koehler's mission, Captain Thomas Lacy of the Royal Engineers, to act as supervisor of the Acropolis project. Lacy was not enthusiastic over this appointment yet he was anxious to free himself from Egypt and the three frustrating years he spent under Koehler. Two days before embarking for Athens, he wrote a sour letter to Hunt: "Congratulate me, for I have at length found means to escape from the Mission and shall now be at leisure to devote myself to my friends. I embark for Athens:

to plunder temples and commit sacrilege. A proper finish to my diplomatic career!"

Throughout his brief stay in Athens Lacy quarreled continually with Lusieri and eventually severed himself from the scene. For the moment Elgin was happy to hear of this; nevertheless, someone was still needed to supervise the artists. Deep down Elgin distrusted Lusieri and suspected that he was consorting with the French agent in Athens, Louis François-Sébastien Fauvel. Although Fauvel had been a political prisoner when the artists first arrived at Athens his influence remained sharply present and within days the Calmuck was accused of concealing drawings and measurements so that he could sell them to Fauvel. Fearing that Fauvel might undermine the whole project, Elgin quickly arranged to have him transferred to Constantinople but even in Fauvel's absence the French managed to slow down the work of the artists: A French doctor cut off the water supply to Lusieri's workshop and thus prevented the washing of the antiquities. This same doctor "made every effort to stop all acquisitions by sowing foolish ideas in the weak minds of the Turks."

But these obstructions did not deter Elgin from his zeal, and he was now more determined than ever to preserve his great moment in Athens. After a long and dreary winter, during which his rheumatism flared up once again, he received encouraging news from Hunt: the firman issued by the Kaimmacam Pasha was now extended to cover a limitless endeavor, and like all official documents of the Porte, its text was so repetitious even the most ignorant of Turks could understand it:

> Under the penalty of death, no interruption shall be given His Excellency, Lord Elgin, nor to his painters who are engaged in fixing scaffolds around the ancient Temple of the Idols. And in modelling the said ornaments, or in measuring the ruins of fallen temples, no obstacle shall be thrown in their way by the Voivode, the Cadi, or any other

officer of the Turkish army. No one shall meddle with the scaffolding or implements, and if the said painters wish to take away any pieces of stone with inscriptions or sculptures therein, no opposition shall be made.

In the above-mentioned manner, see that ye demean and comport yourselves.

Signed with a signet,
Seged Abdullah Kaimmacam

Elgin's spirits were immediately rejuvenated and at the outbreak of spring he decided to pay a visit to Athens and personally supervise his new plans. The thought of another sea voyage resurrected bitter memories for Lady Elgin, especially since she now had a second child. However she over-rode her husband's protest and insisted she make the trip even though she was pregnant for the third time. Before embarking she wrote a jubilant letter to her mother in Scotland:

> Travelling through this country (Greece) while Elgin's ambassadorial titles and pomp remain, is certainly a very great advantage and we mean to take a number of servants to cut a dash. Lord Bruce and Mary Christopher shall come with us and will be looked after by Masterman and Calitza (the Greek Paramana). Doctor Scott goes along with us also.

They left Constantinople in the middle of March, their ship a small brig bound for the Isle of Malta. Even while drifting through the calm waters of the Dardanelles Lady Elgin was overcome with nausea. At Scio (Chios) they encountered stormy winds and had to remain there for almost two weeks. With the first sign of good weather they continued on a swift course as far as Patmos Isle but here too another turbulence erupted, sweeping two crewmen overboard. There was much flooding below and Lady Elgin's bed with all her belongings was immersed in two feet of water.

Only after the brig sailed into sight of Mykonos Isle were the
crewmen successful in bailing out the cabins.

There was yet another delay on Mykonos Isle, and while
they waited for the storm to abate Lady Elgin again wrote to
her mother:

> Hunt is in raptures, for the firman is now perfection. It
> allows all our artists to go into the citadel, to copy and
> model everything in it, to erect scaffolds all round the
> Temple, to dig and discover all the ancient foundations,
> and to bring away any marbles that may be deemed curious
> by their having inscriptions on them, and that they are not
> to be disturbed by the soldiers etc. under any pretense
> whatever.

During their stay at Mykonos Isle Lady Elgin asked to
investigate the place, but the captain warned of pirates and
unfriendly surroundings. Lord Elgin intervened and persuaded the captain to grant them permission. Their party
included two crewmen, Doctor Scott, and Masterman whose
face had blanched at the mention of pirates. That first night
they found a deep cave just off the edge of the sea, and
Masterman prepared their beds. The crewmen then perched
themselves atop a commanding rock high above the cave and
kept a sharp watch for pirates. Meanwhile, Lady Elgin was
relieved that her children were safely on board the brig
under the care of the Paramana.

After Doctor Scott had lit a fire, Masterman brought out
some bread, cheese, and several bottles of wine which they
had obtained from Scio. Against the weird patterns of dancing light on the walls of the cave Doctor Scott talked about
the glories of Athens and especially the construction of the
Acropolis . . . how for one thousand years after she was built
every temple stood as perfect as from the first day. Romans
and Byzantines invaded the city and stripped every stone
—yet the temples of the Acropolis were left untouched. Even
Alaric the Goth showed reverence for these sacred buildings.

But then the destruction began, starting with the Christians. The initial blow was struck when Constantine proclaimed Christianity the official religion of the Empire. Overzealous Christian priests destroyed the east end of the Parthenon to make room for an apse; they also knocked holes in the sides for windows. The Erechtheum was next to suffer, its whole interior torn out and converted into a church. To show their contempt for graven images, these same priests defaced almost every metope and sculpture on the Acropolis.

Another thousand years saw an endless line of conquerors: Franks, Catalans, Navarrese, Florentines, Venetians. Despite these invasions the buildings on the Acropolis miraculously survived until Greece fell to the Turks in 1453. The Parthenon was converted into a mosque and the Erechtheum turned into a harem for the military governor. When war broke out with the Venetians, the Turks used the Propylaea as a gun-powder magazine. In 1645 it was struck by lightning and exploded. The little temple of Athena Nike was then deliberately destroyed by the Turks in order to clear the bastion for a key artillery position. On the 26th day of September, 1687, the Venetians (under General Morosini) laid siege to the Acropolis and one of their cannons made a direct hit on the Parthenon. The roof was blown off, leaving a gaping hole between the long colonnades on both sides. Most of the sculptures were destroyed; and the same blast damaged the Erechtheum.

When Morosini finally evacuated Athens he left the Acropolis in shambles. Word soon circulated around the world, and travelers came flocking to Athens to view her wounded glory. These noble gentlemen then proceeded to pick away at her remains and bring them back into their countries to adorn their estates. When the Turks saw this they wounded her even more, deliberately knocking off heads, arms, legs, noses, and fingers from statues and selling them to eager travelers whose only pride in life was the boastful possession of the authentic remains from the great hand of Phidias.

Lord Elgin was annoyed by Doctor Scott's words, but he stifled his anger. Lady Elgin meanwhile had already fallen into a deep slumber, and Masterman was fretfully pulling a blanket over her shoulders.

Chapter
Three

Greece

THE ELGINS WERE deeply moved by their first view of the Acropolis Hill. The immaculate columns of the Parthenon seemed to reach toward the Grecian sun, their hands splattered with golden eternity as thousands of stones and small chunks of marble worshipped at their feet.

Turkish soldiers were everywhere, their tents pitched at random in the most sacred places while tradesmen of all description sifted through the dense crowd, selling coffee and merchandise. Even the lowest soldier had a servant, a groom, a youthful water-carrier, a cook, and someone to pitch and strike his tent. The place was a turmoil. At the northernmost corner of the Acropolis Hill steady volleys of practice rounds from young recruits resounded against the peaceful Attic sky. In front of each tent Janissaries had hung copper kettles with skimmer and ladle, but not for cooking purposes. Always attended by a guard, these cauldrons were held sacred by the Turks and believed to be their only protection from insidious defeat.

When the Elgin party mounted the last steps of the Propylaea they came upon Lusieri sketching under an umbrella along the west side of the Parthenon. A high scaffold rested against the wall. On it stood two men; one was a humpback. He seemed quite agile on the scaffold and was not afraid to climb to its highest point. The formatori and draughtsmen were busy inside the sanctuary.

In broken Greek, Lusieri informed Lord Elgin that he and his artists had encountered added difficulties. Even with the Kaimmacam's firman in their hand the Disdar had refused to allow them on the Acropolis Hill, claiming the only reason "the artists had built the scaffolds was to look down into the tents of the Harem and spy upon their women." The British Consul Logothetis again came to their rescue and promised to issue the Disdar another firman. In the meantime the artists were forced to work on other sites in various parts of Athens: the Theseum, the Agora, the Stoa of Attalus, and the ancient cemetery of Ceramicus. But here too they confronted problems: there was not one piece of lumber to be found in Athens for more scaffolding; nor ropes to lift their materials. Eventually Lusieri had to arrange for a caique to set sail for Hydra Isle and bring back the necessary lumber. As for the ropes, they had Fauvel to thank.

Fauvel had established himself as Bonaparte's antiquarian agent in Athens when French relationships with Turkey were at their highest. In time he had the run of the place and got anything he requested: statues from every temple in the city, metopes, friezes, vases and jewelry. These were collected and sent to France to be stored in the Louvre under Bonaparte's personal supervision. When Fauvel was driven to demand the sculptures of the Parthenon, the Turks refused. Undaunted, he then bribed the old Disdar and managed to obtain an excellent frieze; also a large metope which was buried in ruins not far from the Parthenon. Later he got his hands on still another metope that had fallen from the Parthenon during a storm. These and more. He shipped everything back to France until suddenly his patron lost favor with the Revolutionaries. Bonaparte allowed Fauvel to remain in Athens with all his equipment, but when Turkey declared war on France after Bonaparte's invasion of Egypt, Fauvel was one of the first to be taken prisoner. Hearing about Fauvel's excellent equipment, Lusieri made an offer to the Disdar which the Turk readily accepted, "giving everything to Lusieri, and especially the large wooden cart that Fauvel used to transport his heavy materials."

The heat of the day still lingered in the deep bowl of Athens when the Elgins came down from the Acropolis Hill. They walked through the Agora then proceeded into a narrow dirt street that was cluttered with squalid houses and adjoining hen-roosts. Small kiosks were everywhere, each raised upon four poles and covered with a thatched roof. Mixed among this filth and disorder were superb buildings of granite and marble.

The Elgins resided with the British Consul Logothetis during their stay in Athens. Lusieri and his artists were also lodged there. It was a dramatic moment when Lusieri and his crew came into the house after a hard day's work on the Acropolis Hill. But Lord Elgin never joined in with their fun and merriment; nor was he satisfied with their efforts. He kept urging Lusieri toward new assignments and projects: "I should wish to have of the Acropolis examples in the actual size of each architectural ornament, each cornice, frieze, fluted column, metope and statue; also specimens of the decorated ceilings and the various architectural orders. I want you to embark at once upon a program of assiduous excavation. History assures me that there are riches of all description in such abundance that this dig is deserving of any labour that can be made under your direction!"

When Lusieri reminded Elgin of the Disdar's interference, Lady Elgin entered the fray. In an obvious attempt to please her husband, she instructed Don Tita "to put about a rumor that Elgin had a new set of powerful firmans which should settle any lingering doubts about the legality of all excavations and removals."

Greece had long been a trouble spot for the Ottoman Empire. Already there were sporadic outbreaks in the Morea,* and there was increased talk of actual revolution. For centuries the Turks had inflicted countless cruelties

* The Peloponnesus.

upon the Greeks: Christian worship in public was forbidden, children were compelled to learn their Greek letters in caves, girls were taken at an early age and put into harems. But after four hundred years of subjugation the time seemed ripe for the expulsion of all Turks from Greek soil.

This was the chief topic of conversation at the British Consul's house during dinner. Occasionally the Calmuck would interrupt with boisterous jabs at Lusieri, chiding Don Tita for being such a slow painter he often had to rub out part of a view because in the interim the growth of trees and alterations to buildings had made the drawing out of date and inaccurate.

Lusieri retaliated by saying the only way he could get the Calmuck to work was by a constant administration of wine. Nevertheless, the Calmuck had great talent and, like Lusieri, was dedicated to detail which pleased Lord Elgin. "It was an easy task to draw sculptures in a state of decay but the Calmuck had the gift of restoring them to their original beauty with one stroke of his brush."

Throughout all these events Hunt was still on his extended tour of Greece and kept sending a steady flow of letters to Elgin:

> I must relate to your Lordship the various excursions I have taken to the ancient cities of the Peloponnesus. But my pen is poor and cannot convey the true picture of Mycenae's glory: her massive walls, the two colossal lions in bas-relief over the main gate, the tomb of Agamemnon etc. etc. I found the door wide open and it grieves me to report that storms of rain have brought in piles of soil and debris, making the entrance difficult. It was impossible to ascertain the true dimensions of the building.
>
> Continuing my inspection of the Morea, I came at last to Patras. There is much beauty in Arcadia and Elia; also at Olympia. The real purpose of my trip however was not entirely consumed by artistic motives, since your Lordship instructed me to make note of all military positions in Greece. Conditions in the Peloponnesus are deplorable.

Turkish troops are five years in arrear with their pay and
there is a general lack of artillerymen, and of competent
instructors. At Nauplia the troops revolted upon more than
one occasion because of poor quarters and foul food.

Lord Elgin went daily to the Acropolis Hill to keep an eye
on the artists. His wife usually accompanied him. Lusieri
presented a comical picture under his constant umbrella and
was forever complaining about the laziness of the artists. But
Lord Elgin assured him that "his presence in Athens now
promised a success beyond his most ardent dreams, and even
ventured to add that his endeavours would one day reach the
same elevation as those of Phidias and Pericles."

Elgin was remarkably patient with his wife's limited
knowledge of ancient Greek art, and he took great pains to
explain everything he knew, flooding her mind with the
deeds of Cimon, Phidias, and Praxiteles. He would stand in
front of one frieze after another and bring it to life before
her eyes: Theseus freshly victorious over a centaur while
hordes of centaurs and Lapithae were embroiled in battle at
the nuptials of Pirithous. At one stage the Lapithae seemed
conquerors; at another, the centaurs. Elgin especially called
to her attention how utterly relaxed the muscles of one
Lapith were after being trampled to death by a centaur.

Within the inner chamber of the Parthenon Elgin would
next remark upon the magnificent finish of the statues. One
of the metopes portrayed a solemn procession during a festival. Many of the figures were on horseback; others just about
to mount; and finally came the foot soldiers. A herd of oxen
led the procession to the altar of sacrifice, while behind them
walked a line of nymphs carrying sacred offerings in baskets
and vases. These were followed by priests, magistrates and
warriors, all dressed in costumes and armor.

Another metope inside the main entrance of the temple
related the history of Athena's birth from the brain of Zeus
as he sat on a throne surrounded by the gods of Olympus. In
loose-fitting robes, the goddess held the horses of the chariot

which introduced her to Olympus—but unlike other statues, she was here represented with the captivating beauty of Venus and the invincible armor of the Spartans. On a third metope there was portrayed a contest between Athena and Poseidon: a fierce struggle from which a name for the city would result. Athena gained the victory by proving that her gift of a peaceful olive branch was more worthy than the warlike offering of the god of oceans: a wild-looking horse whose eyes seemed to reflect every cruel deed imposed upon mankind.

It was impossible to conceive how the marbles were wrought to such depth; each column was so united without the aid of mortar as to make the shafts look like single blocks even to the most scrutinizing eye; the hair of each figure braided in a different manner, with robes so delicate and flowing they actually appeared to move with the breeze. Yet this was only a small portion of what the Acropolis once contained when Plutarch first beheld it: "All the public buildings and temples raised in Rome from the founding of the city to the age of the Caesars cannot be put in competition with the edifices erected on the Acropolis Hill during the brief administration of Pericles!"

Heliodorus wrote so minute a description of each structure on the Acropolis Hill it took up fifteen books, and even after the plunders of Lysander, Sylla, and Nero, there were more than three thousand statues still remaining. All this gave Elgin added reason to persist with his plans "to measure each temple, make elevations and views with the utmost accuracy, mould every block of marble, statue, ornament and inscription." It was an enormous task, and although the amount of work produced thus far by Lusieri and the artists seemed pitifully small, Elgin was determined to carry it through to the end.

Just when the artists had again begun to move forward with a degree of speed and accomplishment, work was halted once more by the Disdar who brazenly ignored the Kaimmacam's warning and demanded five guineas a day from each artist, otherwise no one would be allowed to set foot on the Acropolis Hill. Elgin became incensed and instantly dispatched a message to the Sultan in Constantinople. While he waited for the Turk's reply, Elgin assigned the artists to periodic visits into the city below where they made sketches and drawings of ancient but less important sites. Weeks went by without a word from the Sultan. The Consul succeeded in convincing Elgin that they should all take a holiday: a journey to Delphi and Thermopylae. Upon their return to Athens two weeks later, Elgin expressed a further desire to visit Epidaurus and Tripoli, but Logothetis did not think this wise since there was a constant threat of revolt in that part of the country. However Elgin was not to be dissuaded.

They sailed from the Piraeus on a warm morning in April taking passage on an old Greek brig. Throughout the first day the sea was unruffled and they coasted leisurely along the jagged eastern cliffs of the Peloponnesus. The place was volcanic and its wild mountain peaks were still crowned with patches of snow, but along the massive slopes olive trees were already changing color. Fields of poppies had started to bloom. Approaching the Gulf of Argus, they were immediately surrounded by a rich growth of trees and vineyards; and in the western horizon the summits of Maenalus became plainly visible.

Within a half-hour the brig skirted around the slender promontory and dropped anchor inside the small port of Nauplia. The Elgins found a striking change in the style of dress and the manner of speech among the inhabitants. And yet the Nauplians were conspicuously Greek which was evident from the way they walked, the movement of their arms in conversation, the look in their eyes as they sipped coffee in outdoor taverns.

After a light meal the Consul took them to an old gray fortress on the summit of a high hill overlooking the city. He explained there were many such Venetian fortifications in the Peloponnesus and particularly Mani* which the Turks used for garrison posts. Any movement by land or sea could be easily detected from these advantageous positions. On a sparkling white beach, just a short distance from the fortress, were the ruins of a Byzantine church. Logothetis claimed that it stood on the identical site of an oracular temple to Ceres.† A strange festival was annually celebrated there: a mingling of ancient Greek rite with Christian ceremony. A steer was taken from the fields and brought into the town where it was adorned with garlands of flowers and a wreath of laurel. From there it was led through the streets to the church. Hymns of Apollo were sung and finally the sacrifice was made, the death blow being delivered by the Greek Orthodox priest of the town. Hymns to the Virgin were then chanted, after which the inhabitants made a fervent dash to the altar and soaked their handkerchiefs in the blood, believing it to possess miraculous power.

As soon as they returned to the brig, Lord Elgin suggested they move deeper into the Morea, but the captain grimly reported that a full-scale revolt had broken out in Tripoli, and for once the Greeks had agreed upon a leader: Theodoros Kolokotronis.**

With the first breath of May, Athens took on a new countenance. Houses were whitened, birds sang, the olive leaves glistened, the church bells announced the long-awaited Resurrection of Christ.

In the early hours of Easter morning the Elgins climbed with Logothetis and his family to the Byzantine chapel on the summit of Mount Lycabettus. They joined the noisy procession of priests and worshippers, circling thrice around the church and carrying lit tapers as the bishops chanted: *He is Risen! Christ is truly Risen!* Soon cannon fire was heard from

* The southernmost peninsular of the Peloponnesus.
  † It was an easy matter to transfer religious veneration from goddess to saint in Greece.
  ** A hero of the Greek Revolution.

the distant hills. Cocks began to crow; dogs howled; and eventually the sun's fingers grasped the eastern horizon.

Later that afternoon they all gathered in the parlor of the Consul's house where they were served red eggs and wine. In the ensuing contest, Lady Elgin was proclaimed the egg-cracking champion of Athens by an exuberant Logothetis. The Elgins then joined in with the singing of the Easter hymns which the Greek Paramana had so painstakingly taught them in Constantinople. A huge roasted lamb was at last placed on the table, but first Logothetis offered a toast.

The Easter festivities at the Consul's house continued far into the night. Lady Elgin was late in arising the next morning. A breakfast of fried chicken livers and eggs was prepared, but they were immersed in olive oil and Lady Elgin hardly touched them. In the meantime Madame Logothetis made gossipy inquiries about the social life of Constantinople, the parties, receptions, teas, the costumes of the Turkish women, their jewelry and mode of hair.

When Lady Elgin finally arrived on the Acropolis Hill she saw scores of new scaffolds propped up against the east pediment of the Parthenon. Dozens of workmen labored with ropes and pulleys while many others struggled with windlasses and long wooden beams. On the scaffolds more men were pounding chisels into a large metope which ran between the triglyphs. Within moments the metope was pulled free and hoisted into the air. The magnificent cornice that adorned it was suddenly weakened and it fell to the ground in a thousand pieces, leaving an awesome hole between its columns.

An eye-witness to the destruction on the Parthenon was the ever-present Edward Daniel Clarke:

> Some workmen, employed under Lusieri's direction, were then engaged in making preparation, by means of ropes and pulleys, for taking down the metopes, where the sculptures remained the most perfect. The Disdar himself came to view the work but with evident marks of dissatisfac-

tion; and Lusieri told us that it was with great difficulty he could accomplish this part of his undertaking from the attachment the Turks entertained towards a building which they had been accustomed to regard with religious veneration and had converted into a mosque. We confessed that we participated the Mahometan feeling in this instance and would gladly see an order enforced to preserve rather than destroy such a glorious edifice.

After a short time spent in examining the several parts of the temple one of the workmen came to inform Don Battista that they were then going to lower one of the metopes. We saw this fine piece of sculpture raised from its station between the triglyphs: but the workmen endeavouring to give it a position adapted to the projected line of descent, a part of the adjoining masonry was loosened by the machinery; and down came the fine masses of Pentelican marble, scattering their white fragments with thundering noise among the ruins. The Disdar, seeing this, could no longer restrain his emotions; but actually took his pipe from his mouth, and letting fall a tear, said in a most emphatic tone of voice: *"TELOS!"** positively declaring that nothing should induce him to consent to any further dilapidations of the building. Looking up, we saw with regret the gap that had been made; which all the ambassadors of the earth—with all the sovereigns they represent aided by every resource that wealth and talent can now bestow—will never again repair.

Another witness was the traveler Edward Dodwell:

During my first tour to Greece I had the inexpressible mortification of being present when the Parthenon was despoiled of its finest sculptures, and when some of its architectural members were thrown to the ground. I saw several metopae at the south-east extremity of the temple taken down. They were fixed in between the triglyphs as in a groove; and in order to lift them up, it was necessary to throw to the ground the cornice by which they were cov-

* "The end!" (Greek)

ered. The south-east angle of the pediment shared the same fate; and instead of the picturesque beauty and high preservation in which I first saw it, it is now comparatively reduced to a state of shattered desolation.

The Kaimmacam's firman did not permit Lord Elgin to remove the sculptures and friezes from the Parthenon, but Hunt gave it another interpretation. After his long diplomatic tour of Greece, Hunt returned to Athens and called upon the Voivode, requesting permission to take down the best metopes from the Parthenon. The British Consul Logothetis was present at the meeting and voiced a timid objection, both as a Greek and an Archon of Athens. Hunt curtly reminded him that a Consul should not oppose the wishes of an Ambassador, then, turning once again on the Voivode, insisted that the original firman gave the right to remove sculptures and friezes from the buildings of the Acropolis Hill. Hunt strengthened his case with a "judicious mixture of threats and bribes," and the Voivode finally granted his permission.

When Lord Elgin was in Constantinople, Edward Daniel Clarke visited him. Clarke had just completed a tour to Egypt where he claimed to have found the sarcophagus containing the tomb of Alexander the Great. However his judgment proved to be false, as it was with several other "discoveries," particularly that of a small marble relief which he found at the foot of the Acropolis Hill. Clarke pronounced it to be the certain work of Phidias, but it turned out to be "a coarsely-carved piece of an old gravestone."

A few months later at Eleusis, Clarke achieved a remarkable success: the discovery of an enormous and battered statue weighing two tons and representing a woman with a basket on her head. A traveler who visited Eleusis in 1765 had reported that "this was the site of a shrine to Demeter, the goddess of corn and fertility." He found the inhabitants mired in superstition, fearing that the fertility of their land depended so much on this statue they even lit tapers and votive lamps before it on certain Christian feast days. At the time of Clarke's arrival travelers were warned that "the arm of any person would fall off if he touched the statue with violence." But Clarke (who was now denouncing Lord Elgin for his pillage on the Acropolis Hill) had already made up his mind to take it. However he had to move swiftly and secretly in order to gain the victory over another competitor, the Comte de Choiseul-Gouffier:

> I found the goddess in a dunghill buried to her ears. The Eleusinian peasants, at the very mention of moving it, regarded me as one who would bring the moon from her orbit. *What would become of their corn,* they said, *if the old lady with her basket was removed?* I went to Athens and made application to the Pasha, aiding my request by letting an English telescope glide between my fingers. The business was done.

Clarke was soon confronted with more obstacles: ropes and pulleys had to be obtained; and the jetty at Eleusis needed repairs. On the night before the statue was to be removed an ox broke loose from its yoke and began butting the statue violently with its horns. *A bad omen!* It then ran amuck over the plain of Eleusis, bellowing into the night. At daybreak the peasants accosted the Turkish officer who had proclaimed the firman and a riot resulted. Calm was subsequently restored and the peasants reluctantly agreed to obey the Voivode's command. The village priest then put on his vestments and began clearing away the rubbish from around the statue. At this point Clarke stepped brazenly forward and put both hands on the old lady. Contrary to the ancient fears of the Eleusinians his arms did not fall off, and after long hours of tedious work, a crew of one hundred men and fifty boys at last managed to haul the huge statue out of the village, all the way to the shore where it was loaded into a ship that Clarke had chartered for England.*

Logothetis, who had remained subdued throughout most of the evening, waited until Lord Elgin had finished with his recollection of Clarke's activity at Eleusis and then interjected that the statue should not have been taken. Clarke had no legal authority.

Elgin became defiant and retorted: "All Greeks were peasants. They did not deserve such wonderful works of antiquity and even considered them worthless. It was his divine calling to preserve these treasures unto all ages!"

The next morning Elgin went off in search of more antiquities at Delphi. Before leaving, he had instructed his wife to go to the Piraeus and persuade Captain Hoste of HMS *Mutine* to take on board all the marbles that were lying on the docks. It was a huge shipment and Captain Hoste had already informed Elgin that it would be impossible to take it all. But Lady Elgin used her charms and convinced Captain Hoste. The following day she wrote to her husband:

> I began by saying as the Captain was going straight to Malta, and there being no Enemies to encounter, I ventured to propose his taking them. It would be doing me a very great favour as you were extremely anxious to get them off. Female eloquence as usual succeeded. The Capt. sent me a very polite answer and by peep of Day I send down the three cases.

Lady Elgin came to the Piraeus docks the next morning and in addition to the three cases finally was able to persuade Captain Hoste to take the rest of the marbles. This was accomplished only through her further allurement and with gifts of money for all the crewmen.

* This statue, which no doubt had been worshiped longer than any other in the world, now stands in a corner of the Fitzwilliam Museum at Cambridge. (St. Clair, pp. 106 ff.)

In hopes that I shall be the first to tell you what I have done, know that besides the 5 cases I have already told you of, I have prevaled on Capt. Hoste to take three more, two are already on board and the third will be taken when he returns from Corinth. How I have faged* to get all this done, do you love me better for it, Elgin? And how I have pushed Lusieri to get cases made for these large packages! I beg you shew delight. Lay aside the Diplomatic Character to Capt. Hoste for taking so much on board. I am now satisfied of what I always thought: which is how much more Women can do if they set about it than Men. I will lay any bet had you been here you would not have got half so much on board as I have. As for getting things you wished down from the Acropolis it is quite impossible before you return. Lusieri says, upon his first coming here, he was against the things being taken down but now he is keener than anybody and absolutely wishes you to have the whole Temple of the Carisomething† where the Statues of the Women are.

During the strenuous weeks that followed, Lord Elgin pulled down every important sculpture and frieze from the Parthenon. After the marbles were crated for shipment to England he lashed out at Lusieri, warning him to spare no effort or money toward further acquisitions from all the ancient sites in the neighborhood of Athens. Here Hunt joined in and suggested that the entire Erechtheum could be removed and rebuilt later in England: "If a large Man of War would come here that beautiful little model of ancient art might be transported wholly to England."

True to his nature, Lord Elgin became obsessed with the idea and wrote immediately to Lord Keith, the Commander-in-Chief of naval forces in the Mediterranean:

I have been at a monstrous expense at Athens where I at this moment possess advantages beyond belief. Now if

---

* Lady Elgin should have spelled it "fagged" (exhausted myself).
† The Caryatids of the Erechtheum.

you would allow a ship of war of size to convoy the Commissary's ship and stop a couple of days at Athens to get away a most valuable piece of architecture at my disposal there, you could confer upon me the greatest obligation I could receive and do a very essential service to the Arts in England. Bonaparte has not got such a thing from all his thefts in Italy. Pray kindly attend to this my Lord.

With driving passion, Elgin decided to extend his hand far beyond Athens. Taking Lady Elgin and a crew of workers with him, he went first to Mycenae. Lusieri was left behind with the Calmuck and Ittar the humpback for the purpose of launching a search through every monastery in and around Athens. Elgin further commanded that any artists who could be spared from the Acropolis Hill were to be sent immediately to the Peloponnesus, and chiefly Olympia.

Mycenae's ruins so impressed Lord Elgin he ordered his crew to begin excavations at once and the results surpassed all expectations.

The Elgin visit to Tripoli was unforgettable:

Having received the most pressing and repeated invitations from the Pasha of the Morea, we set off toward Tripoli in the company of the Chiauves* and a very numerous Turkish escort, as well as an Albanian guard in the dress of the ancient Macedonians.

That evening the Elgin party halted at a small village called Aklatho-Cambo. Its houses were merely mud huts covering the side of an almost perpendicular mountain that was interspersed with evergreens and wild pines. After walking among the rocks and groves, they were given lodgings in a poor Albanian hut. At the bottom of the hill, and through the middle of the village, ran a narrow rivulet which had dried up. They were told that the winter rains came down from the slopes in wild streams and inundated the valleys

* Turkish messengers.

below. Lord Elgin noticed "several uncommonly beautiful lassies in this village."

The next morning the inhabitants of Aklatho-Cambo, preceded by their priest and elders, came and entreated Lord Elgin to have the Pasha of the Morea repair their little church which was now too ruinous for the performance of divine worship. Although Elgin promised to comply with their request, he never carried it out.

Before setting out for Tripoli, they were joined by Tartars and other officers of the Pasha. Lady Elgin was placed inside a covered litter that was carried between two mules and guided by six men. The method by which she tried to get into the litter, or *Tarta-Van* as it was fondly called by the Turks, evoked much laughter. A man was summoned whom the Turks called "The Step." He prostrated himself on the ground and Lady Elgin stepped on his back to get into the conveyance. When they approached Tripoli the Tartars hinted it would be more appropriate for Lady Elgin to make her entrance on horseback.

A parade horse was then brought to her and she mounted it. They were eventually met by all the officers of the Pasha's court on chargers richly caparisoned and accompanied by pages and guards who played at the Dgerit.* At this time the Elgins were treated to equestrian feats. Many of the Turkish soldiers who had flung the Dgerit now rode back and picked it up without getting off their horses; others had sticks with hooks at the end by which they pulled up their Dgerits in the quickest manner. Their dexterity was incredible and the performance evoked a hearty cheer from Lord Elgin.

At last they came into the city. Lady Elgin did not imagine that Tripoli would ever see another procession like this: first

* A straight white stick somewhat thinner than that of an umbrella and crooked at the head. It was a sport not entirely without risk, since a blow on the temple could prove fatal. Lord Elgin was told that the Pasha once cut off the head of an officer who had hit him on the shoulder while playing a game. (*The Letters of Mary Nisbet*, p. 187.)

the Pasha, his officers, the Elgins, the pages and guards, the led horses with the most brilliant colors, the Lieutenant-Governor and the First Chamberlain riding in front of the Tartars, and a train of at least seven hundred Turkish soldiers on horseback. Lord Elgin was disappointed when he saw no Greek inhabitants on the streets; not one Greek face greeted them from a window or a door. Meanwhile great cannons from every fort around the walls of the city kept firing away as the First Chamberlain, from out of an embroidered box, started flinging coins into the empty street.

After the procession passed through the center of the city Lady Elgin glanced back and saw groups of bedraggled Greek children clawing for the coins in the dust-filled street. It was a sad sight, and it remained with her even after they had stopped at the house of the Dragoman* for an immense supper "dressed in the Turkish style."

During the Elgins' absence from Athens the Greek Consul Logothetis was given the unpleasant task of keeping a vigil on Lusieri and his artists. A French conspiracy was still feared, especially while the Parthenon marbles awaited shipment and were in plain sight on the Piraeus docks.

When Lord Elgin finally returned to Athens his wife was six months pregnant with her third child, and it was decided they should leave immediately for Constantinople. Elgin burdened Lusieri with still more instructions and in the middle of June they departed from the Piraeus on HMS *Narcissus*.

When the *Narcissus* sailed into the Aegean she called at many islands. Here too Elgin seized any antiquity he could lay his hands on. They stopped on the promontory of Sunium and visited the ruins on its summit. The Temple of Poseidon resembled that of Theseus in Athens, and although the walls had fallen down, shafts of light were pouring through the few columns that were still standing. Several bas-reliefs and ornaments of the frieze had also fallen and were so defaced Hunt could not identify them.

---

* An official interpreter of high rank.

From on board the *Narcissus* they later viewed the Isle of Helen, a barren stretch of rock that sought desperately to give nourishment to a small herd of goats grazing just off the shore. That afternoon they anchored in the harbor of Zea. Mounting donkeys, they then rode into the town over a precipitous road which wound itself around an almost impassable mountain. At times there hardly seemed enough space on the treacherous path for the donkeys to walk.

The town of Zea was situated on the summit of a sloping hill. Its houses were so flat the roofs often served as courtyards. The inhabitants were mostly of Venetian origin. That night the Elgin party was honored with dinner, music and dancing. Their host was Signor Pangali, the Neopolitan Consul. His nine daughters provided marvelous entertainment with their lively renditions of Greek, Italian, and French songs. They also danced minuets and Greek folk dances. Lady Elgin was fascinated by the dress of the women at Zea. Their petticoats only reached to the knee and their stockings were stuffed with cotton so as to make the leg appear more than twice its natural size.

Three days later the *Narcissus* came into sight of Marathon, and even from the ship the Elgins could plainly see the huge mound of Marathon's heroes. Early the next morning they went ashore and pitched a tent on the plain of Marathon. An ancient setting was provided for them when the sailors of the *Narcissus* surrounded the tent with pillars found scattered on the ground. After dinner they visited the mound and discovered it partly open as a result of Fauvel's excavations. Elgin ordered the ship's crew to dig at another site nearby and they unearthed many pieces of pottery, along with numerous articles of silver.

Elgin examined the plain with great care. He agreed with Hunt as to the site of the marshes where the Persians perished in their retreat. Not far from the mound rested the remains of a square building which Hunt identified as the Tomb of Miltiades. Elgin instructed the ship's crew to dig here too, and they found more antiquities. Human bones were also discovered. Near the marshes Hunt came upon the

Temple of Nemesis where the Athenians had placed her statue after seizing it from the fleeing Persians who had overconfidently brought it with them to erect as a memorial of their conquest over the Athenians.

On the first day of July the party landed on Tenos Isle, one of the most flourishing of the Archipelago. Because of contrary winds they had to remain here almost one week, residing in the house of the English Consul, Signor Antonio Vitali. One evening the Russian Consul, M. Vicenzo, gave them a ball and even made a transparency on translucent parchment of Lady Elgin's monogram.

When the stormy winds persisted, making it impossible to sail in an open boat, they were transported to Mykonos Isle in a Martigan, commanded by a French officer who had fled from Toulon. They arrived at Mykonos on a sad day. The Vice-Consul's daughter of seventeen had just died and the Elgins were immediately thrown into the curious ceremonies of a Mykonos death. Three or four times during the mourning period the relatives brought in a number of priests but prior to this a strange composition was created to resemble the dead girl. Prayers were read over it and then it was set on fire while the priests and relatives formed a circle around the flames, wailing over the charred object as though it were the actual body of the girl. Professional wailers were also brought in from a distant village to provoke those who had difficulty in shedding tears. Finally the ashes were collected and carried into the church in a solemn ritual.

The Elgins were happy to depart from this "Melancholy abode, and most barren and wretched island," sailing in the frigate as soon as the wind obliged them. At first sight of Delos Isle they spotted a Latine sail boat giving chase to a large English ship. The frigate fired on the intruder, and she ran off after putting out twenty-two oars. Captain Donnelly gave chase and got as near to the pirate ship as the heavy seas would allow, tacking and retacking, then firing more than three hundred shots at her. The pirates returned the salutation with volleys of musketry which struck the frigate's deck but did not kill or wound any of the crew. By this time the pirate galley was so severely damaged she finally sank. Captain Donnelly dispatched a party of Marines on shore to round up the escaping pirates. They were assisted by a boat filled with soldiers from Mykonos. Together they scoured the island in all directions, taking prisoner the captain of the pirates, Zachary by name, along with twenty-three of the crew. Zachary was a young man of twenty-six, of an open countenance and very bold, but by no means impudent. They confessed to be Maniot pirates but insisted that their only object was the prize and that they had never wantonly killed or even wounded anyone.

These distractions did not deter Lord Elgin from a thorough search of ancient Delos and also the opposite Isle of Rhenea. He found most of the temples demolished and flung over the ground; however, the base of Apollo's statue and part of his body still remained. The theater was in ruins, but the small pond used for sham naval battles was remarkably preserved. Rhenea possessed many beautiful marble altars, one of which Elgin confiscated and brought on board. It was perfectly round and ornamented with festoons of fruit and flowers.

From Delos they sailed to Paros Isle where they stopped to afford Lady Elgin some rest because she had been tossed by the sea from the moment they left Mykonos. She was captivated by the orange groves, the fountains and cascades. All of the marble quarries were in full operation and their glistening walls were adorned with crude sculptures "of nymphs and Bacchanalians dancing."

The marble of Paros disappointed Lord Elgin. It was not as white as the Pentelic in Athens.

Most of the temples at Paros had been destroyed to construct the Venetian fort at Parechia, the Isle's capital. There was a harvest of onions during this time and Captain Donnelly bought a two ton weight at three shillings a hundred.

The whole deck of the frigate was soon covered with this cargo, incarcerating passengers and crew in its repugnant odor all the way to Asia Minor.

After calling at Smyrna, the *Narcissus* sailed on, reaching the Dardanelles in mid-August. Lady Elgin clung tenaciously to her mal de mer throughout the rest of the voyage, but her recovery was instantaneous the moment they came into sight of the shining minarets that glazed the familiar horizon of the Bosphorus.

Chapter
Four

Constantinople

Bouyouk Déré

My very dear Mother:

I open my heart to you and say that Matilda (the Elgins' third child) was today innoculated* and took the vaccine without the slightest complaint . . . .

It was fortunate for the Elgins that fresh vaccine was sent from Vienna which Doctor Scott had previously tried with much success. He had already innoculated scores of people in Constantinople and at Belgrade where hundreds of children were dying each day.

The plague did not stop Lord Elgin, however, and he persisted in his strong desire to possess every valuable antiquity in Greece. The Parthenon had now been entirely stripped and not one inch of ground on the Acropolis Hill had been spared from excavations. The removals were taking place daily. Already six more slabs of the Parthenon frieze had been pulled down, along with all the metopes. Still another slab of the frieze was unearthed in excavation. Four slabs from the Temple of Athena Nike which had been built into the fortification of the Acropolis Hill were dug out and removed. All these and more: examples of the architectural details from the capitals, bases, cornices, and pieces of the

* A smallpox plague was raging through the Near East at this time.

91

pillar at the Erechtheum—plus those from the Propylaea, the Erechtheum, and the Temple of Athena Nike. One piece of the Parthenon column had to be sawn in two so that it could be removed.

Not one day passed that did not bring a new windfall of treasures as a result of the Elgin tour to the Peloponnesus. On the day of their departure from Athens Elgin gave a horse and green cape to the Voivode who responded immediately with his own gift: the colossal headless statue of Dionysus that stood above the monument of Thrasyllos on the south side of the Acropolis Hill. Even before they boarded the *Narcissus* Lusieri suggested "that Elgin might be able to remove the Monument of Lysicrates in its entirety if he offered enough money to the Capuchin Abbot, and Elgin urged him to try."

The whole venture had already cost Elgin thousands of pounds and still there was no end in sight, nor any promise from the British Government that he would ever be reimbursed.

Soon after their arrival in Constantinople Lord Elgin learned that all the crates which held these new acquisitions were scattered along the quay at the Piraeus, awaiting shipment. For weeks Lord Nelson had refused to dispatch any of his warships for Elgin's benefit because of the war. Thus Elgin was obliged to send the marbles piece-by-piece, and with any ship he could find. The frigate *La Diane* took a great number of cases; also HMS *Mutine*. But the treasures were piling up so rapidly Elgin worried about their safety and had to purchase his own ship, a good-sized brig named *Mentor*.

Elgin now ordered Lusieri to put absolutely everything on board the *Mentor* that the captain could be persuaded to accept, and if necessary to charter other vessels in order to get the marbles and statues off for England. Along with scores of Greek laborers and Turkish soldiers, Lusieri worked unceasingly, hauling the marbles to the Piraeus docks and loading them into the *Mentor:* fourteen more pieces of the Parthenon frieze, four sections of the frieze from the Temple of Athena Nike, and countless other sculptures too numerous to mention. The largest pieces which contained the figures from the pediments had to be left behind, since the captain refused to enlarge the hatches of the ship to get them in.

The *Mentor* sailed out of the Piraeus at last—but within two days she ran into a violent storm and struck rocks at the entrance to the harbor of Cerigo.* Because of her excessive weight, she sank at once in twelve fathoms of water and only by good fortune were Lusieri and the crew able to scramble ashore. The exact spot of the sinking was marked well however and Lusieri quickly posted guards on shore to keep vigil. By this time the *Mentor* was beyond salvage. Huge holes had to be cut in her decks by sponge divers from a neighboring island and every case of marble was saved. The marbles were then buried in a sandy beach and covered with seaweed and large stones to conceal them from French eyes.

A second ship was subsequently dispatched with special instructions to pick up everything at Cerigo. This was done within a few weeks, and finally the entire shipment was on its way to England. Hamilton went with it while Lusieri returned to Athens and proceeded with Elgin's instructions to continue with more acquisitions and excavations.

In Constantinople Lord Elgin was beside himself with joy, and for the first time felt that the real purpose of his mission had at last been accomplished. He daily boasted to his wife that he had successfully overcome the indifference of the Greeks, the treachery of the Turks, and the envious intrigues of Bonaparte. On Christmas Day he promised his wife that if all went well they would leave Constantinople before the end of January. Lady Elgin tearfully exclaimed that she could not wait to set foot once again upon Scottish soil; to catch that first glimpse of the sun on Aberlady Bay, on the Firth, and on Archerfield.

The children's growth was incredible, and Lady Elgin

* A small island off the southernmost coast of the Peloponnesus.

had all she could do to sustain Bruce from dashing out of the sight of the Greek Paramana. Mary yearned to follow him but failed nobly; fortunately the babe Matilda was too busy eating to pay either of them any heed.

Meanwhile, Lord Elgin's appearance had now deteriorated beyond all help. His nose was completely eaten away and he had grown shockingly gaunt of body. He ate sparingly and slept hardly at all. Many nights Lady Elgin was awakened by his nightmarish commands to Lusieri, his curses upon Bonaparte, and by his violent rage with the British Government. As was often the case, Lady Elgin had no one to turn to but her mother:

> The plague still continues, and by way of hiding it, the Turkish authorities carry the dead bodies during the night which so far is lucky for us, since we have the less chance of meeting them ... pray for us, dearest mother!

January brought unceasing rains to Constantinople, making the weather so unusually mild the Turks took it as a bad omen. A woman who resided in a house alongside the Embassy Palace died suddenly after complaining of swollen glands and high fever, and before nightfall of that same day a dozen similar cases were reported in that quarter of the city. Within a few more days Constantinople was gripped by panic. Stricken houses were marked with black strokes of paint over which were scribbled the words: "Allah have mercy!" Doctor Scott hesitated before diagnosing it as the plague, but Lady Elgin had seen its dreadful hand in Edinburgh when she was twelve: the vomiting, giddiness, intolerance to light, numbing pain of limb, sleeplessness, apathy, delirium, and finally death. Although she feared for her children, she was even more concerned about Elgin whose weakened state made him susceptible to the contagion. Already there were traces of redness in his eyes, and he was suffering painfully from constipation. His speech had become thick, and upon more than one occasion Lady Elgin saw him staggering across the floor in a daze.

Doctor Scott submitted the entire household to daily examinations, particularly Lord Elgin, and was thoroughly convinced they were in no danger. Scott was disturbed when he learned that Elgin was severely troubled by his bowels, and to cure the problem he prescribed a strong cathartic. The redness of Elgin's eyes resulted from lack of sleep, according to Scott, and as for Elgin's occasional thick speech and uncertainty of gait, Scott hoped to effect the cure by a daily application of six leeches to each temple for a period of one week. After dinner each evening Scott took it upon himself to lecture the household, cautioning everyone that common sense was needed and that panic had to be avoided.

Scott had already formulated a theory concerning the plague which was based upon extensive scientific studies while he was at Glasgow. For hundreds of years the plague had been victorious over mankind because the medical profession had focused its attention only upon the symptoms and not the cause. In previous years up to this time most medical observers were disposed to lay the full blame for the propagation and spread of the plague to the rat. Scott believed it was incontestable that a great mortality among rats was reported during epidemics of plague; however a comparison made by him between rat-infested and rat-free districts in Glasgow showed a much higher incidence of plague in the latter. Plague rats were rarely found in ships sailing from infected ports, and although millions of rats had been transported backwards and forwards from quay to quay between the great ports of the world, they somehow never brought the disease ashore.

Scott concluded that the contagion was not caused by rats but by rat fleas. In twenty-one experiments out of thirty-eight he noticed that more than half the percentage of healthy rats living in flea-proof cages had contracted the disease after receiving fleas collected from rats that were either dead or dying from septicemic plague. This same experiment also proved that close and continuous contact of plague-infested animals with healthy ones did not infect the latter if fleas were not present. Rats could even become infected through the faeces of a flea that had been fed on plague-infested rats. Thus Scott warned everyone to be specially careful about clothing and linens, since these were prime conveyors of the disease. He established a complete smoking system* in the household. Anyone returning from business outside had to be thoroughly smoked from head to toe before entering the house. Scott also admonished Lady Elgin for the daily strolls she had been in the habit of taking through the Gardens of Pera. These were to cease immediately.

One evening Captain Maling called on Elgin "to dispel the rumor that eighteen men on *La Diane* had succumbed to the plague." However he did admit the disease was most violent on board several Russian ships that had recently returned from Egypt. Maling was also aware that Lord Elgin had completed arrangements with the Sultan to gain the release of all Maltese slaves who had been in bondage for more than thirty years. "For centuries the Knights of St. John had employed the Maltese as crewmen for their ships in crusades against the Turks." The Ottoman Empire never forgave the Maltese; and those unfortunate enough to fall into Turkish hands were either kept in chains at Bagnio prison or used as slaves in the dockyards at Tophana.

Elgin impressed upon the Sultan that Malta was now a British possession, which made the Maltese British subjects. Accordingly he demanded their instant release. It was granted without any conditions, and the following day Elgin arranged to have all these slaves present for the laying of the foundation stone at the new British Palace. The Sultan did not take to this at first, but he finally acceded to Elgin's

---

* Fumigation, for the purpose of disinfection, was common practice in the eighteenth and nineteenth centuries. The best protection was afforded by exposing the body, or a portion of it, to the fumes of ammonia, sulphur or mercury. Fumigation, by the injection of tobacco smoke into the great bowel, was also a recognized medical procedure in Lord Elgin's day.

strong persuasion that he do it out of compliment to the Queen of England upon the occasion of her birthday.

Elgin attired himself in dress uniform for the ceremonies, and before leaving the house he and all the others in the household were cautioned by Doctor Scott to cover their noses and mouths with cloth protectors. It was raining hard when they stepped outside. Elgin requested chairs and the entire party was transported to the new Palace. As soon as they came inside the gate they saw the Maltese slaves strung out in two long lines, and Elgin was given three lusty cheers. "The joy these slaves showed surpassed all expectation. They cried, laughed, and embraced one another, and said that as long as they lived they would pray for the Elgins."

The ceremonies were brief. Even though tents had been pitched and a large dinner prepared, gusty winds and rain drove them inside where speeches were delivered and gifts handed out. Each of the slaves received new clothes and forty-eight piastres from the Sultan. During the long reception that followed, many dignitaries from foreign countries came forward to praise Elgin for his benevolent action.

On the sixteenth of January Lord Elgin left the British Palace at daybreak to make his final visit to the Porte. The embassy had been shut down for three days and all records put on board *La Diane,* together with trunks of clothing, books, gifts, and furniture. The entire embassy staff was anxious to return to England. Lord Elgin was more impatient than anyone else. He had achieved all the objectives of his mission. And now he was faced with the difficult task of putting his huge collection of marbles in order. He also planned (personally) to promote his political career.

Soon after returning from the Seraglio he went from room to room to make certain that nothing was left behind, and then he dispatched a hurried message to Lusieri:

> If I had still three years and all the resources needed, I would employ them all at Athens . . . the slightest object from the Acropolis is a jewel!

The carriage ride to the docks was a happy one. Constantinople's tile rooftops clashed brilliantly against the clear winter sun, and the populace, aware of Elgin's departure, overflowed the street along both sides of the carriage and shouted: *"Elkin! Elkin!"* Even the most phlegmatic Turks waved and bowed while the women gazed through veiled eyes.

There was a final reception on board *La Diane*. Gifts were exchanged with the Sultan, music was played, guns sounded. Moving out of the frenzied harbor at last, *La Diane* was escorted by the *Selim III,* while on both sides of the shore crowds cheered and waved miniature English flags. Elgin seemed pleased. Yet it irritated him to know that the Turks had waited until he was leaving their country before according him proper respect.

An English brig sailed alongside *La Diane* as a precaution against pirates. A Ragusan vessel trailed behind, carrying the Maltese slaves back to their country. *La Diane* was a large enough ship to carry the full embassy including Doctor Scott, Masterman, Duff, Reverend Hunt, Elgin's two secretaries: Hamilton and Stratton, and even the enormous Greek Paramana who emotionally announced that she was to dedicate the rest of her life to the care of the Elgin children.

Later that afternoon, after a slow passage through the Dardanelles, they dropped anchor off the Isle of Tenedos, and though the sea was calm Lady Elgin insisted they spend the night on shore. A fire was lit and Duff pitched a tent. They awoke early the next morning amidst a fierce storm and had to fight their way through churning waves to get back to the ship. Lady Elgin went below and huddled the children into their beds. She did not remain in her cabin however, choosing instead to go on deck with Masterman and the jug of vinegar.

The storm persisted for four days, but Captain Maling's seamanship brought them successfully into the Bay of Mantria where the party went ashore. Hunt was sent to procure horses and asses from a neighboring village. After giving it much thought, Elgin decided that Captain Maling should continue to the Piraeus without them. Everyone on board, with the exception of the captain, had been severely stricken by the sea during the storm and Elgin thought it best that they now proceed by land. Athens was not too distant from Mantria and could be reached within two days.

They mounted their beasts and soon set off. The Greek Paramana preferred to walk, but after a few hours of battle with the invincible hills she gave in and was assigned to the sturdiest ass. In time they arrived at a small village. There was much bickering and bargaining before Elgin could secure the appropriate lodgings in a Han* which consisted of one large room. A small fireplace hugged the wall near the door. Masterman attended to the beds while Hunt arranged for food to be brought in. They supped then fell into their beds exhausted. Almost immediately they were assailed by fleas and the children had to be "danced out of their beds every two minutes." But to no avail. The enemy greatly outnumbered them.

In the morning, after a breakfast of goat's milk and cheese, they resumed their journey. Duff contrived a way to carry the children by slinging a large straw basket on each ass and then strapping the conveyance securely around its middle. Both Bruce and Mary were so delighted with this they too had to be strapped down for fear of falling out of the basket. Matilda snuggled warmly in the Paramana's embrace. Before departing, they were told by the owner of the Han that Athens was nine hours distant.

At noon they came upon a sparkling white village that was perched high on one side of a mountain. Although at first the inhabitants glared at them with great suspicion, they soon proved to be remarkably hospitable and offered whatever food they had. They were particularly taken by the

---

* A shepherd's hut of mud and thatched roof.

children, addressing Bruce as *The Blond Angel,* and insisting that both Mary and Matilda—with their raven hair and brown eyes—were Greek waifs whom the Elgins had adopted.

After a nap the party resumed its trek, skirting around the towering mountain and trudging wearily across a bleak valley of limestone and sand. The place was utterly devoid of life. As dusk began to settle, a heavy rain fell. The children were bundled up and told to remain quiet until Duff pitched the tent. But it turned out to be only a squall, and when the rain stopped Lord Elgin commanded everyone to move on.

Chapter Five

Athens

IT WAS SOLIDLY dark when they entered Athens. The Greek Consul Logothetis was pleased to see them, and despite the late hour he ordered his servants to bring in food and wine. After the children finished eating, all three were carried by the giant Calmuck to their bed chambers on the second floor. Meanwhile, Lord Elgin peppered Lusieri with incessant questions concerning his activities in Athens, and he learned that all remaining cases of the Parthenon marbles were now on their way to England, thanks to the voluntary assistance of Captain Clarke of HMS *Braakel*. Soon after the *Mentor* had sunk, Captain Clarke was called upon by both Hamilton and Lusieri for his help which he gave willingly, loading the marbles into his ship with great care, "but as the *Braakel* churned out of the Piraeus harbor she ran aground and was in danger of sinking for lack of hands to unload her and pull her free."

Hunt had been in Athens at this time, and in the early hours of the next morning he paid a hurried visit to the Voivode, requesting the Turk to send one hundred men to the Piraeus at once. At first the Voivode was reluctant, but Hunt's persistence won out. It turned out to be a day of wild excitement during which almost everyone in Athens flocked to the Piraeus "to watch the spectacle." Happily for Hunt and his party, the *Braakel* was saved. Yet, hearing about this near-disaster, Lord Elgin gave vent to his anger and asked

101

Hunt: "How was the weather?" The Chaplain sheepishly replied: "A Naval person can hardly believe that the *Braakel* ran smack on a boldish shore with a wind off the land—in a clear night, and fine weather. It is attributed to a terrible obstinacy on the part of the Master who had the Midnight watch when it happened."

Without Captain Clarke's help,* nevertheless, Lord Elgin's prized possessions would never have left the Piraeus. The operation lasted five whole weeks, and no less than forty-four cases of the Parthenon marbles were embarked, which was by far the largest and most important shipment to date. But many others were to follow. Lusieri next informed Lord Elgin about his excavation achievements. He had unearthed an area not far from the Parthenon and found colossal sections of that same pediment which had been thrown down by the explosion of 1687. Among these were included the torso of Zeus, the Nike, Hermes and numerous others. Excavations were launched on the southern side, uncovering a thesaurus of fallen metopes and parts of the frieze. These marble blocks were so heavy and cumbersome, Lusieri had to send out for saws to cut off the sections on which the sculptures were carved and only thus were they able to transport them to the Piraeus docks.

Elgin was horrified to learn that these marbles still lay on the docks in plain sight of Bonaparte's agents, but Lusieri assured him they were well-guarded day and night. At this point the Consul Logothetis rose to his feet, glass of brandy in hand, and "announced they were all invited to the wedding of his daughter on the coming Sunday." Elgin submitted his regrets, reminding Logothetis that Captain Maling and *La Diane* were awaiting them at the Piraeus, but Madame Logothetis declared that it would be a great honor if the Elgins attended. It was agreed. More toasts were offered, and after everyone had retired to his bed chamber Elgin

---

* Captain Clarke was the brother of Edward Daniel Clarke, the crowning point to this bizarre affair.

suggested to Lusieri that he was to remain under his employ until further notice. He then instructed Lusieri to give reimbursement and releases to all the artists. They had no further commitments in Athens and were now free to return to their countries.

Lady Elgin enjoyed a sound sleep that night, her first in nearly a fortnight. Lord Elgin did not take breakfast the next morning. He left immediately with Lusieri instead to inspect the cases of marbles on the docks at the Piraeus. Madame Logothetis invited Lady Elgin to join her daughter and herself on a visit to the seamstress, but Lady Elgin graciously declined, complaining of fatigue. Throughout the rest of the morning she read from the Aesop fables to Bruce while the Paramana looked after Mary and Matilda.

The household took a nap after the noon meal. Lady Elgin awoke and found the sun already dropping behind Mount Lycabettus. She put on a white linen dress and black lace hat then left orders with Masterman and the Paramana to feed the children promptly at five o'clock.

In the dusty street Greek and Turkish faces flitted past her. Noisy children played in bedraggled clothes while beggars squatted everywhere with outstretched hands. Soon she was alone on Hymettus and surrounded by the delicious fragrance of an orange grove.

It was almost dusk when she returned to the street. On her right hand the sun had already sped toward Eleusis, leaving its purple wake on the gravestones of Ceramicus. At the base of the Propylaea steps she looked up toward the Parthenon for a moment and then moved on until she reached the Consul's house.

On the morning of the wedding the Elgins attired themselves in their best dress. Lady Elgin attended the bride inside the tiny Byzantine church of St. George on the summit of Mount Lycabettus. The ceremony was unbearingly long and the guests almost suffocated in the dense clouds of incense.

In the reception that followed at the Consul's house, the Elgins seated themselves in one corner of the spacious parlor as guests and dignitaries greeted the wedding party. Reverend Hunt chose this occasion to tell Lord Elgin about a letter he had just received from Ioannes Benizelos who was the master of a school at Athens maintained by wealthy Venetians:

> I am sure if you saw Athens today you would be very unhappy. One thing only would make you sad as it does all those who have some understanding of these things: *the last deplorable stripping of the Temple of Athena on the Acropolis and of the other relics of antiquity.*
>
> The Temple is now like a noble and wealthy lady who has lost all her diamonds and jewelry. Oh, how we Athenians must take this event to heart, and how we must praise and admire those ancient heroes of Rome (Pompey and Hadrian) when we look on these things!

This was the first Greek objection to Lord Elgin's pillage. A short time later John Cam Hobhouse added his voice:

> I have said nothing of the possibility of the ruins of Athens being (in the event of a revolution in favour of the Greeks) restored and put into a condition capable of resisting the ravages of decay; for an event of that nature cannot, it strikes me, have ever entered into the head of anyone who has seen Athens, and the modern Athenians. Yet I cannot forbear mentioning a singular speech of a learned Greek of Ioannina who said to me: "You English are carrying off the works of the Greeks, our forefathers. Preserve them well because we Greeks will someday come and redeem them!"

Hunt's reference to the letter from Benizelos did not disturb Lord Elgin because he had always felt that the modern Greeks bore no resemblance to their ancient heroes. "In fact, they had nothing whatsoever in common with them and for centuries had permitted the Turks to enslave them. Far worse, these same modern Greeks looked upon the superb works of Phidias with ingratitude and indifference. They did not deserve them!"

And so, the destructions continued, much to the distress of Lusieri who was seen shivering one day at his post on the Acropolis Hill—but not because of ill health:

> As he observed to us, he is always thus attacked whenever an English or a French frigate anchors in the Piraeus. The young midshipmen are then set loose upon the venerable monuments of Athens, and are seldom deterred by the religion of the place from indulging in the most wanton devastation of statues, cornices and capitals, from which they carry off mementoes of their Athenian travels.

Incidents of this nature became more frequent by the day yet no one lifted his hand in protest:

> The last time I visited the citadel, I was much displeased at seeing an English traveller, an officer of the Navy (for such his uniform bespoke him to be) standing upon the base of one of the Caryatids, clinging with his left arm round the column while his right hand, provided with a hard and heavy stone, was endeavouring to knock off the only remaining nose of those six beautifully sculptured statues. I exerted my eloquence in vain to preserve this monument of art.

Still another eye-witness observed:

> When Elgin's agents removed the Caryatid from the Erectheum, Athena wept. But there were louder lamentations from the remaining Caryatids as they looked upon their ravished sister. And later, as Elgin's labourers were hauling the last of the marbles to the Piraeus, they had to stop suddenly and drop them to the ground; nor could they be prevailed upon to carry them further, protesting that they could hear the doleful moan of Athena deep within each vein of marble!

Lord Elgin regarded all this as foolish talk, the superstitious offspring of weak and deluded minds.

La Diane called at Cerigo Isle six days later. Lord Elgin and Hunt went ashore to inspect the remains of the *Mentor* while Lady Elgin and the children watched from the deck of the ship. When Elgin at last returned he reported that any hope of ever raising the *Mentor* should now be abandoned since winter storms had dashed the vessel to pieces. Throughout the rest of that day he immersed himself in a black mood and stayed away from everyone. At dinner that night he ranted about the enormous weight of his expenses and how the salvage operations had cost him over six thousand pounds, not to mention the loss of the *Mentor.*

A powerful wind grasped hold of their sails and sent them to Candia* sooner than expected. Anchoring off the harbor of Canea, they eventually went ashore in the captain's barge and found the climate unusually mild for mid-February. They walked with caution along the sandy beach and within an hour encountered a sizeable colony of lepers, many of whom sat near the shore and stared across the sea. No one dared go near them. The party walked for another kilometer and then pitched tents. Several of the crewmen went inland to search for wood and soon a good fire was lit. Masterman saw to the cooking: a soup of black-eyed beans, together with goat cheese, olives and dark bread. The children were quickly bundled up after the meal and put into makeshift beds on the sand.

In the morning they were awakened by voices and scuffling feet. Several hundred men had encircled the two tents. They were attired in long pantaloons and wore leather bands around their foreheads. Lady Elgin was frightened by their fierce looks. Their leader stepped forward and introduced himself as Nouri Bey, the Governor of Crete. He was afraid to come near Elgin for fear of contagion, but Doctor Scott

* The Isle of Crete.

assured him there was no cause for alarm and that Elgin's features had not been scarred by leprosy. Nouri Bey was not convinced; nor his men, and throughout the reception that followed, the Cretans kept a safe distance from Elgin.

Nouri Bey then called for chairs and the party was transported to the Governor's Palace, a large mansion of white stone guarded in the front by seven Doric columns which Nouri Bey proudly boasted had once belonged to the Temple of Venus at Canea. At this time Nouri Bey's harem made its appearance, coming specifically to meet Lady Elgin. They had been carried across the yard "in covered boxes, two of which were slung across a mule like Gypsy panniers." Over their heads were curtains of scarlet cloth to protect them from the eyes of the throng that had already converged around the palace. The women of the harem seemed amused by Lady Elgin's manners and dress. One of them came forward and presented her with a gift of rose water while the others brazenly touched her hair, her jewels, her slender arms. Throughout the long inspection Masterman stood at Lady Elgin's side in nervous despair.

Before dinner Nouri Bey accompanied the Elgins on a carriage ride through the narrow streets of Canea. It disturbed Lord Elgin when he received no applause from the inhabitants and he was particularly upset by their scornful looks. At dinner he again fell into a black mood. Meanwhile Nouri Bey did his best to please the party, entertaining them with dancers and magicians. But it was hopeless. Elgin's gloom had infested everyone by this time. Fearing that the Governor might take such conduct as a personal affront, Lady Elgin offered the weak excuse that Elgin's health had been impaired by the bad climate at Constantinople. But she could see that Nouri Bey did not believe her.

They returned to *La Diane* early the next morning and after leaving the harbor sailed under the lee of Crete and were carried on a straight course toward Malta, arriving there on the twenty-third day of February. Almost immediately the authorities on that Isle ordered them "to per-

form twenty days quarantine." They were permitted, however, to land and stay at the ruins of Boghi Palace, which was
once Malta's finest building until the French destroyed it.
Elgin was told that a large segment of the British fleet lay at
anchor in Malta, and he went directly to Pratique House with
Captain Maling for a talk with the commanders. The quarantine was immediately lifted and elegant quarters were provided for the whole party in a large villa owned by a wealthy
Italian shipowner. But this convenience came a trifle late.
Matilda had not taken to life inside a damp tent and fell prey
to chills and fever. Malta was a filthy place, a stepping-stone
of the Mediterranean. Her houses were tightly packed and
her inhabitants weak with sickness and hunger after a prolonged war with the French. For this reason Doctor Scott
deemed it necessary to put Matilda on board *La Diane* as soon
as possible.

They remained on the Isle of Malta only two days.

Their farewell was somewhat strained. Now that the Maltese slaves were safely home Elgin was accorded the Isle's
highest honor in a long ceremony on the deck of *La Diane*,
but whereas in Constantinople he had been deeply moved by
the respect and gratitude of the slaves, he presently became
annoyed with the whole business and seemed anxious to take
leave of the place. At sea he kept entirely to himself and even
chose to dine alone. Doctor Scott took notice of this and
warned about the dire consequences of such behavior, but
Elgin ignored him.

Lady Elgin meanwhile was in a state of bliss, engrossing
herself in nostalgic memories of Scotland. They were out of
Malta three full days before she realized that the sea had not
affected her; but now it was suddenly starting again, even
though she tried to put her mind elsewhere: upon Lusieri's
comical appearance on the Acropolis Hill, the breath-taking
view of the Bosphorus, the last shipment of Parthenon marbles aboard the British frigate which Lord Nelson had reluctantly sent to the Piraeus just before they departed from
Athens.

That evening Elgin made his appearance at the captain's table, but he partook more of the wine than the meal. Hunt then armed himself with a bold audacity and began narrating some of his experiences in Epirus. Tea was served. Elgin became restless again and without bothering to excuse himself, got up from the table and retired to his cabin. Lady Elgin listened to Hunt a while longer then walked on deck for a few moments. The wind was bitter cold, and although the sea churned mightily under her feet she felt no discomfort other than a resurging heartache for Archerfield and her parents.

They did not put into Sicily but continued on a direct course for Naples, docking there three days later. The Italian authorities had been holding a packet of letters for Lord Elgin. One was from Lusieri with news of still more excavations at Delphi and a windfall of acquisitions; another message came from his mother, the dowager Countess of Elgin:

Please be advised that the *Braakel* docked recently at Portsmouth and unloaded fifty cases of marbles which I arranged to have stored (along with the previous shipments) at the house of the Duchess of Portland in Westminster. After a fortnight she became irritated because they were cluttering her grounds and she begged me to move them elsewhere. Fortunately the Duke of Richmond arranged to have them transported to his estate but soon he too shewed his vexation about having so many cases totalling one hundred and twenty tons of marble scattered about his grounds and thus I was obliged to rent a large house at the corner of Piccadilly and Park Lane which has a spacious garden.

In rapid time a sizeable shed was built and after the workmen unpacked all the marbles we arranged them in the best manner possible, considering their gigantic weight. It was impossible to lay out the collection in a systematic way. This shall have to await your arrival. And so I report to you that the sculptures, inscriptions, metopes, friezes and architectural fragments are now housed inside this shed. In the center stands the Caryatid, the other figures having been placed around her according to size and shape. The torso of Hermes is perched atop an inscribed column and is splendidly balanced at the other side of the room by the horse's head from the Erectheum.

There are additional cases of marbles at the docks. Shipments keep arriving at steady intervals and I have employed agents to be at the London Customs House to look after each piece. Many of these antiquities have battered noses, broken arms and legs, missing heads. We have a man here whose name is John Flaxman and is called *"The English Phidias."* Although he says the restored parts would be inferior to the original, which might bring about a constant source of dispute, nevertheless he is of the opinion that the restoration should be done, since it would increase the financial worth of the collection. He estimates the cost to be in the vicinity of twenty thousand pounds.

While Hunt went to summon a carriage Elgin wrote a hasty reply to his mother and warned her not to spend another farthing on the marbles. *Twenty thousand pounds for an English Phidias!*

It was decided by Doctor Scott that the children should not leave the ship. Naples was an unclean city and there was mounting concern over a contagion that had already gripped most of the surrounding towns. Scott suggested that the Elgins continue overland through Italy and into France, leaving the children on board *La Diane* and under his care. After the ship's arrival at England Captain Maling would subsequently entrust them to Elgin's mother. It was a bitter decision for Lady Elgin to accept, but she had to agree that Scott was right. There were tearful embraces and sad farewells; final instructions were then given to both Hamilton and Stratton concerning the many cases of marbles that still awaited clearance and duty payments at the London Customs House.

As soon as *La Diane* pulled out of Naples harbor Lady Elgin was again on the verge of tears until her husband reassured her that they had decided upon the best course of

action, especially if war should break out again. Elgin had
learned from the Italian authorities at Naples that Count
Sébastiani had been sent to the Levant by Bonaparte, which
made it quite obvious that if war did break out again
Bonaparte would surely invade Egypt. The Elgins had acquainted themselves with Sébastiani during their stay in
Constantinople. Lady Elgin was particularly impressed:

> There is a smart French Beau just arrived from Paris to
> sign a Treaty of Peace with the Turks. He arrived two days
> too late. He has called upon us and was excessively civil;
> there is another young man come with him; they are both
> equipped *parfaitement à la mode* and are both handsome. I
> wish you could see the fuss everybody makes of them.

Since Bonaparte had recently made the brash claim "that
only six thousand men would be needed to reconquer
Egypt," Sébastiani's presence in the Levant was looked upon
with much apprehension and suspicion by the British Government. As Marshal of France his mission certainly implied
that he intended to inquire into the current state of the
Egyptian and Turkish armies.

During the long carriage ride to Rome, Elgin seemed
relieved to be free of the children and talked enthusiastically
about visiting the many galleries of Florence. Hunt and Masterman accompanied the Elgins on this overland journey;
the Greek Paramana was to remain on board *La Diane* with
the children.

In Rome Hunt wished to go on a tour of the city, but
Lady Elgin complained of fatigue. Within a few hours suita-
ble lodgings, not too far from the Colosseum, were found
and the wife of the owner cooked them a meat dish thick
with tomato sauce. After the dinner Hunt persisted with his
desire to tour the city, but Lord Elgin decided against it.

Hunt was disappointed again the following morning.
Reasoning that Florence was at least a journey of three days,
Lord Elgin suggested they leave Rome immediately. He ar-
ranged for the hire of a post chaise drawn by two horses and

they set off shortly after breakfast. Inside the conveyance Lady Elgin quietly told her husband that she was pregnant with her fourth child. Hunt, in the meantime, was still sullen because of their hasty departure from the city and made a last-minute request to follow a course along the street of St. Gregory and perhaps catch a fleeting glimpse of the ancient sites near Palatine Hill. Elgin thought this unwise and commanded the driver to head northward, along Via Del Corso.

The tight confinement of the post chaise was oppressing to Lady Elgin and the road beyond Rome was rough and gutted with holes. They made good time, nevertheless, and by mid-afternoon arrived at Spoleto-on-the-Tiber where they ate and rested. Elgin had miscalculated the distance to Florence, and it was now his firm conviction that if they continued at a rapid pace they might reach the city in only two days. Hunt disagreed.

A new team of horses was fitted to the post chaise, and they moved on, reaching Perugia shortly before dusk. With the help of the village priest, Hunt found lodgings in a small inn, but there were only two available rooms. Masterman and Hunt were given separate bedding on the floor, which Masterman regarded as highly improper, and consequently Lord Elgin had to persuade the inn-keeper to put a small partition between the beddings.

Lady Elgin felt some fatigue the next morning, but she braced herself and managed to eat most of her breakfast. Fortunately the road out of Perugia was well-paved, and they passed through many little towns, following the Tiber all the way into Arezzo where again they stopped to eat and rest. Hunt were given separate bedding on the floor, which Mas- they indeed would make Florence as he had estimated.

After another exchange of horses they set off once more. Lady Elgin's malaise seemed to be getting worse, but she was determined not to complain. By this time Hunt had completely liberated himself from the depression of spirit which had preyed upon him since Rome and he gave a long narration of his recent tour of Greece, particularly Mycenae,

Olympai, and the Morea. Suddenly Masterman surprised everyone by breaking into song:

> A highland lad my love was born,
> The Lawland laws he held in scorn;
> But he still was faithful to his clan,
> My gallant braw, John Highlandman.

She was joined in the chorus by all the others, even Lord Elgin:

> Sing, hey my braw, John Highlandman!
> Sing, ho my braw, John Highlandman!
> There's not a lad in a' the lan'
> Was match for my John Highlandman!

It had just stopped raining when they entered Florence. Behind the fast-moving clouds, the dim light of the dying sun could be seen reflected on the red tile rooftops of the city. They encountered no difficulty in finding lodgings, and after they had dined, Hunt was eager to launch out on a tour, but again Elgin dampened his hopes, advising that it would be best to wait until morning.

Hunt was first to arise. The air felt raw and everyone dressed warmly. Already the streets were swarming with people; church bells pealed; priests and nuns swept past them as they approached the ancient cathedral of Santa Maria Del Fiore.* Matins had just ended and a throng of worshippers poured down the marble steps. The Elgins waited for the church to clear and then walked inside, examining each work of art on the walls, the windows and altar. Although construction of Santa Maria Del Fiore had begun in the late thirteenth century, its marble facade was still unfinished. Wars, internal bickering, strife, yearly floods and earthquakes delayed its completion. Alongside it, was the magnificent bell tower of Giotto. Lord Elgin was much im-

---

* The Duomo, largest and most important church in Florence.

pressed by its numerous bas-reliefs and even climbed its four hundred and fourteen steps to the terrace, from which there was a commanding view of Florence.

Across the cobblestone street stood the baptistery, its exquisite bronze doors clashing against the sharp rays of the morning sun. The scenes depicted on the Ghiberti panels recalled ten events of the Old Testament: from the creation of Adam and Eve, to the reception of King Solomon by the Queen of Sheba.

They walked directly to the Uffizi Galleria and went first to the paintings of Raphael. From there they examined the works of Andrea del Sarto, Perugino, Ghirlandaio and Botticelli. Each painting was arranged in strict chronological order. Lord Elgin's favorite was Michelangelo's "Holy Family;" Lady Elgin preferred a canvas by Botticelli which contained the life-like portraits of the important members of the Medici family.*

They stopped to dine in a small inn just off the Piazza San Firenze and then spent the rest of the afternoon at the Pitti Palace, the residence of the Duke of Florence.

It was dark when they finally returned to their lodgings. Masterman had a hot meal waiting; and shortly before the hour of sleep, the maid drew a hot bath for Lady Elgin.

* "The Adoration of the Maji."

Chapter
Six

Paris

THEY TRAVELED FROM Leghorn to Marseilles by ship. It was a calm crossing and the French coast enchanted the Elgins. From Marseilles they continued by barge up the Rhône and into Lyons where Lord Elgin arranged for the hire of a carriage. On the following day they set out for Paris, but less than two hours from their destination they were apprehended by a detachment of soldiers under the command of a lieutenant. Elgin was unaware that war between France and England had been declared once more or that the First Consul Bonaparte had issued the following decree:

> All the English enrolled in the Militia from the age of 18 to 60 holding a commission from his Britannic Majesty, who are at present in France, shall be made Prisoners of War, to answer for the Citizens of the Republic who have been arrested by the vessels or subjects of his Britannic Majesty before the declaration of war. The Ministers, each as far as concerns him, are charged with the execution of the present decree.

In their zeal to carry out Bonaparte's instructions, the Ministers reasoned that all British male subjects had an obligation to serve their country and theoretically might become officers. Consequently they felt that every male British subject should be considered a prisoner of war. Lord Elgin was

one of the first to be seized. After being told that he was
under arrest, he was further informed that he and his party
were to be detained at the Hotel de Richelieu in Paris until
further notice. Lady Elgin was heartbroken:

> We intended remaining a week or ten days at most in
> Paris . . . I must have made some sad mistakes in writing to
> you if you did not understand that. We were most positively
> assured by all the French Generals and Commanders and
> Ministers between Leghorn and this, that even should war
> be declared, we might go through France in the utmost
> security. We only knew that war was declared when it was
> too late to turn back—and with assurances, how could one
> imagine that an ambassador would be arrested; never since
> the world began was such a thing done before. The night
> we arrived here, Elgin—finding Lord Whitworth (the
> British Ambassador in Paris) gone—immediately wrote to
> M. de Talleyrand* to ask whether he had better set off for
> London instantaneously or whether we might remain a few
> days to rest after our long journey. M. de Talleyrand's an-
> swer was that we might remain as long as we pleased and
> that we should have our passports whenever we pleased.
> The very next day Elgin was declared a prisoner of war.
> Who could expect that?

* Charles Maurice de Talleyrand-Périgord (1754-1838) was Foreign Minister
under Napoleon from the first days of the Revolution. Before accepting the post,
Talleyrand weighed the matter very carefully because he had to be certain about the
aims and ideals of the Republic. His greatness was attributed to both parents, who
were descended from the most noble and powerful families of France. They were in
constant attendance at the Court of Louis XV and, as was the case with most
aristocracy, neglected their son by entrusting him to the care of a nurse in Paris.

At the age of four Talleyrand fell from a high chair and so injured his foot it
crippled him for life. In his adolescent years he was sent to a seminary to prepare
for the priesthood, but he could not conceive any fondness for discipline and doc-
trine, and in his spare time he plunged into a passionate reading of Voltaire, whose
radical thoughts had already begun to undermine the authority of the church.

As a sub-deacon Talleyrand witnessed the coronation of Louis XVI at Reims. He
was ordained a priest four years later, and while in Paris found every opportunity to
mix in the circles of philosophers who frequented the salon of Madame de Genlis.
His ideas about political and social reform were born here, and at an annual assembly of the clergy, he made a proposal to redress the glaring grievances of the
underpaid priests. His efforts were rewarded with the bishopric of Autun, a position which carried much prestige. At this time the first rumblings of the Revolution
were being heard throughout France.

The treaty of Amiens had been tossed to the wind. Bonaparte now demanded that England not only abandon Malta but Egypt and Gibraltar as well. Elgin objected to his detainment, emphasizing that he was a diplomat and not a soldier. It was a firm convention of all wars that only soldiers participate. Civilians were always free to go about their business, and even during the eighteenth century wars, the Dover to Calais packet continued to run uninterrupted, its gentlemen on the Grand Tour suffering only minor inconveniences.

Their carriage was escorted into Paris by four soldiers on horseback. Through its open windows Lady Elgin followed every move they made. They did not look like soldiers: faces unshaved, layers of mud caked over their boots and breeches, uncouth peasants. The whole episode was unreal to her, and when at last they entered into the capital they saw many curious faces crowded along both sides of the wide boulevard, staring at the horsemen. The French women seemed to be unconcerned. Parasols in hand, they continued their stroll, heads erect and long dresses flowing in the wind while dozens of screaming children dashed after the carriage.

The Hotel de Richelieu was a red granite structure with flower boxes along its entire front. Two tall cypresses guarded a colossal metal door, while directly above their heads an iron balcony jutted over the street. A uniformed attendant came to escort them inside, but he was pushed away by one of the soldiers. In the meantime, his companions had removed all the baggage from the carriage and were carrying it inside.

The lobby of the hotel had thick red carpeting which continued up a circular staircase. The Elgin party followed the soldiers to the top of the stairs, turning sharply to the right and then walking down a dimly-lit corridor until they reached the very last door. Before entering their suite, they were issued a warning: "They were free to move about in the hotel and also in the gardens but, upon arising each morning and before retiring at night, they had to register their names with the soldier standing guard outside their door. Under no condition was anyone permitted to leave the hotel without written authority!"

Everyone was crestfallen when the soldier finally closed the door. Feebly Hunt tried to assure them that their detainment would be only for a short duration, but no one believed him. Elgin was furious, and while Masterman began rearranging some of the old furniture and complaining about the dust everywhere, he went to the writing desk near the window and angrily wrote a letter to Talleyrand, demanding their immediate release. Later that afternoon Masterman confided to Lady Elgin that she was anxious to return to Scotland because her father had given assent to her marriage in a promise that could not be broken. Lady Elgin assured the maid that when the time was proper Lord Elgin would attend to the matter of her release.

After dinner Hunt reported to the soldier standing on guard outside their door and requested permission to take a short stroll through the gardens of the hotel. He came back moments later to report that the place was crawling with English détunus, all very wealthy. Lord Elgin made no comment, but his wife was quick to express a sincere yearning that "surely there must be at least one good whist player in the lot!"

The next morning they registered their names with the soldier on guard and walked into the gardens. It was a mild day; birds frolicked in the magnolia trees; the scent of jasmine filled the air. They were soon joined by several other détunus: Mrs. Fitzgerald, Mr. and Mrs. Cockburn, Colonel Crawford, and Mr. Sterling; all of them English to the core. The Cockburns seemed to be a devoted couple and held hands throughout the conversation. Mrs. Fitzgerald was well along in years, but pleasant and sociable. Colonel Crawford walked with a pronounced limp and constantly complained about the absence of Lord Whitworth who deserted the embassy on the very day that war was declared. Sterling was a middle-aged man of delicate nature.

Before returning to the hotel, Mrs. Cockburn extended an invitation to all for dinner at her suite that evening. She had also invited a young scientist named Robert Fergusson, who came from Scotland and was a bachelor. With a glint in his eyes, Colonel Crawford boasted to Lady Elgin that he himself never had experienced the need for a wife, adding in a jocular voice, that in every relationship between a man and woman only one point should be borne in mind: the brief encounter. To expect or demand more than this was absurd since a woman's virtue lay neither in beauty nor charm, but in novelty. His remarks mortified Mrs. Cockburn. Waiting until the old Colonel had hobbled up the stairs, she felt obliged to explain to the Elgins that he was approaching senility, but Lord Elgin doubted this and inquired as to the cause of his limp. Mrs. Cockburn tartly replied that Colonel Crawford claimed it was from an old wound, however everyone suspected he had the gout. Later, as Lord Elgin and Hunt dressed for dinner, Lady Elgin asked Masterman to step into the corridor and ask the guard for her Imperial.* The soldier brought it in himself and stood alongside as Lady Elgin opened it. She deliberated a moment before deciding to wear her pink lace gown. She looked for the matching pearls but could not find them; nor the rest of her jewelry. Everything of value was missing!

After registering their names with the soldier in the corridor, they went directly to Mrs. Cockburn's suite. With the exception of Colonel Crawford, who sat in a wicker chair, the other guests had formed a semi-circle in front of the wide window and were sipping sherry from their glasses. Mrs. Cockburn's two maids were serving. A long table was laid out in the center of the parlor and the place settings were meticulously arranged. Just as dinner was about to be served, a tall young man was received at the door by Mrs. Cockburn.

* A large valise.

He had a blond moustache and a thick crop of hair; a black cloak was thrown over his broad shoulders. He conversed with Mrs. Fitzgerald for a moment and was then introduced to the Elgins. Lord Elgin remembered him as a young lad, and the young man, Robert Fergusson, responded by recalling frequent visits to Broomhall with his family.

"And how is your father?" Elgin asked.

"In excellent health, my Lord."

"He must be near seventy."

"Seventy-three, my Lord."

"And yourself, Robert?"

"Twenty-six, my Lord."

Fergusson had already made certain contributions to science as a geologist and was also a Fellow of the Royal Society. France was to be the last stop of an extended tour through the continent, upon which he had embarked more than a year before his detainment. As the tea was being served, Fergusson talked at length with Lord Elgin about Bonaparte. At the height of the conversation the young bachelor looked up and noticed that Lady Elgin was staring at him.

Talleyrand's reply to Lord Elgin's letter came in three days. The Foreign Minister of the French Republic regretted the inconvenience of their detainment in Paris, but since the order had been issued directly by Bonaparte there was little that Talleyrand could do except offer his sincere hope that their detention would be of short duration.

Elgin was thrown into despondency and refused to take his morning stroll into the gardens. For almost two weeks he ate very sparingly and shunned all conversation. One afternoon, shortly after Lady Elgin had taken her nap, she came down into the gardens and learned from Colonel Crawford that Count Sébastiani was in Paris. As the new Marshal of the French Army, Sébastiani would be influential with Bonaparte. Lady Elgin quickly extended a written invitation to him, and on 12 July Sébastiani made his appearance at the Hotel de Richelieu. Prior to his arrival Masterman busily tidied up the place. Fresh flowers were placed in clean vases and a dessert was prepared. Meanwhile Elgin's hopes were once again revived and he sat down and wrote a lengthy dispatch to Lusieri, alerting him to keep a constant watch on the large collection of Parthenon marbles which still lay on the Piraeus docks at the full mercy of the French.*

Sébastiani was escorted to their suite precisely at noon. He looked even more handsome to Lady Elgin than the time of their first meeting at Constantinople. He was attired in a red and blue uniform weighted down with medals and decorations. From the outset he was pleased to see them and tried to make jest of their plight by saying he could not understand why Elgin was turning the world upside down to get out of such a beautiful country as France. Surely they had been accorded the deepest courtesy, but Elgin did not find this very amusing and again demanded their immediate release. Sébastiani smilingly reminded him that their countries were at war. England was detaining hundreds of French civilians and until they were released, all British subjects in France had to be detained as well. But aside from this, Bonaparte's animosity toward Elgin could never be appeased now that Elgin had successfully stolen the Parthenon marbles which Bonaparte had wanted for the Louvre.

It was an easy matter for Lady Elgin to overwhelm Count Sébastiani with praise and flattery. And like a true Frenchman he proved receptive. Putting on his hat and gloves, he kissed her hand then promised he would call upon Bonaparte and discuss with him the possibility of their release. "But despite his repeated assurances Lord Elgin nourished a strong suspicion that Sébastiani was not to be trusted."

Sébastiani called upon them within a few days but with the sad news that Bonaparte refused to consider their release at this time. Furthermore a decree was about to be issued for

* Lord Elgin's credit was considered too risky at this point by most European bankers. His last hope lay in Malta, where he hoped to borrow the necessary money for this last shipment.

the expulsion of all English détunus from Paris, after which they were to be transferred to the country and put to work on farms. Through Sébastiani's persuasion Bonaparte took heed of Lord Elgin's health and agreed to assign him to Barèges, a summer resort high in the Pyrenees, whose hot baths were a mecca for tourists.

Lord Elgin protested strenuously, seeing this as a plot to delay their eventual departure from France. But Lady Elgin was more practical. Mindful of her husband's chronic attacks of rheumatism, she reasoned that the baths at Barèges might be beneficial and that they should regard the change as a vacation, not confinement. Two carriages were put at their disposal the next morning and Sébastiani came to see them off. Lady Elgin chose this occasion to request a safe passage for Masterman to England but Sébastiani was not in a position to grant it. Masterman's wedding plans would have to be delayed at least until the end of the summer season.

Chapter
Seven

Barèges

Barèges is the most dreary place I ever saw; immense high hills without a tree. There is a ride which one can call practicable, and it continues going down a hill for an hour and a half. There are many beautiful spots at an hour or two's distance from this but Barèges itself is most miserable. However I firmly believe it has saved Elgin's life. He feels better every day; he gets up at six or seven o'clock in the morning and goes out a shooting for four or five hours with the Duke of Newcastle, (another British détunu) then about one o'clock he goes out a riding with me. He has now begun to take the baths twice a day: when he returns from shooting, and at 11 o'clock at night. He remains almost an hour each time.

The baths in Barèges held no interest for Lady Elgin. They were frequented primarily by gossipy ladies who had nothing better to do but pry into each other's lives. Her evenings "were spent at dinner parties, concerts, and whist. Social life at the spa was different from that at home or at Constantinople."

Toward the end of August one of the foremost collectors of antiquities in Europe came to visit the Elgins:

Le Comte de Choiseul-Gouffier is here. He is very pleasant. Poor man, he had been most unfortunate; after having lost almost all he possessed, he had just money

123

enough to buy a Villa near Paris and set his heart upon placing the marbles etc. that he had collected at Athens. He has just received information that the Frigate on board which his Antiquities were placed, has been taken by the English. The tears were really in his eyes when he told us. He said after having lost his fortune and very nearly all the Antiquities he had with so much trouble and expense collected . . . and having hid these for so many years, and having now sent for them, he is completely overcome by the loss.

Because of his allegiance to the king of France, Choiseul-Gouffier was treated unkindly by Bonaparte. However, after Choiseul-Gouffier returned from exile, Bonaparte forgave his disloyalty and even granted him the small villa near Paris. But his entire collection of antiquities was confiscated by Napoleon and placed in the Louvre. Choiseul-Gouffier was able to withstand these misfortunes, but the loss of one piece particularly distressed him: a section of marble from a Parthenon frieze which his agent had successfully hauled to the Piraeus and brought on board the French frigate *l'Arabe*. The ship was only one day out of port when war broke out. She was captured and taken as prize by the English warship *Maidstone*. Since it was the law that the value of any enemy property taken should be divided equally among the crew, *l'Arabe* and all her contents were sold at auction in Malta, with the exception of the Parthenon frieze, which was confiscated by Lord Nelson and ordered to be sent to England.

Lord Elgin was surprised to learn that this frieze was still being held at the London Customs House. He was more astonished when Choiseul-Gouffier appealed to him for assistance, confident that two gentlemen of noble tradition should have no bitterness toward each other. The Frenchman was willing to pay for the return of the frieze, but Elgin assured him this was not necessary and gave his solemn word that he would dispatch an immediate message to Lord Nel-

son, requesting that the frieze be sent at once to Choiseul-Gouffier's villa.

The next day's post brought a short letter from Captain
Maling: "he had delivered the children in perfect health" to
the Nisbet family at Archerfield. Nothing else. Not one word
about the shed at Park Lane, nor Choiseul-Gouffier's frieze
which was now open prey at the London Customs House.
Surely if Captain Maling had kept his eyes on the alert he
would have spotted it.

For the first time in their marriage Lady Elgin expressed
her agitation over Elgin's lack of concern for his children.
From the day the Parthenon marbles were taken down and
shipped to England the entire household had not known one
moment of peace. But far worse, Lady Elgin did not know
where she might find the strength to endure the aching loss
of her children. And so her thoughts fled to Archerfield
once again: to her father's house looming over the Firth, the
tall oaks in the north fields, the spring grass lush and fra-
grant, the sandy shores of Aberlady Bay. In the soft hush of
silence she could hear voices: Bruce, Mary, and Matilda run-
ning toward her, shouting: *Mitéra! Mitéra!**

Count Sébastiani paid them a visit in September and reported that Bonaparte had agreed to Masterman's safe passage back to England, but the Elgins and Hunt were to
remain in France as prisoners of war. Sébastiani tried to
assuage Elgin's anger by offering the weak excuse that
Bonaparte wanted Elgin to remain in France because he considered him the unofficial ambassador, now that Lord
Whitworth had abandoned the post. The Marshal of the
French Army then spoke about the wave of rumors circulat-
ing throughout France and the continent which accused
Elgin of deliberate ill-treatment of French prisoners in Constantinople:

* The Greek word for mother.

Ah, c'est ce Milord Elgin qui a si maltraité nos compatriotes à Constantinople!

One story which bothered Elgin emphasized that he had caused a French diplomat named Beauchamp to be put to death, whereas Elgin had intervened successfully with the Porte to relieve the sufferings of not only all the French prisoners confined in the Seven Towers but in addition had rescued Beauchamp from the hands of Sir Sydney Smith who wanted him beheaded as a spy. Elgin furthermore gave the French diplomat money and a passport to return to his country.

Another rumor claimed that Lord Elgin had attempted to deceive the French at El Arish, even though Elgin was one of the few to come out of that muddle with honor. Finally, and perhaps most insultingly, a warning was initiated by Bonaparte that no one in France should dare come near Elgin for fear of contamination from the pox.*

Two days after Sébastiani's visit a contingent of French soldiers stormed into the Elgin cottage at Barèges and seized Lord Elgin. They commanded him to dress then took him under heavy guard to the fortress at Lourdes, a few miles to the south. The order for his arrest was issued by Alexandre Berthier, Prince of Neufchâtel and Wagram, Vice-Constable of France. Berthier was Bonaparte's Chief of Staff and constant companion, dining with him and traveling in the same carriage. He previously had served with Lafayette in the American War of Independence.

Lady Elgin was stunned by her husband's arrest:

> Elgin is to be confined at the Castle of Lourdes, the most dreadful place you ever saw. The Castle is situated on a high rock close to the Pyrenean Mountains . . . and is so remarkably unhealthy and cold the soldiers at Barèges say how much they pitied the poor English who were to be confined there.

* Syphilis.

Lady Elgin was not present in the cottage when the soldiers seized her husband. They permitted him, however, to leave her a brief note of explanation:

> I am to go to Lourdes; it is fortunate that we know (and particularly you) the Commandant so well. The officer who is come has been remarkably polite . . . and now, my Angel, I may speak of my feelings: God knows the wretchedness I have had from this, on your account; I dare not think of you. At first the stupefaction of the blow stunned me. But when I found it necessary to burn your letters I never felt such misery before. When I think of all you have suffered from Constantinople: my ill health, and this detention, I am unable to bear myself. Our marriage has been a continued scene of suffering to you and I can't make it up. God in Heaven bless my Dearest Angel.

Bonaparte's animosity toward Elgin had become even more inflamed when a French general named Boyer was captured and thrown into prison in England. There were stories of ill-treatment which so enraged Bonaparte he issued an order that an officer of Boyer's rank should be arrested "in retaliation." Elgin was selected.

Now that Masterman had been granted permission to leave the country Lady Elgin felt obligated to escort her maid as far as Paris. This decision had deeper implications however: in Paris Lady Elgin would seek a personal audience with Talleyrand to plead her husband's case; she also hoped to call upon several of her acquaintances from the Hotel de Richelieu.

Reverend Philip Hunt accompanied Lady Elgin and Masterman on this long journey. They got as far as Rabastens the first day and after an overnight stop there, resumed their trip and made excellent time into Cahors despite the poor roads and a steady downpour. When they awoke the next morning they found that the storm clouds had disappeared and the sun was shining brightly. The French countryside was suddenly transformed: houses and trees glittered under the penetrating rays of the sun; birds sang; children played in the green pasturelands. Toward mid-afternoon the carriage pulled into Limoges.

Reverend Hunt secured lodgings in that town's only hotel, an ancient structure of two stories which was badly maintained and reeking with cooking odors. Lady Elgin's bed was so abominably uncomfortable she abandoned it and reclined instead on a lumpy sofa. Not a soul was at the desk when they prepared to leave the next morning. Hunt argued that they should not be required to pay for such gross inconvenience, but Lady Elgin restrained him and Hunt begrudgingly left twelve francs on the desk.

At this time Lady Elgin was five months pregnant with her fourth child. Nevertheless her energy was remarkable and both Hunt and Masterman found it difficult to keep up with her. By midday they were inside the village of Ambazac where they enjoyed a breakfast of toast and tea. Meanwhile, Hunt arranged for a new team of horses, which brought them into Orléans before nightfall. Lady Elgin implored Hunt to be more sagacious in his choice of sleeping quarters, and he came back moments later with the cheerful news that he had procured the residence of the mayor who had been called into Paris on urgent business. The mayor's wife was an overbearing creature who eventually calmed herself after Lady Elgin offered Masterman's service in the preparation of supper.

The horses were sprightly throughout the next day, pulling the carriage into Chartres exactly at noon. Hunt located a small cafe on the left bank of the Eure, high atop a hill crowned by Chartres' ancient cathedral. He described the city to them while they ate . . . how it was founded in the eleventh century on the very site of an earlier church which had been destroyed by fire, and how another conflagration laid waste the new structure even before it was completed.

Horse, from the East pediment of the Parthenon.

Combat of the Centaurs and Lapiths, Doric frieze of the Parthenon.

Dionysos, from the East pediment of the Parthenon.

Group on horseback, from the Panathenaic procession; Ionic frieze of the Parthenon.

Lord Byron at the age of twenty-six (1814). Portrait by Thomas Phillips; from the Roe-Byron Collection in Newstead Abbey.

Newstead Abbey
Nottingham Public Libraries

British Museum

English reaction to the purchase of the Elgin Marbles (from a cartoon by Cruikshank in the British Museum).

The Elgin Marbles at the British Museum in 1819, from a painting by A. Archer.

A watercolor of the Parthenon in 1776, with a small mosque inside the ruins. By William Pars.

A current photograph of the Parthenon.

Lord Nelson, engraved by W. Barnard, from a painting by L. F. Abbott, and formerly in the possession of Lady Hamilton.

British Museum

Lady Hamilton, from a painting by George Romney.

National Portrait Gallery, London

Lord Elgin, from a drawing by C. P. Harding.

Lady Elgin, from a painting by Hoppner.

But clergy and congregation set themselves to work and finished its final construction in the year 1240.

Below them were spread out the farmlands of Baeauce which were commonly called the granaries of France. The Eure divided into three branches and travelers usually crossed into the plains by several bridges, ancient and fringed with the remains of many old fortifications. The greatest attraction of Chartres, in addition to its cathedral, lay in the sharp contrast between the steep and narrow streets of the ancient town and the modern tree-filled boulevards whose width could contain at least ten carriages riding abreast of each other.

Lady Elgin entertained the notion of bribing Talleyrand, but Hunt cautioned against this. Here the chaplain broke out with one of his rare smiles and reminded Lady Elgin that she already possessed the best weapon in the world, one which Talleyrand could not ignore: motherhood.

Lady Elgin was not permitted to see Talleyrand until the third day after their arrival into Paris. His rooms were inside the old Palace of Luxembourg which was constructed to resemble the Pitti Palace at Florence. A spacious garden stretched out from the south facade and was abundant with trees and flower beds. There was much activity inside the Palace: men scurrying from room to room, officers waiting outside every door, soldiers snappily attired and casting flirtatious looks at any woman who happened to pass by. Lady Elgin was led into an inner office where a thin-shouldered man sat hunched over a large desk of oak. He was not aware that someone had entered the room and the adjutant had to touch him on the arm.

It seemed to Lady Elgin that Talleyrand's fragile body was held together only by his extremely tight-fitting clothes. However he was most attentive to her request and promised to do his utmost about obtaining Elgin's release from the prison at Lourdes. It was a cordial and friendly meeting.

Lady Elgin captivated the Foreign Minister "by protesting her helplessness," and before taking leave of him, she asked for Masterman's passport. Talleyrand assured her that it would be delivered to the Hotel de Richelieu where she was again staying.

After dinner that night Lady Elgin wrote to her husband:

> I have this moment dined and drank my beloved Elgin's health from the bottom of my heart. How does my Elgin do? This morning I was awaked by the firing of an amazing number of guns. I hear the First Consul returned last night to St. Cloud, and the report is that the expedition is landed in Ireland—50,000 men . . . At this moment I am in a fever with indecision. I am very very unhappy at being separated from you. I am told that the opinion of the world about you is much changed. People know the mistakes they have made about things at Constantinople. One man in particular, who was most violent, now owns his mistake and says so publickly. But still you *have* enemies.
>
> I want you sadly; you have no idea how deserted I feel, tho' I must say everybody pays me as much attention as possible. The weather is dreadfully bad, very rainy and blowy. . . .

Masterman's passport arrived at noon of the next day. The maid had her luggage packed and waiting in the corridor, and when the moment for her departure was at hand she fell to her knees before Lady Elgin, weeping and exclaiming that it was wrong to leave at such a time, with Lord Elgin in prison and Lady Elgin's baby expected in a few months. But Lady Elgin insisted that she go. It was too late and too dangerous to alter Talleyrand's decision.

Lady Elgin did not have the strength to walk downstairs with Masterman. Instead she waved good-bye from the window and sadly watched the carriage pull away. For the rest of that day she prayed to be delivered from a gnawing loneliness:

> I am in sad distress today, for I have just parted with M. I never thought I could have felt so furlorn [sic] but she is a

great favorite and I am sure much attached to me. The parting as you may imagine was sad. What a loss she is to poor me!

Hunt returned later in the afternoon and announced that he had scoured the whole capital before procuring a new maid, a capable young lady of twenty-one who carried the best recommendations, having been employed for six years in the household of the American Ambassador. Her name was Félicité: a demure little thing with dancing brown eyes and raven hair that was cut scandalously short, like that of a young lad.

It was decided that they should leave for Barèges early the next morning. Lady Elgin joined the other détunus in the Hotel that evening and was disappointed to hear that Robert Fergusson had left the capital for a fortnight's visit to Le Havre. Before retiring, she "sent out streams of letters to all her acquaintances, English and French, whom she thought might help" in effecting her husband's release from prison. She also wrote to the British Foreign Secretary; and to her father, asking him to "stir up political support."

She dreaded the return journey to Barèges, and once she stepped into the waiting carriage her mind rushed to Elgin, shivering inside a damp and unhealthy prison when only yesterday he had been feted by kings and queens while whole armies stood at rigid attention . . . sad and lonely Masterman, sitting in the cold silence of that carriage, eaten away by fear and apprehension . . . and her poor waifs, hundreds of miles from her arms, so destitute for her love!

Chapter
Eight

Pau

Through the bay window of her bedchamber Lady Elgin had a clear view of the snow-covered Pyrenees. October had already spent itself yet there was much warmth in the air. Leaves still clung to the trees and a powerful scent of grapes in harvest permeated the atmosphere. Talleyrand was true to his word and had not only negotiated Elgin's release from confinement at Lourdes, but he also supplied them with a fine winter house at Pau.

Lady Elgin became upset when she saw her husband after arriving from Paris. He was waiting in the large parlor, looking wretched, gaunt of body, his whole face pale except for the raw blotch of skin where his nose had been. He expressed no concern over the presence of a new maid, and after they had finally settled themselves around the dinner table he grew melancholic and kept staring at the floor.

While confined at Lourdes, Elgin wrote a long memorandum to King George III, explaining in great detail the incidents of his arrest and imprisonment. He had been on parole in the neighborhood of Pau when early one morning during the period when Pichegru, Moreau, and Georges* were in prison at Paris, an aide de camp of the general commanding the division arrested him under an order "that he was to be sent into close confinement in the

---

* These three generals were implicated in a plot against Napoleon.

Prison of Lourdes situated in the Pyrenees, in retaliation for severities said to have been exercised in England against the French General Boyer who had been taken prisoner in the West Indies."

On the day of his arrest Elgin received intelligence by post from Paris about a French officer arriving from England who entirely explained away the odium which had been thrown on the British Government by exaggerated misrepresentations on the occasion of General Boyer's transference (for misconduct) from Mansfield to Norman Cross in England. Elgin was immediately placed in the custody of Gens d'Armes and brought to the town of Pau where he made his report to the Prefect of the Department, the Count de Castellane, a gentleman no less in sentiments and manners than by birth. After hearing of Elgin's arrest, the Count exclaimed: *"J'aurais volontiers donné cinquante mille écus de ma poche que ceci ne fut pas arrivé chez moi!"**

Encouraged by the Count's example, the Receiver General of the Department gave Elgin a public breakfast on his passage through Pau, "which was the means of so deranging the measures that had been regulated for transporting him to prison, that the first escort was forgotten and they proceeded so wholly unattended they reached the village of Lourdes without being perceived by a strong detachment of Gens d'Armes who had been posted to relieve those who were expected to have brought them on their way."

Elgin was left at the Inn that night under guard. The Pyrenees at this time were completely under snow and the weather very severe. Most of the windows at the Inn were broken and the walls had no plaster. "Nor was there a bed or a single article of furniture provided. While in the Inn, the Paris papers of the day were brought in to me and it was a no less striking than alarming coincidence that the paper edited by Barriere, a native of that district in which it was of course

---

* I would willingly have given fifty thousand crowns that this matter had not come to my house.

much circulated, contained a most gross and impudent declaration, purporting that I had been guilty of the greatest atrocities towards the French Prisoners in Turkey."

The commandant of the prison at Lourdes happened to be a close friend with whom Elgin had spent the preceding summer at Barèges in great intimacy and fellowship. Elgin expected to get the same treatment at Lourdes; but instead of his former good manners, the commandant proved to be a stern and austere jailor. "I was not removed to Prison till it was dark. The procession was conducted with a very marked ostentation of rigour and a studied endeavour to heighten the gloom and impressiveness of the scene. I was led up by many windings along the side of the rock on which the Prison stands, and through a number of old Gates which were opened with much solemnity and guarded by numerous Detachments of Soldiery. At length I was lodged in a dreary and intensely cold room."

The commandant and his lieutenant continued with Elgin for some hours, expatiating with much show of sympathy on all the horrors that would attach to his situation, appealing to his feelings for his family and children, and alluding to the unfortunate extremities to which it was sometimes necessary to resort in great revolutions. "In point of fact, from the moment of being arrested I had abandoned all expectation of being released from this imprisonment in life. I had even destroyed all my papers and made my Will. I professed my conviction that the sentence of death was virtually pronounced against me and asked for nothing but that when the blow was to be struck, the Commandant would give me the satisfaction of being befriended by these honourable feelings of an Officer of the *ancien régime* which I knew him naturally to possess. They left me at a very late hour with evident reluctance."

In the course of a few days a sergeant of the guard came quite mysteriously to Elgin's cell and drew from under his coat a letter from a person styling himself "a fellow Prisoner who intimated that though confined *au secret* and unable to come to me, nevertheless he would receive me and *faire passer mes ennuis** whenever I was disposed to go and converse with him at the window. I immediately tore the letter to pieces; gave the Sergeant a Louis d'or as an expression of my thanks to him but warned that if he or any of his comrades brought me any further communication—verbal or in writing—I should instantly deliver it to the Commanding Officer in their presence."

Throughout most of Lord Elgin's confinement at Lourdes the commandant called upon him, but always under much reserve. On one of his visits the commandant spoke incidentally of the above-mentioned prisoner and added that a consultation of medical men had been called with a view to afford the prisoner the benefit of exercise since his health was obviously impaired. The very next day, to Elgin's surprise, this same prisoner was walking along a terrace near Elgin's window, evincing every disposition to enter into a conversation which Elgin successfully resisted.

Lord Elgin's confinement at the prison of Lourdes continued for a number of weeks under many severities until early one morning the commandant came to him with a messenger bearing his official discharge. No explanation was given concerning the reason for his arrest; and quite remarkably "no sooner was the messenger dismissed than the Commandant resumed all his former gaiety and freedom of intercourse."

Although she had held off until this time, Lady Elgin now decided to tell her husband that Talleyrand was willing to grant them a safe return to Scotland on the condition that Elgin cede the entire Parthenon collection to Bonaparte and the Louvre. Elgin's response was a morbid silence.

Lady Elgin's fourth child (William) was born at Pau on the fourth of March, and a short time after this she became involved with the festive life of the town:

* Assist me through my vexations.

The situation (in Pau) is most delightful: such a variety of beautiful rides and drives, you would be quite enchanted. We are allowed to remain perfectly quiet and only go to town to present ourselves occasionally to the Authorities. I have not seen a soul; almost all the other families are in the country. In winter Pau is the greatest of places: balls, great dinners and suppers, and plenty of card playing—tho' unfortunately only for sous. Elgin, with all his luck, says of a long evening that he could never contrive to lose more than half a crown.

Toward the end of the month Lord Hawkesbury finally replied to Lady Elgin's letter which was written from Paris concerning Lord Elgin's possible exchange for General Boyer:

Downing Street,

MADAM:

I have received the honour of your Ladyship's Letter, which I lost no time in laying before His Majesty. It would have given His Majesty the most sincere satisfaction to have contributed to the release of Lord Elgin by allowing his Exchange for General Boyer—but a sense of duty renders it impossible for Him in any way to admit or sanction the principle of exchanging Persons made prisoners according to the Laws of war, against any of His own Subjects who have been detained in France in violation of the Law of Nations and of the pledged Faith of the French Government.

The Account of the imprisonment of General Boyer was wholly without foundation. That Officer has never been in Confinement but has been considered merely as a Prisoner of war on Parole, and is at present residing at Chesterfield in the enjoyment of as much liberty as is ever accorded to Persons in similar Situations.

I can assure your Ladyship that it is with very deep regret that I find myself unable to render you the Assistance you desire. I should have felt the greatest pleasure in contributing by any practicable means to Lord Elgin's release and to the deliverance of your Ladyship and Him from the very unpleasant Situation in which you have been placed by arbitrary Proceedings of the French Government.

I have the honour to be etc.,

Before the end of March their acquaintances from the Hotel de Richelieu were assigned to Pau: the Cockburns, Colonel Crawford, and Mr. Sterling. Mrs. Fitzgerald had passed away during the summer. Lady Elgin inquired about Robert Fergusson and learned that he was back again in Paris.*

During their detainment in Pau Lord Elgin learned that a furor had been touched off in England concerning the presence of the Parthenon marbles at Park Lane.

The chief protagonist against Lord Elgin's activities in Athens was Lord Byron. The young poet had a close correspondence with the British Consul in Athens and had written to Logothetis to inform him that he and his friend John Cam Hobhouse were leaving Falmouth for a grand tour of the East. They expected to reside with Logothetis.

Byron had just received his Master of Arts, which he considered a nobleman's degree and a farce. To celebrate the event, the two college friends indulged themselves at Newstead Abbey, fitting up several apartments to entertain their guests in strange rites with monkish costumes.

They were delayed in Italy after leaving Geneva where Byron entered into an aesthetic relationship with the poet Shelley. In Venice he fell in love with Teresa Guiccioli, the young wife of an elderly Count; he also seduced at least one hundred women of the lower class.

Byron then traveled to the Dardanelles, and on a warm spring morning he and a British Lieutenant named Ekenhead swam across the Hellespont, a distance of eight treacherous kilometers. The water was bitterly cold, and the

* As a scientist, Fergusson could move about without fear of prison.

violent current from the melting mountain snows made the effort extremely difficult.*

> If, in the month of dark December,
>   Leander, who was nightly wont
> (What maid will not the tale remember?)
>   To cross thy stream, broad Hellespont!

Logothetis awaited Byron's arrival with great anticipation. In one of Byron's letters to the Consul several paragraphs were devoted to the young poet's tendency toward obesity and how he was able to maintain his beauty only through a strict diet of biscuits, rice and vinegar.

But Byron's promiscuities had already left their scars on his psyche:

> I am so changeable, being everything by turns but nothing for a long period of time . . . I am such a strange mélange of good and evil, it is impossible for anyone to really know me.

When the news of Byron's debarkation at the Piraeus reached Logothetis, he frantically began stocking his house with food and drink. After three days had passed without Byron's appearance, Logothetis was deeply affronted. In desperation, he ordered two of this servants to launch an immediate search throughout the city. They did not return until well past midnight. Most of the household had retired, with the exception of Logothetis and Lusieri.

For some mysterious reason, Byron had chosen to lodge himself inside the Monastery of the Capuchin Fathers which was about one kilometer from Logothetis' house. The Consul

---

* Byron wanted to commemorate the ancient story of Leander, who swam across the Hellespont each day to visit Hero, the priestess of the goddess Venus. It took Byron one hour and ten minutes to accomplish the feat; Ekenhead did it in one hour and five minutes. But two attempts were necessary. Their first try came on May 1st and they had to call a halt after one hour because of the current. Two days later they were transported by ship to a point near the Asiatic fort and this time they succeeded.

deemed this unpardonable and set out at sunrise to go after
Byron. Lusieri accompanied him. They stopped for a moment before the gate of the monastery: "Hymettus looming
before it, the Acropolis Hill behind. A monument of Lysicrates stood at the entrance, while just off the side to the left,
lay a peaceful grove of orange trees."

In the quadrangle they came upon a group of hooded
monks, within whose circle two young novices were flailing
away at each other, their white bodies bare to the waist. Loud
cries of approval came as each blow was landed; most of the
cheering emanated from the eldest of the group, a gray-
haired abbot whose hood had fallen over his frail shoulders.
A third man stood between the young fighters. He was of
medium height and shockingly thin. When he saw
Logothetis he broke away from the circle and ran to embrace
him. The Consul chided him for scorning his hospitality and
then inquired about the young fighters who were ready to
resume their positions, arms raised and fists clenched. Byron
laughed and exclaimed that the two novices were embroiled
in a bitter and ancient battle: "a contest between East and
West. Patriarch and Pope!" For the moment the Papal representative appeared to be winning which caused Logothetis
to rush toward the Greek novice and demand that he avenge
himself and his noble race. Although the young man's face
was puffed with red welts, and blood was trickling from his
nose and mouth, Logothetis' challenge somehow infused
him with new strength and he threw a desperate blow at his
adversary's stomach causing him to double over in pain. The
Catholic abbot suddenly stopped the fight, at which point
Byron roared: "Hail Byzantium!"

The monks slowly dispersed to their cells and within
moments the quadrangle reverberated from the loud clang
of the chapel bell announcing the noon meal. Byron invited
them into the refectory where bowls of bean soup were being
served. It was a sagging structure with low ceiling and
cracked walls. The monks stood impatiently behind their
benches as the abbot invoked his blessing. Before he had

finished, they plunged at the food, slurping loudly and shoving large chunks of dark bread into their mouths. Byron seemed to enjoy this. He led his guests to the furthest corner of the refectory where two men in European dress sat alone, toying sourly with their soup. Byron did not bother with introductions but seated himself and between mouthfuls talked of his travels: "And when we left Falmouth, Hobhouse here took one hundred pens along, together with two gallons of ink and a year's supply of paper. Wretched soul! He fashions himself a writer . . . and I never heard such grumbling in my life until William Fletcher, there on my right hand, decided to travel with us. He was my valet at Newstead and wanted desperately to join us even though he had just been married only a few days prior. Throughout most of the voyage he wept and wished he were back with his Sally. Meanwhile the ocean was unkind to Hobhouse and even induced him to vomit first his dinner then his boring impressions of the entire journey. I caught everything flush between the eyes!"

At Lisbon the travelers encountered a continent at war. The English had just taken over the city from the French and she was in a deplorable state: dead bodies lay exposed in the churchyards with saucers on their breasts, their burial delayed until enough money was put into the saucers for the gluttonous priests. Yet there was enchantment in Portugal. Byron loved the orange trees that sprinkled the green valleys with necklaces of gold. He swam the Tagus. He rode on an ass. He conversed with the monks in Latin. He swore in Portuguese. He suffered with diarrhea and bites from mosquitoes but never complained: "Comfort must not be expected by folks that go a pleasuring!"

They journeyed from Lisbon to Seville on horseback, across a country where death and love mingled together like clouds in a storm. The women of Seville were the most handsome in the world. Their black eyes and fine forms obsessed Byron. After being lodged in a house with two such creatures and it came time to leave, Byron was embraced by the

younger of the two, who cut off a lock of his hair then presented him with one of her own which measured three feet
in length. Her last words were: "Adieu, you pretty fellow.
You please me much."

Both Hobhouse and Fletcher remained silent while
Byron talked. Hobhouse was in his late twenties, very fair
with intense features. Fletcher had the appearance of a
dwarf who had aged before his time.

After a while the monks finished with their food and,
following a quick benediction from the abbot, began filing
out of the refectory. Byron helped himself to another bowl
of soup as he continued to talk: "We then boarded the Malta
packet from Gibraltar and walked the deck, staring at the
sea, breathing in the wondrous poetry of the Gibraltar cliffs.
With the lighting of the lamps I would go forward and sit on
a roll of sailcloth, remaining there for hours and watching
the moonbeams dance on the waves. No doubt my fellow
passengers mistook my yearning for solitude as cold arro-
gance and judged me harshly. Far worse, once I had assumed
this attitude of detachment I had to stay with it because I was
still enraptured by the immature thought that it was noble to
seek such melancholy pleasure."

At Malta Byron took lessons in Arabic from an old Egyptian monk; "also in platonic love from the wife of Elgin's
arch-enemy, Sir Spencer Smith." At last they reached Albania, a barbarous land whose fierce mountains reminded
Byron of Scotland. The goatherds even wore skirts to the
knee. When the Pasha of Ioannina heard of their arrival he
invited them immediately to his house where they dined in
elegance, surrounded by Albanians with embroidered tunics,
Tartars in tall hats, rows of black eunuchs, and a steady
chorus of drums. Meanwhile the muezzin chanted from
every minaret in the city: "There is no other God than
Allah!"

The Pasha was seventy full years and had a thick white
beard, always smiling, and with the manners of an English
gentleman. Yet he thought nothing of roasting his enemies

at the stake, or throwing ten women off a cliff if they annoyed his daughter-in-law. Such conduct intrigued Byron. He strongly believed that holiness and virtue were more prevalent in a band of rogues than under a priest's cassock. Despite the apparent frailty of Byron's body, a surging strength of spirit transformed him into a titan. His eyes were alive, passionate, daring . . . as though embracing humanity itself in pools of universal love.

Byron, Hobhouse, and Fletcher plodded up those impossible Albanian mountains, and when they finally left the country and boarded a Turkish man-of-war to head for Greece, Fletcher called upon his Sally to save him from the terrible storm and the incompetence of the sailors. It was a fiasco: the Greeks on board praying to their saints; the Turks to Allah. Their invocations fell upon deaf ears and the sails were torn to shreds as Fletcher whimpered: "We shall all find a watery grave!"

After the storm spent itself the man-of-war lay stranded on a beach, surrounded by a wild-looking band of Suliotes.* Captain and crew were afraid they would be harmed, but instead the Suliotes dried their clothes, fed them, entertained them with their klephtic† songs, and as they were about to depart Byron offered their chief a few coins. The old Suliote admonished him: "I wish you to love me, not to pay me!"

Before going to the Capuchin Monastery, Byron stopped at the house of a widow for a visit and while there immediately fell in love with her three daughters, all of them under fifteen. But over Teresa, the youngest, he became enamored:

> Maid of Athens, ere we part
> Give, oh give me back my heart;
> Or since that has left my breast

* Inhabitants of northern Greece.
† Mountain songs of independence.

Keep it now and take the rest.
Hear my vow before I go:
Zoë mou, sas agapo!*

A few days later Lusieri and Logothetis paid another visit
to the Monastery of the Capuchin Fathers. The day was un-
bearably hot; the air sticky. When they came into the swelter-
ing quadrangle they saw Byron stripped to the waist, absorb-
ing punch after punch from a young novice monk twice his
size. As soon as the monk noticed the Consul he dropped
his arms and raced toward him, explaining that Byron asked
to be thrashed; that he had burst into the novice's cell at
daybreak and commanded him to do it:

> In one fleeting moment faces glide past me . . . faces
> that once brimmed with life, with joy. But now they are
> gone. Alas, there is something incomprehensible about
> death. In all this world I had but two people who cared for
> me. Really cared. And they are both gone! And you, charm-
> ing but cynical Matthews, how often did I admonish you:
> 'Matthews, you swim badly. If you persist in keeping your
> head so high you will surely drown yourself!' Charon† what
> have you dealt me? My mother and my best friend! But
> peace be to the dead; let us resume the dull business of life
> . . . as to immortality, if people are to live again then why
> die? If our carcasses are to rise again are they worth rising?
> And if mine is, I hope it shall have a better pair of legs than
> these!

Byron came to his senses after a glass of brandy.
Logothetis assisted the monk, and they brought him into the
cool shade of his cell where Byron's disjointed words eventually came together: Fletcher had left for England to settle the
estate of Byron's deceased mother; Matthews had drowned in
the Cam, caught in the waterweeds. Just before setting off

* My life, I love you. (Greek)
† Ferryman.

for Greece, Byron had arranged a party at Newstead Abbey for Matthews, Hobhouse, and himself. They passed the first few days in foolery. "At the front entrance, directly off the stairs that led into the main hall, they chained a live bear; and to the left, a wolfhound. If a visitor ambled in unannounced the sight of that bear and wolfhound was enough to paralyze him; and if by chance he was able to survive that shock he then had to contend with the rapid fire of their pistol practice beneath the vaulting." They got up late every morning. But it did not matter. Breakfast always remained on the table until each of them had come down. Then they read, fenced, pistol-practiced, went for a ride, rowed, and even played with the bear and wolfhound. After dinner they passed around a human skull filled with brandy, the pate of some unfortunate monk whose skeleton had been struck by the gardener's spade. Byron had it mounted as a cup by a Nottingham jeweler, with the inscription:

> I lived, I loved, I quaff'd like thee;
> I died, let earth my bones resign.
> Fill up. Thou canst not injure me;
> The worm hath fouler lips than thine.
>
> Better to hold the sparkling grape
> Than nurse the earth-worm's slimy hood,
> And circle in the goblet's shape
> The drink of gods, than reptile's food!

Logothetis again demanded that Byron leave the monastery and come stay at his house, but Byron threw him a helpless gaze: "If you could but look into my soul and see its torment! I am like a tiny vessel in a storm. My life has no meaning, no direction. When Father D'Yvree* gave me permission to inhabit one of the cells here, I kissed his crucifix in tears."

Religion, like everything else, had to be a violent experience for Byron.

---

* The abbot of the Capuchin Monastery in Athens.

In the middle of his lamentations Byron suddenly turned
on Lusieri and denounced Lord Elgin, threatening to shame
him before the world unless he called away his despoilers
from the Parthenon. "What right had he to remove the precious stones of a weak nation? What right had he to raise his
hand against a building that had stood whole for two
thousand years?"

> But who of all the plunderers of yon fame
> On high, where Pallas lingered, loth to flee
> The latest relic of her ancient reign,
> The last, the worst, dull spoiler, who was he?
> Blush, Caledonia! Such thy son could be.
> England! I joy no child he was of thine;
> Thy free-born men should spare what once was free,
> Yet they could violate each saddening shrine
> And bear these altars o'er the long-reluctant brine.
>
> What! Shall it e'er be said by British tongue
> Albion was happy in Athena's tears?
> Though in thy name the slaves her bosom wrung,
> Tell not the deed to blushing Europe's ears;
> The ocean queen, the free Britannia, bears
> The last poor plunder from a bleeding land;
> Yes, she whose generous aid her name endears
> Tore down those remnants with a Harpy's hand,
> Which envious Eld forbore and tyrants left to stand.
>
> Cold is the heart, fair Greece! that looks on thee,
> Nor feels as lovers o'er the dust they loved;
> Dull is the eye that will not weep to see
> Thy walls defaced, thy mouldering shrines removed
> By British hands which it had best behoved
> To guard those relics ne'er to be restored.
> Cursed be the hour when from their isle they roved
> And snatched thy shrinking gods to northern climes
>   abhorred.

Shortly after this, Byron returned to England. He awoke
one morning and "found himself famous." Four editions of

Childe Harold's Pilgrimage had already gone through the press and he was besieged by London's society at teas and dinner parties. A large part of the second canto of *Childe Harold's Pilgrimage* was a bitter attack on Lord Elgin.

Lord Elgin had been forewarned about Byron—both by Lusieri and Logothetis. Elgin, however, refused to give the poet serious thought—at least not openly—but in a letter to Hobhouse written in the summer of 1811, Byron made a startling disclosure:

> Lord Elgin has been teazing to see me these last days. I wrote to him at his own request all I knew about his robberies, and at last have written to say that, as it is my intention to publish in Childe Harold on that topic, I thought proper since he insisted on seeing me, to give him notice so that he might not have an opportunity of accusing me of double-dealing afterwards.

Elgin may have wanted this publicity even though it was unfavorable. In any case, he was firmly influenced by his secretary William Richard Hamilton who, after being advised of Byron's animosity toward his employer, remarked:

> I do not consider him (Byron) a very formidable enemy in his meditated attack and I shall be much surprised if his attack on what you have done does not turn out one of the most friendly acts he could have done. It will create an interest in the public, excite curiosity, and the real advantage to this country and the merit of your exertions will become known and felt as they are more known.

It was a bad mistake for Hamilton to make. Elgin never dreamed he would be eternally stigmatized in a poem. Only once throughout the entire work does Byron attack an individual and that person is Lord Elgin. *Childe Harold's Pilgrimage* lifted Byron into prominence. Within a few short months an unknown dreamer and versifier had become a great romantic poet who was seriously read in every drawing room in Great Britain and the continent.

When the Prince Regent joined Byron's forces it gave rise to a wave of personal assaults upon Lord Elgin. Edward Daniel Clarke, always present and willing, leaped into the fray, congratulating Byron on the publication of *Childe Harold*. Clarke chided Elgin's agents for "want of taste and utter barbarism. Removed from their original setting, the Parthenon marbles have lost all their excellence!"

Lord Elgin soon learned that a host of other voices were speaking out against him, most of them travelers freshly returned from the East:

> It appears to me a very flagrant piece of injustice to deprive a helpless and friendly nation of any possession of value to them . . . I wonder at the boldness of the hand that could venture to remove what Phidias had placed under the inspection of Pericles.

A large number of these travelers were despoilers themselves. Dodwell had no call to fault Lord Elgin's "insensate barbarism and devastating outrage which will never cease to be deplored." Hughes too spoke of Elgin's "wanton devastation and avidity for plunder." And Eustace had the audacity to condemn Lord Elgin "without even having been to Athens."

These mounting attacks of condemnation did not come from England alone. The French too added their indignation. The usually gentle Chateaubriand affixed his support to the melee, "even though he too had a piece of the Parthenon in his pocket when he left Athens."

It did not end here.

Lord Elgin was subjected to an avalanche of cruel jokes and jibes, "and even the ugly disfigurement of his nose was not spared. It was viciously attributed to venereal disease:"

Noseless himself he brings here noseless blocks
To show what time has done and what the pox.

But the sharpest attack of all came from Byron's most
recent poem: *The Curse of Minerva*. One of Lord Elgin's
friends tried to prevent its publication and for a time it
seemed that Byron would oblige. While in Athens, Byron
was visited by Edward Everett of Massachusetts. Everett
asked him "whether his poem which he speaks of as printed
but not published would ever be given to the world. 'Oh, no!'
Byron replied. 'It is a satire upon Lord Elgin which a particular friend has begged me to suppress!"

Byron nevertheless printed a few copies and sent them to
select friends, including Clarke. A pirated copy found its way
into *The New Monthly Magazine* and the poem was soon
brought to the attention of the world. It begins with the poet
sitting disconsolately within the ruined walls of the Parthenon as evening is falling over Athens. Suddenly Minerva
(Athena) appears, but she does not look like the goddess at
all: her aegis has no power, her armor is dented, her lance
broken:

'Mortal!'—'twas thus she spake—'that blush of shame
Proclaims thee Briton, once a noble name;
First of thy mighty, foremost of the free,
Now honour'd less by all, and least by me:
Chief of thy foes shall Pallas still be found.
Seek'st thou the cause of loathing? Look around.
Lo! here, despite of war and wasting fire,
I saw successive tyrannies expire.
'Scaped from the ravage of the Turk and Goth,
Thy country sends a spoiler worse than both.
Survey this vacant violated fane;
Recount the relics torn that yet remain:
These Cecrops placed, *this* Pericles adorn'd.
That Adrian rear'd when drooping Science mourn'd.
What more I owe let gratitude attest—
Know, Alaric and Elgin did the rest.

That all may learn from whence the plunderer came,
The insulted wall sustains his hated name!*
For Elgin's fame thus grateful Pallas pleads,
Below, his name; *above,* behold his deeds!'

Moving deeper into the poem, Venus vows to avenge Minerva and she invokes her own curse upon Elgin:

'Yet still the gods are just, and crimes are cross'd:
See here what Elgin won, and what he lost!
Another name with his pollutes my shrine:
Behold where Dian's beams disdain to shine!
Some retribution still might Pallas claim,
When Venus half avenged Minerva's shame.'

Minerva now begs the poet to carry her curse home to his native country. Elgin's deed is so damnable it is not enough that he alone suffer. England too has to be punished. She will be plagued by a succession of horrible wars which eventually shall destroy her. "Her tyrant empire will be shaken to its base!" Her trade will languish; famine and pestilence will break out over her land; and finally she will be invaded and ravaged. But the main brunt of the curse is to fall upon Elgin and his family:

'First on the head of him who did this deed
My curse shall light—on him and all his seed:
Without one spark of intellectual fire,
Be all the sons as senseless as the sire!'

The Scottish novelist John Galt was unquestionably the most vicious of Elgin's antagonists. He was present at Athens when the Parthenon and Erechtheum were being ravaged by Lusieri and his crew of laborers. "Galt was also an eye-witness

---

* The names of Elgin and Mary Elgin were carved deeply and clearly about half-way up one of the columns of the Parthenon in a place which Hunt had specially reserved. Elgin's name was soon erased but that of Mary Elgin could still be read in 1826. (William St. Clair, *Lord Elgin and the Marbles,* p. 193.)

to the struggle between Lusieri and Fauvel for the possession of the Parthenon marbles, and even intervened in an attempt to prevent a Hydriote ship from loading the marbles into her hold":

> Two circumstances occasioned this interference on my part: an Italian artist, the agent of Lord Elgin, had quarrelled about the marbles with Monsieur Fauvel, the French consul . . . Fauvel was no doubt ambitious to obtain these precious fragments for the Napoleon Museum at Paris; and certainly exerted all his influence to get the removal of them interdicted. On the eve of the departure of the vessel, he sent in a strong representation on the subject to the governor of the city, stating (what I believe was very true) that Lord Elgin had never any sufficient firman or authority for the dilapidations that he had committed on the temples. Lusieri (the Italian artist alluded to) was alarmed and called on me at the monastery of the Roman Propaganda where I then resided; and it was agreed that if any detention was attempted I should remonstrate with the governor and represent to him that such an arrest of British property would be considered an act of hostility.

Meanwhile Lusieri had armed himself with still another firman from the Kaimmacam to the Voivode. Along with this, he had additional support: the presence of HMS *Pylades* which was sent specially from Smyrna to the Piraeus for the purpose of escorting the Hydriote ship with her prize collection of marbles.

Fauvel was finally rejected by the Voivode and Lusieri dispatched a triumphant message to Lord Elgin:

> Covering up all my past woes with eternal oblivion, I wholly give myself up to joy when I see the antiquities on board the polacca ready to set her sails for Malta. I regret that I cannot follow them as I am obliged to stay here as a surety for paying what I owe and carrying out my promises to the Voivode.

John Galt took passage on this same Hydriote ship, but only as far as Hydra Isle. Prior to this, he wrote to his banker at Malta and instructed him to buy all the marbles as soon as the Hydriote vessel reached port. "Galt anticipated that Lord Elgin's bankers would allow no further credit, since he was already heavily in debt to them":

> Here was a chance of the most exquisite relics of art in the world becoming mine, and a speculation by the sale of them in London that would realise a fortune.

Fortunately for Elgin, Galt's scheme failed and thus another collection was on its way to the museum at Park Lane: forty-eight cases of marbles, including the best of the Parthenon sculptures. Galt of course was itching to strike back at Elgin, and as soon as he returned to Scotland he wrote a cruel satire which he called *Atheniad*. As with Byron's *The Curse of Minerva*, Lord Elgin tried to suppress its publication, using the influence of his former secretary William Richard Hamilton who now held the position of curator at the museum in Park Lane.*

The Atheniad is "an amateurish piece of mock heroics, good-humoured enough on the whole, but where *The Curse* becomes bitter against Lord Elgin, the *Atheniad* merely shows bad taste."

Galt disguises his main characters in the poem. Lusieri is "Dontitos" and Lord Elgin is called "Brucides." The poem begins as Dontitos calls upon Brucides and tells him he must rescue the Parthenon marbles from the Turks. Hoping this would make him famous, Brucides undertakes the task, but in the midst of his endeavors the gods of Olympus show their wrath and immediately begin to take their revenge. Neptune sinks Brucides' ship at Cerigo. Soon after this, Brucides loses his post at Constantinople because Minerva has taken his military and diplomatic dispatches and transposed them into

---

* Hamilton later became Under Secretary at the Foreign Office.

garbled nonsense. The goddess then follows Brucides into France and, disguised as Talleyrand, persuades Bonaparte to detain all the British there as prisoners of war. Mars also takes his revenge and stirs up horrible wars in Egypt and Russia.

The final act of revenge is left with Athena: Brucides' marriage is destroyed, his children die, and Cupid sends a flaming torch into his face, disfiguring him so badly that he becomes a noseless statue.

Although Byron refused to admit it, he borrowed many ideas from the *Atheniad*. In one glaring example, Galt calls Eratostratus "the bold youth that fired th' Ephesian dome;" *The Curse of Minerva* has it, "the fool that fired the Ephesian dome."

But Elgin's enemies were not confined to poets and novelists. The main brunt of the attack against him was leveled by Richard Payne Knight in England. Knight's influence as a patron of the arts was strongly felt everywhere. As a youth he wrote a diary of a journey to Sicily which so impressed Goethe, immediate arrangements were made to have it published in Germany. Knight's best book, *An Analytic Inquiry into the Principles of Taste*, was a penetrating study of sense, idea, passion and truth. Claiming that ideal beauty does not exist, Knight did concede to "certain standards of excellence which all cultures have recognized in theory, even though they have departed from them in practice. Accordingly, the precious remains of Greek sculpture afford true beauty, grace and eloquence in the human form. Their perfection can never be questioned."

Knight was one of the first to inspect the Parthenon marbles at the museum in Park Lane and wrongly concluded they were not Greek in origin but Roman. Benjamin West (the venerable president of the Royal Academy who tried to find an English artist for Elgin's embassy) took a contrary view and came quickly to Elgin's defense:

I have found in this collection of sculpture so much excellence in art, and a variety so magnificent and boundless, that every branch of science connected with the fine arts cannot fail to acquire something from this collection. Your Lordship, by bringing these treasures of the first and best age of sculpture and architecture into London, has founded a new Athens for the emulation and example of the British student.

The leading artists of England praised Lord Elgin for his labors. Many of them requested permission to enter the museum at Park Lane to make sketches and paintings of the marbles. Included in this group was the landscape painter Joseph Farington who saw the marbles as "the highest quality of Art, a union of greatness and nature." Sir Thomas Lawrence, the British portraitist, was also a frequent visitor; as was Nollekens,* and even the group of painters who were all rejected by Elgin at Broomhall in 1799. All of them now admitted that they had missed out on a great opportunity. Turner in particular took the time and wrote to Elgin, "to pay my homage to your Lordship's exertions for this rescue from barbarism."

Artists, statesmen, foreign dignitaries, and every important name in London society requested permission to visit Lord Elgin's shed at Park Lane. The Elgin Marbles soon became the main topic of conversation in London, and their most notable champion was the young historical painter Benjamin Robert Haydon who up until this time had been unsuccessful in his endeavors to prove that he was predestined to form a new and brilliant school of English historical painting. Through the influence of a friend, a pass was obtained for Haydon, and his impressions were jotted down into a diary which later was to be his autobiography:

> To Park Lane then we went, and after passing through the hall and thence into an open yard, entered a damp, dirty pent-house where lay the marbles ranged within sight and reach. The first thing I fixed my eyes on was the wrist of a figure in one of the female groups in which were

---

* Joseph Nollekens (1737-1823). The most fashionable portrait sculptor of his day. Among his many busts were those of Pitt, and George III.

visible, though in a feminine form, the radius and the ulna.
I was astonished, for I had never seen them hinted at in any
female wrist in the antique. I darted my eye to the elbow
and saw the outer condyle visibly affecting the shape as in
nature. That combination of nature and idea, which I had
felt was so much wanting for high art, was here displayed to
mid-day conviction. My heart beat! If I had seen nothing
else, I beheld sufficient to keep me to nature for the rest of
my life. But when I turned to the Theseus and saw that
every form was altered by action or repose—when I saw
that the two sides of his back varied: one side stretched
from the shoulder blade being pulled forward, and the
other side compressed from the shoulder blade being
pushed close to the spine as he rested on his elbow with the
belly flat because the bowels fell into the pelvis as he sat
—and when, turning to the Ilissus, I saw the belly pro-
truded, from the figure lying on its side—and again, when
in the figure of the fighting metope I saw the muscle shown
under the one arm-pit in that instantaneous action of dart-
ing out, and left out in the other arm-pits because not
wanted—when I saw in fact the most heroic style of art
combined with all the essential detail of actual life, the thing
was done at once and forever. Here were principles which
the common sense of the English people would understand; here were principles which I had struggled for in my
first picture with timidity and apprehension; here were the
principles which the great Greeks in their finest time established; and here was I . . .

Oh, how inwardly I thanked God that I was prepared to
understand all this!

For many months after this, Haydon "spent every spare
moment of his life drawing in Elgin's chilly museum. He
drew for ten or fifteen hours at a time, continuing by can-
dlelight until the porter came to close up at midnight."

Then often have I gone home, cold, benumbed, and
damp; my clothes steaming up as I dried them; and so
spreading my drawings on the floor and putting a candle

there, I have drank my tea at one in the morning with ecstacy as its warmth trickled through my frame, and looked at my picture, and dwelt on my drawings, and pondered on the change of empires, and thought that I had been contemplating what Socrates looked at, and Plato saw—and then, lifted up with my own high urgings of soul, I have prayed to God to enlighten my mind to discover the principles of those divine things—and then I have had inward assurances of future glory, and almost fancying divine influence in my room, have lingered to my mattress bed, and soon dozed into a rich balmy slumber.

Despite his long hours of labor, Haydon religiously fed entries into his diary:

8 September: Drew at Lord Elgin's from ten till half-past two, and from three to three-quarter-past five ... walked about and looked at those matchless productions. I consider it truly the greatest blessing that ever happened to this country, their being brought here.

Lord Elgin's original aim in undertaking the Constantinople post certainly must have found gratification with Haydon's entry for 5 November:

Drew at Lord Elgin's—six hours. My taste thank God is improved wonderfully.

But even with the support of all these artists, Lord Elgin's reputation suffered greatly from the steady assaults of Richard Payne Knight. As the leading spokesman for the Society of Dilettanti (which had come a long distance from its original goal "of meeting once a month in the Star and Garter, and drinking toasts to 'Grecian taste and Roman spirit' "). Knight was relentless in his battle with Elgin and even volunteered to write the text of the Society's newest publication, *Specimens of Antient Sculpture*, which included excellent engravings of at least sixty works of art belonging to various members of the Society. (Knight himself possessed twenty-three of these works. His collection of bronzes was reputed to be the largest in Europe.)

In writing the text for *Specimens of Antient Sculpture,* Knight spared no feelings on the Elgin Marbles, although quite surprisingly he did not mention Elgin's name:

> Of Phidias' general style of composition, the friezes and metopes of the Temple of Minerva at Athens, (published by Mr. Stuart and since brought to England,) may afford us competent information; but as these are merely architectural sculptures executed from his designs and under his directions probably by workmen scarcely ranked among artists, and meant to be seen at the height of more than forty feet from the eye, they can throw but little light upon the more important details of his art . . . The relief in the metopes is much higher, so as to exhibit the figures nearly complete, and the details are more accurately and elaborately made out; but they are so different in their degrees of merit, as to be evidently the works of many different persons, some of whom would not have been entitled to the rank of artists in a much less cultivated and fastidious age.

Confined in France throughout all this time, Elgin was not too disturbed over Knight; nor Byron or Clarke or John Galt. His mind was on still another collection of marbles that was under guard on the docks of the Piraeus, awaiting the long-delayed arrival of a British warship which the Admiralty had promised to dispatch.

Félicité took admirably to her duties, complex and demanding as they were. She was exceptionally competent with William and spent most of her free moments with him. Lady Elgin was quite busy at Pau during these long winter weeks. Occasionally Mr. and Mrs. Cockburn joined the Elgins for whist, but Mr. Cockburn was a poor player and Lady Elgin doubted if he would ever grasp the game. Once each week the détunus dined together, but this proved burdensome for Lord Elgin and his heart was not in it. Not a day passed that he did not manifest his anxiety over the Parthenon marbles at the Piraeus docks. He sent a flood of letters to Lusieri, coaxing him toward even more acquisitions and excavations, no matter what the cost. In January alone he wrote three times to his mother and alerted her to spare no expense in confiscating Choiseul-Gouffier's frieze from the Parthenon "which all this time was being held under heavy duty charges at the London Customs House."

On the second day of February Lady Elgin received word from her own mother in Scotland. Mrs. Nisbet had finally warmed to the Greek Paramana and even went so far as to admit there were no English nurses to compare with this obese Greek peasant who took exactly the same care of the children whether Mrs. Nisbet was present or absent. But the Greek Paramana's fondness for garlic and thick sauces was still frowned upon by Lady Elgin's mother.

Lady Elgin was pleased to learn that Bruce was keeping diligently to his study of Greek. Tearfully, she recalled his daily greeting in Constantinople, so clear and brimming with love: *"Kali 'mera, Mitera. S'agapo!"**

And Mary trying her best with Matilda to imitate him, their thin lips moving along with each syllable, stumbling but never giving up. True Scotsmen!

William's health bothered Lady Elgin. The child ate like a sparrow and was of very delicate constitution. But Lady Elgin was exceptionally attached to him:

> William has cut his first tooth without the least fever or anything to annoy us. He is really the finest child I ever saw. Such long eye lashes—so firm, so good a skin—and then he has such a merry little intelligent face of his own, as would quite captivate you I am sure. I don't know what we should do without him; he is the life of the whole house.

* Good morning, mother. I love you!

Mrs. Cockburn recommended a physician in Pau who was considered an authority on childrens' ailments and after a lengthy examination he pronounced William fit, much to the vexation of Lady Elgin who was convinced the child was seriously ill. To improve William's appetite the French physician prescribed a teaspoonful of red wine before each feeding. Lady Elgin was also encouraged to submit the child to regular visits at the baths in Barèges as soon as the season began.

They never got to Barèges.

In the first week of April the French authorities at Pau notified the Elgins that they were now free to return to Paris. That evening they visited their friends and everyone seemed in fine humor, even Mr. Sterling. Colonel Crawford added to the festivities by narrating some hoary tales of military life in Egypt.

Hunt left the house early the next morning and made negotiations for the hire of two carriages. By noon everything was ready. After the drivers had attended to the luggage Félicité stepped into the first carriage, carrying William in her arms. Lady Elgin joined her in the rear seat while Hunt and Lord Elgin shared the front. At the outskirts of Pau their driver turned toward the Bordeaux road, but Lady Elgin had already traveled it many times and suggested they go via Toulouse and Lyons. The route or the stops were insignificant to Lord Elgin. He was happy enough to be leaving Pau. Even William seemed content and lay snuggled in his blanket, a pink glow on his face.

As the carriages sped across the countryside, hamlets and towns flitted past them like clouds tossed about in a storm. Lady Elgin observed a surging look of joy in her husband's eyes which probably was brought about by a rekindled hope of imminent freedom and the promise of seeing Scotland at last. Toulouse skipped by before they realized it: a few squalid houses of white stucco, a solitary church, cows grazing in a quiet meadow. It was a long journey, and Hunt wondered if they should have taken the Bordeaux road after all, but Lord Elgin could see no point in turning back. Besides, he had always wanted to visit Lyons.

Just before dusk they entered a small village. Lady Elgin became suddenly alarmed over her son. The child's brow felt hot and he had started to fret while they were passing through Toulouse. They decided to stop here. The name of the village was Burlats and they took lodgings at a remote inn. William was given some warm milk and eventually fell asleep. He awoke the household in the middle of the night, however, violently ill with vomiting and high fever. Hunt summoned one of the carriage drivers and together they hurried into the neighboring village of Brassac in search of a physician. It was almost dawn when they returned. The old doctor took one look at the child and immediately subjected him to an application of eight leeches to each temple, followed by an additional ordeal of cupping and blood-letting.

By mid-afternoon William's fever subsided and he was able to take a little beef broth which the innkeeper's wife had prepared. Lord Elgin was reinforced and declared they should continue with their journey but both Lady Elgin and Hunt prevailed upon him to wait another day until William was more fit for travel. Elgin sulked momentarily, but at dinner he recovered enough to engage in a heated political discussion with the innkeeper.

They left Burlats at daybreak.

Lyons truly astounded them: the baths, tombs, relics of an ancient theater, three aquaducts, and even traces of a subterranean canal that once conveyed the waters of the Rhône into a lake specially constructed for miniature sea battles. From the moment they entered the city Hunt began to deluge them with his depth of learning, carrying the Elgins as far back as the Gauls and Segusians, explaining how Lyons was once wedged between the Rhône and the Saône, and bordered by fine quays that were joined by twenty-four bridges. Agrippa had made Lyons the starting point of four great roads; and Augustus gave the city a senate, making it the seat of an annual assembly of deputies. Although it was burned to the ground just after the birth of Christ, Lyons was successively adorned by Trajan, Hadrian, and Antoninus. St. Irenaeus met his martydom here during the savage persecution of Septimus Severus; and in the thirteenth century two ecclesiastical councils convened inside the Cathedral de Nôtre Dame de Fourviere.

Lady Elgin was half listening to Hunt. William's fever seemed to be acting up again, and she warned her husband that they should look for a physician.

Paris

Pray for me, dearest mother. Take me in your arms. Your prayers will be heard tho' mine were not listened to. I have lost my William, my angel William. My soul doated upon him; I was wrapt up in my child. From the moment of his birth, to the fatal night it pleased God to call him, I have devoted myself to him. I resigned to the Will of the Almighty but my happiness is destroyed forever. My William, my adored William is gone, and left me here!

Lady Elgin refused to have the child buried in France, and while Elgin pleaded their case to Talleyrand she arranged to have William embalmed and placed in a bier. Several weeks went by before Talleyrand finally sent word: Bonaparte had relented and agreed to grant Lady Elgin and Hunt permission to return to England so that William could be buried in Elgin's family vault at Dunfermline. But Lord Elgin was to remain in France for the duration of the war.

Although Lady Elgin fell into a dilemma about abandoning her husband at a time like this, she could not bear another day in France; and to add to her misery, she was pregnant with her fifth child.

Passage was arranged for embarkation in three days on an English brig that was docked at Calais. Robert Fergusson was also returning to England on board the same ship.

On the morning of Lady Elgin's departure French soldiers came to the Richelieu and ordered Lord Elgin out of bed. He was arrested and taken to the prison at Melun:

> When I was a prisoner in Paris—I received a mysterious
> letter from an English traveller which complained of
> Lusieri's taking down of the frieze of the Parthenon. The
> next morning a common gens d'arme came and took me
> out of bed, and sent me into close confinement away from
> my family. Such was the influence exercised by the
> French . . . .

The channel crossing was perilous. Stormy winds en-
gulfed the brig from the moment she left Calais, forcing
Hunt to confine himself to his cabin throughout the voyage.
Lady Elgin remained on deck, bundled up with several blankets and refusing to look back at the despised French coast.

At first sight of Dover, the storm abated and the brig
drifted peacefully around Folkstone, putting herself on a
straight course for Portsmouth. A favorable wind soon
found her sails and she continued swiftly past Hastings and
Brighton, coming finally into Portsmouth harbor. Before
leaving the ship, they dined that evening at the Captain's
table. Robert Fergusson spoke at length with Lady Elgin.
Because she was in a weak physical state, he offered to as-
sume full responsibility for the burial of William at
Dunfermline.* She assented.

When they reached London, Hunt parted with Lady
Elgin. His hopes of ever realizing an independent fortune
were all but shattered. Lord Elgin had not reimbursed him
with one farthing up to this point and Hunt was now compelled "to transfer his services to the Duke of Bedford." This
revelation was a blow to Lady Elgin and she begged Hunt to
reconsider, but he was too embittered and wanted no more
of Lord Elgin.†

On the carriage journey to London, Lady Elgin was given
a newspaper that carried a story demanding the immediate
return of the Parthenon marbles to Greece. The article was
spurred by the deplorable report that a famous prizefighter

---

* Fergusson escorted the bier to Scotland and was present at the funeral.

† Hamilton alone, out of all the party that sailed to Constantinople, was to
remain loyal to Lord Elgin until the very end.

named Gregson was induced to stand naked in Elgin's museum at Park Lane and pose for two hours in various attitudes so that his anatomy might be compared with the statues. "A considerable number of English gentlemen paid as much as a guinea to witness this performance. A month or so later, three actual boxing matches took place inside the museum between the best pugilists of the day."

Throughout her stay in London, Lady Elgin resided in a small house at Number 60 Baker Street. Her parents owned a palatial house at Portman Square which was nearby and they entreated her to live there, but Lady Elgin was in dire need of rest and recuperation. She asked her parents to escort the children back to Scotland and promised to join them as soon as her health permitted. Mrs. Nisbet's maid, Mrs. Gosling, remained with Lady Elgin at Baker Street, along with two servants.

Lady Elgin gave birth to her fifth child here, a girl named Lucy. A few days after the child was born Lady Elgin wrote to her husband in France:

> I have suffered so much from this event that I shall never subject myself again to that intercourse with you which might be productive of such effects!

Fergusson returned to London after the funeral and was a frequent visitor at Number 60 Baker Street.

Throughout her long recuperation, Lady Elgin felt many stabs of conscience about her husband and to atone for this disposition of mind she wrote a long letter to King George III, imploring him to intercede in Elgin's behalf. She also wrote to the King of Prussia and to the Emperor Alexander of Russia.

A short time after this, the following article appeared in *The Times* of London:

> One of Bonaparte's confidential ministers recently disclosed that any high intercession from kings or emperors

relating to Lord Elgin's imprisonment in France might very well prolong his Lordship's captivity since Bonaparte could not deny his pride by rejecting it. However it was observed that if the application came from any learned Society in England on the ground that his Lordship was an enlightened and liberal patron of the arts, and had recovered many remains of antiquity at a great personal expense, it is not improbable that the application might succeed.

Lady Elgin felt it was worth a try, and since Fergusson was a Fellow in the Royal Academy of Science, he was willing to submit the application:

TO THE FELLOWS OF THE FRENCH INSTITUTE:
   The rage of war ought not to interrupt the intercourse of men of science and we rejoice in the progress and success of your labours. Being always ready on our part to lend assistance to your scientific men who may visit our country, we beg leave to represent the following case for your consideration:
   A British Nobleman, an Ambassador imbued with the love of the arts and sciences, has—at a great expense —remitted to England a very large collection of ancient Greek art. But these precious remains have neither been published nor exhibited, to the great disappointment of artists and the learned world because, in his absence, it is impossible to form any arrangements for that purpose. These noble fragments of antiquity remain packed in large cases and moulder in obscurity, exposed to the dangers of negligence and accident. Withdrawn from the destructive ignorance of the Turks who have already converted into lime too many similar works of Grecian genius, they have passed now into learned hands without conferring any of the numerous advantages that might otherwise have been expected to arise from their study and inspection.

Lady Elgin had been instructed by her husband to make a full inventory of the collection at Park Lane, but she had delayed this as long as possible. Shortly before departing for Scotland she braced herself for the ordeal and walked to the museum which was just off a small street behind Piccadilly. She passed through a small garden whose trees and flowers looked depraved and neglected, and came finally before the large shed. Its front door was open and several groups of visitors were huddled around the many metopes and statues. She made a record of each piece and even described its exact position and arrangement.

When she stepped before the Caryatid it was as though she had come into a tomb. She walked nervously across the floor, past the torso of Iris which was taken from the west pediment of the Parthenon, then on to that of Ilissos and the huge metope of the Centaur doing battle with a Lapith. Before leaving the shed, Lady Elgin cast a final look at Aphrodite as she reclined on her mother's lap, the folds of her garment clinging to her skin.

Lady Elgin slept fitfully that last night at No. 60 Baker Street. A carriage was waiting for her early the next morning and only after she had stepped into it did she feel a moment of comfort, knowing that at last she was on her way to Scotland. Mrs. Gosling attended to the infant Lucy and rode in the post chaise with Lady Elgin while the other servants followed in a cabriolet.*

It was raining when the carriages pulled free of London. The storm became more severe when they reached Waltham Abbey and they were forced to stop at Cambridge for the night. In the morning they fought their way through rain and mud, and arrived at Wainfleet where they found accommodations in a small but comfortable inn. The horses made their best time on the third day. Mrs. Gosling negotiated for a change of horses that same afternoon, and they continued along a road that weaved between the banks of the Witham. Lingering at York for tea and biscuits, they continued as far as Richmond and secured lodgings at a spacious inn which lay in the center of the town.

---

* A two-wheeled, one-horse carriage with a folding top, capable of seating two persons.

Darlington was reached the next day. They ate their noon meal at a remote inn alongside the River Tees and Lady Elgin was pleased by her child's appetite and tolerance of travel. On the opposite bank lay Stockton, its grimy chimneys pouring thick columns of purple smoke into the English sky. After crossing the old wooden bridge into Stockton, the carriages came into Newcastle just as dusk was descending.

They moved off again early the next morning. Lady Elgin sat back against the seat and fastened her eyes on the unwinding hills. There was much greenery everywhere, even though April had just shown its face. It moved her heart to see heather once again; and for a moment she closed her eyes. When she awoke she discovered it was much later than she had imagined. The sun had already sunk behind the western hills and a chilling mist was settling over the earth. The carriages made swift time into Berwick-upon-Tweed, but the town was buried in darkness and Lady Elgin saw nothing except the lighting of the lamps in the windows.

She slept hardly at all that night. Archerfield and her children were less than thirty miles from her heart; and she could already feel her mother's comforting arms.

Chapter
Nine

Scotland

Lusieri assumed that the Elgins had reached Scotland after all this time and his long dispatches kept arriving at Archerfield with monthly regularity:

Athens,

My dear Lord:

Immediately after your departure from Athens I set forth plans for further removals and excavations, as your Lordship instructed. We soon amassed still another collection of marbles and succeeded in hauling them to the Piraeus for shipment—but during this time Count Sébastiani persuaded the Turks to break their alliance with Russia in favor of the French. The British heard about it and sent their fleet to the aid of Russia. However when their ships passed through the Dardanelles to make a show of force in Constantinople, the Turks fired at them from the forts in the Straits, inflicting heavy losses.

This had a devastating effect on our shipment of marbles. The Voivode prevented us from putting them on board the waiting warship and I was forced to flee Athens, leaving our treasures at the mercy of the French. The cases which contained a large assortment of vases were broken into and then sent overland to Epirus,* from whence they were forwarded to France and the Louvre. But the real prize, your Lordship's fine collection of marbles, presented

---

* A region in north-west Greece.

a more difficult problem for the French. Because of their excessive weight, the muleteers from Ioannina* refused to haul them over the mountains, and here the French Admiralty was called upon for assistance, but fortunately for your Lordship not one French ship could be spared from the war effort.

After many tribulations, I managed to reach Sicily. At Palermo, I negotiated with an agent of the Levant Company to act as your representative and we arrived at a plan to save the marbles, which involved not only the persuasion of Lord Nelson to dispatch another war vessel to the Piraeus but also the more daring scheme of seizing the French agent Fauvel by force of arms and holding him as ransom until the marbles were safely embarked. I equipped your Lordship's representative with large sums of money which I had to borrow from several sources until such time as your Lordship can reimburse them. Much of this money went toward the purchase of silver pistols and English watches, since additional bribery was to be expected from the Turks. Lord Nelson was then warned that any warship sent to the Piraeus should also be accompanied by a strong transport ship, along with horses, tackle, ropes and carts.

Your Lordship's representative went at once to Constantinople and obtained a firman which allowed me to return to Athens. I presented it to the Voivode and then took repossession of my house. I found the doors and windows broken. A ladder was attached against the garden wall, enabling anyone to enter at will. Everything of value had been stolen: vases, scaffolding, ropes, and all my equipment. My first concern however was the shipment of marbles on the Piraeus docks. To my complete astonishment, they still remained there untouched. Working swiftly, I obtained permission from the Voivode to embark the collection on a chartered vessel from the Isle of Hydra. The marbles were put on board and the ship was about to set sail when an order arrived from the Porte, demanding that all the marbles be unloaded at once. Again Bonaparte and his agents had thwarted us, and as each case was

* The capital city of Epirus.

hauled out of the ship and put on the docks Fauvel stood there, cane in hand and gloating.

The next day Nelson's warship and transport vessel arrived at the Piraeus. I called upon the Voivode and showered him with gifts but he refused to permit us to load the marbles into the ships. Within a fortnight however the Turks became thoroughly disenchanted with the French and began veering once again toward an alliance with Britain. Your representative in Constantinople wrote to me a short time after this and said he had succeeded in obtaining the Sultan's order to the Voivode for the embarkation of your Lordship's collection of marbles. The firman reached Athens on 2 June, but by that time Nelson's ships unfortunately had sailed out of the Piraeus. Needless to say, Fauvel found great delight in this. But Lord Nelson once again came to your Lordship's assistance and sent the most available warship to the Piraeus directly from Smyrna. Even in this last hour the French tried to block our plans through Fauvel's bribery and intrigue—but the Sultan's firman was sovereign and thus the marbles were hauled on board the warship and she finally set sail for Malta, and thence to England.

I must now report to your Lordship the rebellious scene which took place on the docks as the warship was being loaded. The trouble was instigated by the pen of Lord Byron. His poems have ignited the heart of Greece against your Lordship's taking of the Parthenon marbles. I include herein an article printed by him in an Athenian journal:

"It is to be lamented that a war more than civil is raging on the subject of Lord Elgin's pursuits in Greece. We can all feel or imagine the regret with which the ruins of cities, once the capitals of empires, are beheld—but never did the smallness of man nor the vanity of his very best virtues of patriotism and of valor to defend his country appear more conspicuous than in the record of what Athens was, and the certainty of what she now is. This theatre of contention between mighty factions: the struggles of orators, the exaltation and deposition of tyrants, the triumph and punishment of generals . . . is now become a scene of petty intrigue and personal disturbance between the bickering agents of Lord Elgin and Bonaparte. The wild foxes, the owls and serpents in the ruins of Babylon were surely less degrading than such as these. The Turks have the plea of conquest for their tyranny; and the Greeks have suffered the fortune of war incidental to the bravest. But how are the mighty fallen when two lascivious men contest the privilege of plundering the Parthenon, each triumphing in turn according to the tenor of succeeding firmans! Sylla could not punish; Philip subdue; and Xerxes burn. It remained for one paltry Scotch nobleman and his despicable painter to render Athens contemptible as themselves."

Lusieri finished his letter by asking to be released from the bonds of his contract with Lord Elgin. As with his previous messages to Elgin, he again reminded his employer that "he had yet to receive any of the salary promised him." Like Hunt, Carlyle, and all the others, he too had not collected one penny for his labors. Far worse, the world was now looking upon him with hatred and contempt.

Shortly after this time, Lord Elgin obtained his release from prison and returned to London:

His Lordship's release was brought about in large measure by a direct plea to Bonaparte by Lord Grenville during the brief period of his service as Prime Minister. Before obtaining his safe passage from France, Lord Elgin was obliged to sign a document in the presence of Talleyrand, promising that he would return to France whenever the French Government required it.

Elgin was elated to be back home. It was now common knowledge that he had compiled an enormous expense in bringing the Parthenon marbles to London. But he was hopeful of retrieving these losses, and he immediately put before Parliament the proposition of purchasing his collection for the British Museum.

He also decided to bring a civil action against Robert

Fergusson. Elgin had in his possession many letters which Fergusson and Lady Elgin had exchanged during their detention in France:

> I can boast of loving you with a passion never felt before and I hope the time of our union approaches. Good God! how can you submit to that man's gross conversation! how can such language be addressed to a wife? Your husband's conversation is abhorrent to you, and you must break your fetters.

Another letter from Fergusson to Lady Elgin was even more inflammatory:

> You must prove and act upon your disgust; you must exasperate him; you must consider his approach as a violation of your person and force him to a separation!

In still another letter, there was a powerful declaration of Fergusson's love for Lady Elgin:

> If ever love reigned in all its purity, it is in our hearts. I shall die with thy image upon my heart, and shall hold up my face to heaven, and declare my most faithful love, even when expiring.

Through the help of his former secretary at Constantinople, William Richard Hamilton, Lord Elgin had impounded most of the letters that Lady Elgin had written to Fergusson:

> Elgin was very much agitated indeed, but he said nothing. After tea he got up suddenly and went into his room for a couple of hours. He coughed dreadfully, which he always does when he is annoyed. I told him of my wish to go and see where my beloved William is laid, and that I wished to go alone. It is something I cannot account for, but I feel as if he was our own. Elgin went out early this morning. I have not met him. I must do him the justice to say he has

taken upon himself to keep his promise, to allow me to proceed to England without him, but I hardly think it possible he can go on with it. I shudder when I dare think of it and too thoroughly I feel I cannot live without you.

Lord Elgin had confiscated additional letters, most of them written in the same manner, with detailed instructions about how the illicit affair should be conducted. Elgin's own friends were passing the letters between Lady Elgin and Fergusson.*

Lord Elgin's jealous nature demanded instant retaliation, and although he won a quick civil action in London, he was now compelled under English law to undergo a second and very expensive trial in Edinburgh. Divorce was permitted by Scots law, whereas in England it was granted only by a private Act of Parliament. Fergusson did not contest the civil action in London and thus the decision went against him by default. However both he and Lady Elgin were determined to plead their case in Edinburgh.

The Nisbet household was oppressed by turbulence in the weeks that followed. Lord Elgin's decision to bring shame and disgrace upon his wife bordered on madness since he would be dragging his own name into the mess. A deeper motive for his action was soon revealed when the following account appeared in *The Times*:

> Lord Elgin's operations in Athens have left him penniless. Accompanying his proposal to Parliament for the purchase of the Parthenon marbles, his Lordship referred to his huge personal expenditures:
>
> Pay of the Artists at Athens £9,200
> Conveyance of the Artists to and from the East . .£1,500
> Pay of Workmen at Athens and elsewhere £15,000
> Storage of Marbles at Malta £2,500
> Cost of the *Mentor*, its salvage etc. £5,000
> Cost of moving the Marbles to England etc. £6,000
> Total   £39,200

* Alexander Stratton, a secretary to Lord Elgin in Constantinople, was one of the letter carriers.

This staggering sum pertained only to the first collection of marbles brought to England. A comparable figure was to be attached to the subsequent shipments, making a total of seventy-four thousand pounds!

Parliament was not anxious to pay such a price and during its long deliberations two incidents occurred which gravely affected Elgin's case. The first concerned John Tweddell, a young scholar of exceptional ability who took a grand tour of Switzerland, Germany, Russia, Turkey, Egypt, Palestine, and Greece. He compiled five huge books of journals; also four volumes of Greek inscriptions, seven portfolios of drawings, eight books of etchings and paintings, and numerous other works of artistic and academic value. In addition to all this, Tweddell engaged the painter Preaux who had formerly been employed by both Choiseul-Gouffier and Edward Daniel Clarke. Tweddell was determined to surpass Clarke's massive accomplishments and even purchased many choice drawings from Fauvel—but he suddenly died of a fever in Athens and Fauvel arranged to have him buried in the Theseum.* A large collection of Tweddell's papers had been assigned to Thomas Thornton of the Levant Company for safe keeping in Constantinople, but these were mostly destroyed in a fire. The rest of the papers were sent by the British Consul at Athens (Logothetis) to Sir John Spencer Smith who was Ambassador in Constantinople at the time, with the request that they be forwarded to Tweddell's heirs in England.

Lord Elgin had just succeeded Sir John Spencer when the papers eventually arrived in Constantinople after a hazardous journey in which the ship carrying them was wrecked in the Sea of Marmora. However most of the boxes were saved although they reached the British Embassy in a wet and damaged condition. Elgin had all the papers laid out in the cellar of the British Palace to dry; and he assigned Hunt and

---

* Fauvel's motive did not stem from loyalty. By digging out Tweddell's grave, he hoped to unearth the tomb of Theseus.

Professor Carlyle to the task of sorting and cataloguing those papers that were still in good condition. After this tedious work was done, Elgin ordered the papers to be packed and sent to England at his expense. But somehow a mistake occurred and the papers were never dispatched. Inexplicably, many of the drawings found their way to the home of William Nisbet in Scotland; and Hunt later admitted "that he had copied some notes from Tweddell's journals, hoping they would be useful on his visit through Greece."

These matters were brought to the attention of Sir Spencer Smith who wrote to Tweddell's family and laid the blame entirely on Elgin. Tweddell's brother, Reverend Robert Tweddell, immediately decided to investigate the whole affair. He wrote to Lord Elgin, politely asking him to relate the complete circumstances regarding the loss of his brother's papers. He covered up his real purpose by claiming he intended to write a biography. Elgin responded with a full account of everything that he could remember, upon which Reverend Tweddell wrote again, requesting that Elgin clear up certain points that had arisen. Elgin once more obliged, supplying Reverend Tweddell with a steady stream of letters for a period of six months.

Reverend Tweddell employed the same tactics with Thornton of the Levant Company; also with Philip Hunt. Since Carlyle had unexpectedly died, Reverend Tweddell approached one of the Professor's friends and was successful in extracting many valuable recollections. The information was then handed over to a lawyer. When Edward Daniel Clarke received news of it, he too added his voice to the debate:

> That the literary property of this gentleman, after being in the undisputed possession of the British Ambassador at Constantinople, should absolutely have disappeared *in toto* and eluded the most diligent inquiries of his family and friends, presents a subject for the deepest regret, and is a circumstance of the most unaccountable nature. Upon this

point, however, the author refrains from saying all that he might in the expectation of seeing this strange mystery unfolded by a kindred hand which may justly aspire to the best information.

It is to be feared that if any other part of Mr. J. Tweddell's observations upon Greece ever see the light, it will be in the garbled form of extracts made from his writings by those who had the ransacking of his papers which will be published, as perhaps they have been already, without any acknowledgment being made of their real author.

All this publicity proved to be destructive during Lord Elgin's negotiations with Parliament, and when the sad matter finally came to an end his prospects of arriving at a satisfactory sale were severely dampened.

The second unfortunate incident related to the valuable manuscripts which Professor Carlyle had borrowed from the Greek monasteries before departing from the East. They were lent to him by the Patriarch of Constantinople on the written condition that Carlyle "promise to return them to the Patriarch when the purposes for which they were borrowed were completed or whenever the Patriarch should demand them." As a secretary to Lord Elgin's embassy, Philip Hunt affixed his signature alongside Carlyle's, thus making the British Government a responsible party to the contract.

These ancient manuscripts ranged in date from the tenth to the fifteenth century and contained priceless texts of the New Testament. Six were taken from the monastery of St. Saba in Syria; four came from the Library of the Patriarch of Jerusalem at Constantinople; eighteen were borrowed from various monasteries in the Princes Islands near Constantinople. It was Carlyle's hope to have them collated in England so that he might produce a revised edition of the New Testament. Up until this time, many scholars had attempted unsuccessfully to get their hands on these rare manuscripts, but the Greek monasteries strictly forbade it; and their monks were bound to an oath which was administered before taking their vows: to preserve and protect all property of the monastery.

Overcoming these preventive measures, but only through the sanction of Elgin's embassy, Carlyle undeniably obtained these manuscripts by irregular means, and when he finally reached England he realized that his collection "amounted to near a tenth part of all manuscripts of the New Testament that have yet been examined in Europe." He quickly assembled a group of scholars and theologians to assist him in the gigantic task of collation and, to make their work less burdensome, he printed a memorandum: *Hints and Observations Which Mr. Carlyle Takes the Liberty of Suggesting to the Consideration of the Gentlemen Who Have Kindly Promised Their Assistance in Collating the Greek Mss. of The New Testament.* Thus the manuscripts from St. Saba were marked "S," the four from Constantinople bore the reference "C," and the eighteen from the Princes Islands were designated "I."

Just as the work was being launched and moving toward a sound goal, Carlyle fell suddenly ill and died. His family was heartbroken. Carlyle's trip to the East had cut into his entire fortune, and the manuscripts were the only things of value left in his family's possession. To offset this loss, Carlyle's sister arranged to have published a posthumous edition of Carlyle's poems; she also decided to sell the manuscripts, but before doing so, she wrote to Philip Hunt and asked his advice. Hunt suggested they should be deposited with the Archbishop of Canterbury in the Library at Lambeth. This had never occurred to Miss Carlyle, and she gratefully replied to Hunt:

> As to the manuscripts, I think that as the survivor you have an undoubted right to dispose of those brought from Constantinople in any way you please; nor could you have fixed upon any place more agreeable than under the patronage of the Archbishop of Canterbury. It would give me great pain to separate what has cost us so dear to collect together. At the same time, I do not conceive myself au-

thorised to refuse any compensation for them which the Archbishop, after inspection, may think proper to make me. My brother, the day before he died, said to me that, as his unfortunate journey had been attended with a great pecuniary loss to his family, I must make what I could of his manuscripts.

Elgin suffered bitterly from Hunt's blunder. While his proposition for the sale of the Parthenon marbles was being considered and debated in Parliament, a curt letter was sent to the British Government from the English Ambassador at Constantinople, stating that the Patriarch had formally requested the return of the borrowed manuscripts. Fearing a scandal, the Foreign Secretary asked the Archbishop to honor the Patriarch's request, but the Archbishop balked. Several months later a second letter arrived from the Ambassador at Constantinople, angrily declaring "that the National character suffers by this neglect and that the Patriarch looks on the transaction as a breach of confidence!" The message ended with a sharp criticism of Elgin's embassy.

The Archbishop finally acceded—but he sent back only the four manuscripts that Carlyle had marked "C" for Constantinople, whereas the Patriarch's request included the six manuscripts from St. Saba and the eighteen from the Princes Islands. This touched off a long argument. Elgin's reputation was now at stake, and he pleaded with the Archbishop, but it was hopeless. The Archbishop refused to comply.*

In addition to these disturbing incidents, Lord Elgin had to combat the assaults of Richard Payne Knight. To bolster his cause, Elgin offered one hundred and twenty pounds to Ennio Quirino Visconti, Director of the Louvre, to come to London and examine the Parthenon marbles. Aside from the fee, the famous Visconti was to stay in London for a fortnight at Elgin's expense and then prepare a memorandum of his examination before returning to France. Visconti accepted and his memorandum was a triumph for Lord Elgin:

* To this day, the manuscripts are confined inside Lambeth Library.

Neither Stuart's drawings, nor Choiseul-Gouffier's fragment and casts, had been able to give me the idea of the works of Phidias which the sight of the actual objects has done. The frieze, the metopes, the pediments ... all showed every perfection and were every bit as excellent as the famous statues of Italy. There can be no doubt that the Parthenon marbles were executed under the supervision of Phidias himself; and if the classical statues of Italy were an inspiration to the Michelangelos and Raphaels of the sixteenth century, will not the Elgin Marbles inaugurate a new era for the progress of sculpture in England?

Lord Elgin set about at once and ordered a printed edition of Visconti's letter to be included in his own *Memorandum on the Subject of the Earl of Elgin's Pursuits in Greece,* and as soon as it was published he distributed copies to each member of Parliament, with the suggestion that the whole matter be referred to a select committee of the House of Commons which would then investigate his expenditures and decide what price the government should offer for the marbles. During the hearings of the select committee, Visconti sent a full report of his appraisal which apparently struck a hard blow upon Knight's claim that the sculptures were not done by Phidias:

In their new situation, in the midst of an enlightened nation particularly disposed to afford encouragement to sculpture, the Elgin Marbles will rouse the talents of the young artist to exertion and will direct him in the road which leads to perfection in his art. We have only to regret that the noble idea which induced Lord Elgin to rescue them from the daily ravages of a barbarous nation was not entertained a century and a half earlier.

The select committee consisted of eighteen members of Parliament, each with different shades of opinion. Only two had any substantial knowledge of Grecian art and sculpture: F. S. N. Douglas and J. H. Fazakerley. Elgin presented his case in a convincing tone of voice, recounting how the idea of improving the British arts was first suggested to him by his architect Thomas Harrison; how he went ahead at his own expense to obtain the services of artists, draughtsmen, architects and formatori; and how his real purpose for rescuing the Parthenon marbles was spurred by the great destruction perpetrated daily on the Acropolis Hill by the Turks, unscrupulous travelers, and the ravages of time and weather.

He reminded the committee that when it came to the subject of the Parthenon marbles he never skimped, producing authentic accounts which showed every penny spent from the first day of his embassy to the very last. His many gifts to the Turkish authorities at Athens alone amounted to seven thousand pounds. The interest on the large sums of money borrowed from his bankers at Malta came to 17¾%. On top of this, there were the artists, the costs of transporting the marbles to the Piraeus, the price of three ships, and the loss of the *Mentor*. A heavy sum was attributed to the museum at Park Lane; and to the staggering duty charges leveled at the London Customs House.

Richard Payne Knight led the opposing forces and did his utmost to discredit Elgin's endeavors by exclaiming at one point: "You have lost your labour, my Lord Elgin. Your marbles are overrated. They are not the works of Phidias. They are Roman, of the time of Hadrian!"

Lord Elgin brought in the most eminent names in the art world to give testimony. Nollekens said: "the Elgin Marbles are the finest things that ever came to this country." Flaxman (the English Phidias) agreed: "The finest works of art I have ever seen." Sir Thomas Lawrence showered his praise on the marbles: "There is in them an union of fine composition and very grand form, with a more true and natural expression of the effect of action upon the human frame than there is in the Apollo Belvedere or in any of the other most celebrated statues."

Benjamin West was too ill to attend the hearings; nevertheless he sent his opinions in writing, strongly supporting Lord Elgin. Furthermore, West agreed that the Elgin Marbles should not have been restored by Flaxman or anyone else. West closed his remarks by saying that the acquisition of the Elgin Marbles would bring a great improvement in the fine arts of Great Britain.

Throughout the long interrogations Benjamin Haydon "stood patiently by, waiting to be called, but the day passed and he was not." Three days later he wrote a stinging letter which was printed in London's leading newspapers. He titled it: "On the Judgment of Connoisseurs Being Preferred to That of Professional Men," and it was of course an indictment against Richard Payne Knight and the elite group of the Dilettanti Society whose opinion (rather than that of professional artists) was given priority by the select committee.

> In no other profession is the opinion of the man who has studied it for his amusement preferred to that of him who has devoted his soul to excel in it. No man will trust his limb to a connoisseur in surgery; no minister would ask a connoisseur in war how a campaign is to be conducted; no nobleman would be satisfied with the opinion of a connoisseur in law on disputed property; and why should a connoisseur of an art be preferred to the professional man?

Haydon's article did more good for the artist than for Lord Elgin. "It was widely published and even translated into several European languages." Members of the select committee claimed they were not influenced by it and had already drafted their report when the article appeared; nor were they carried away by Richard Payne Knight's last efforts to sway them from the surging tide of Lord Elgin's supporters. In fact Knight injured his case when he appeared as a witness before the select committee:

> *Are you acquainted with the Elgin Collection?* Yes. I have looked them over, not only formerly, but I have looked them over on this occasion with reference to their value.
> *In what class of art do you place the finest works of this Collec-*

tion? I think of things extant, I should put them in the second rank—some of them. They are very unequal. The finest I should put in the second rank.

Do you think that none of them rank in the first class of art? Not with the Laocoön and the Apollo and those which have been placed in the first class of art. At the same time, I must observe that their state of preservation is such I cannot form a very accurate notion; their surface is gone mostly.

Do you consider them to be of a very high antiquity? We know from the authority of Plutarch that those of the Temple of Minerva, which are the principal, were executed by Callicrates and Ictinus, and their assistants and scholars; and I think some were added in the time of Hadrian.

In what class do you rank the fragments of the draped female figures? They are so mutilated I can hardly tell. But I should think most of them were added by Hadrian . . . they are but of little value, except from their local interest, from having been part of the Temple.

Soon after his testimony, Knight delivered a paper to the select committee, in which a figure was finally put against the main items of the Elgin collection. The total came to less than twenty-five thousand pounds, and Knight's last remarks were an open insult to Elgin: "The amount is far more than twice what these marbles could fetch on the open market!"

Knight's opinions were damaging. After two whole weeks of examination and study, the committee's report was prepared and made public. It recommended an unyielding price of thirty-five thousand pounds, which was less than half of what Elgin had personally expended. When Elgin submitted his firm figure to the select committee he made one last emotional plea:

I beg once more to repeat that I do not offer this view of my expenses as a criterion of the intrinsic value of my Collection. I ever have been persuaded that, in justice to the Public, this should be calculated on other grounds. But it is, I trust, sufficient to prove that in amassing these remains of antiquity for the benefit of my Country, and in rescuing them from the imminent and unavoidable destruction with which they were threatened, (had they been left many years longer the prey of mischievous Turks who mutilated them for wanton amusement, or for the purpose of selling them piecemeal to occasional travellers) I have been actuated by no motives of private emolument; nor deterred from doing what I felt to be a substantial good, by consideration of personal risk or the fear of calumnious misrepresentations.

But it was of no avail. The select committee had arrived at a decision and refused to budge. During the long negotiations Lord Elgin was unexpectedly released from one of his debts:

Giovanni Battista Lusieri fell victim to a horrible death in Athens, brought about by the rupture of a blood vessel. He had borne the weight of Greek animosity against Elgin and had to barricade his house every night in fear of his life. On the day of his death the neighborhood was surprised to find him absent from the Acropolis Hill. They invaded his house and discovered him lying on the floor in a pool of blood. A black cat was seated on his chest. Scattered about the place were some tattered clothes, his ever-present umbrella, and scores of drawings—all of them unfinished.*

Despite the great pressure of his marital problems and heavy debts, Lord Elgin was gratified to know that scores of visitors came daily to view the Parthenon marbles at Park Lane. He was specially pleased by the revival of Grecian art which he had brought about in England. The foremost painters of the time visited Park Lane and made full-scale drawings of the marbles. Benjamin Haydon was always in attendance and often obliged royal dignitaries and visiting artists with an outward show of enthusiasm over the presence of the Elgin Marbles in England.

* Lusieri was buried in the grounds of the Capuchin Monastery at Athens. Several English benefactors erected a monument for him which can still be seen alongside the tombstone of John Tweddell on one wall of the English Church in Athens.

Parliament was still buzzing over the sale and many of its members seriously questioned whether Lord Elgin had the right to use his position as ambassador to acquire the collection.* Newspapers throughout Great Britain were furious over the sale. Lord Brougham, a frequent contributor to the *Edinburgh Review,* chided the British government for ignoring the real wants of the people: "If we cannot give them bread, we ought not to indulge ourselves in the purchase of stones!" Cruikshank† used this theme to create one of his most famous cartoons.

In the midst of all this furor Haydon brought his young friend John Keats to see the marbles for the first time and the poet wrote two sonnets on the occasion:

* The most powerful attack in the select committee came from one of its leading members, Hugh Hammersley:

> It was to be regretted that the government had not restrained this act of spoliation; but, as it had been committed, we should exert ourselves to wipe off the stain, and not place in our museum a monument of our disgrace, but at once return the bribe which our ambassador had received, to his own dishonour and that of the country.

In the heated debate which ensued, Hammersley proposed the following amendment:

> This committee therefore feels justified, under the particular circumstances of the case, in recommending that £125,000 be offered to the earl of Elgin for the collection in order to recover and keep it together for that government from which it has been improperly taken, and to which this committee is of opinion that a communication should be immediately made, stating that Great Britain holds these marbles only in trust till they are demanded by the present, or any future, possessors of the city of Athens; and upon such demand, engages, without question or negotiation, to restore them, as far as can be effected, to the places from whence they were taken, and that they shall be in the meantime carefully preserved in the British Museum.

Hammersley's proposal was defeated. (Hansard, xxxiv, pp. 1027–40, 7 June 1816)

† George Cruikshank (1792-1878), an English artist, caricaturist, painter and illustrator, whose talents were recognized even in his youth. By the time he was twenty Cruikshank had already established a broad reputation throughout England and Europe. For one whole generation his drawings delineated Whigs, Tories and Radicals with a sharp impartiality. An extreme patriot, Cruikshank was unrelenting in his attacks on the enemies of England. He was an outspoken champion of the poor and underprivileged, and fearlessly exposed the follies of royalty. John Ruskin considered him to be in the highest rank of artists and compared his work with the all-time masterpieces of etching.

ON SEEING THE ELGIN MARBLES

My spirit is too weak—mortality
Weighs heavily on me like unwilling sleep,
And each imagin'd pinnacle and steep
Of godlike hardship tells me I must die
Like a sick Eagle looking at the sky.
Yet 'tis a gentle luxury to weep
That I have not the cloudy winds to keep
Fresh for the opening of the morning's eye.
Such dim-conceived glories of the brain
    Bring round the heart an indescribable feud;
So do these wonders a most dizzy pain,
    That mingles Grecian grandeur with the rude
Wasting of old Time—with a billowy main—
    A sun—a shadow of a magnitude.

The second sonnet overflows with lavish praise for
Haydon and contempt for Richard Payne Knight and his
party of connoisseurs:

TO B. R. HAYDON, WITH THE FOREGOING SONNET ON THE
ELGIN MARBLES

Haydon, forgive me that I cannot speak
Definitely on these mighty things;
Forgive me that I have not Eagle's wings—
That what I want I know not where to seek:
And think that I would not be over meek
    In rolling out upfollow'd thunderings
    Even to the steep of Heliconian springs,
Were I of ample strength for such a freak—
Think too, that all these numbers should be thine;
    Whose else? In this who touch thy vesture's hem?
For when men star'd at what was most divine
    With browless idiotism—o'erwise phlegm—
Thou hadst beheld the Hesperean shine
    Of their star in the East, and gone to worship them.

Although these are not Keats' best poems, the Elgin Marbles certainly inspired him to create two masterpieces: *Ode on*

a Grecian Urn and *Hyperion*. "For the young poet who knew no Greek, the Elgin Marbles opened a vision of the classical world."

Keats visited the Elgin Marbles "again and again, and would sit for an hour or more at a time beside them, rapt in revery. Severn, the great painter, came upon him on one such occasion. Keats' eyes were shining so brightly and his face was so lit up by some visionary rapture that Severn quietly stole away."*

Among the hordes that visited the museum, it was not an uncommon sight to find a stern riding master instructing his students to sit properly on horseback by studying a certain frieze of the Parthenon. This same frieze became a motif of Regency wallpaper; and of the vase in Buckingham Palace Gardens commemorating the Battle of Waterloo.

The Dilettanti Society soon recognized its grave mistake and officially censured Richard Payne Knight. Lord Elgin was then informed in writing that he had been elected a Member, an honor which had escaped him all these years because of Knight's antagonism. Elgin's reply to the secretary of the society camouflaged the deep pain he had suffered:

---

* Thomas Hardy also visited the museum to view the Elgin Marbles, but his reaction differed sharply from that of Keats. Hardy envisioned the Marbles as prisoners who were sadly conversing on Christmas Day:

> We are those whom Christmas overthrew
> Some centuries after Phidias knew
> 　How to shape us
> 　And bedrape us
> And to set us in Athena's temple for men's view.
>
> Oh it is sad now we are sold—
> We gods! for Borean people's gold,
> 　And brought to the gloom
> 　Of this gaunt room
> Which sunlight shuns, and sweet Aurore but enters cold.
>
> "For all these bells, would I were still
> Radiant as on Athena's Hill"
> 　—"And I" "And I"
> 　The others sigh,
> Before this, Christ was known, and we had men's good will.

No one knows more intimately than you, that the impulses which led me to the exertions I made in Greece were wholly for the purpose of securing in Great Britain, and through it to Europe in general, the most effectual possible knowledge and means of improving, by the excellence of Grecian art in sculpture and architecture. My success, to the vast extent it was effected, will never cease to be a matter of the utmost gratification to me. If, when it was first made known to the public, it had been thought that the same energy would be considered useful to the Dilettanti Society, most happy should I have been to have contributed every aid in my power. But as such expectation has long since past, I really do not apprehend that I shall be thought fastidious if I decline the honour now proposed to me at this my eleventh hour.

Lady Elgin was overcome by the swift turn of events in her life. She left her father's house many mornings without breakfast, walking in deep thought through the frozen meadows while the strong winds of winter howled against the shivering sky. No matter how hard she tried, she could not free her heart from the terrible nightmare of her husband's wrath.

One afternoon she returned from Aberlady and learned that the children had been whisked away to Broomhall: a court order had been issued, remanding all four children to Elgin's custody pending the outcome of the divorce proceedings. That same evening she was handed a summons by the constable of Dirleton which instructed her to be at the main courtroom of Parliament House in Edinburgh at ten o'clock the following morning.

The carriage was ready at daybreak. Above Archerfield, the sky was burdened with storm clouds, and a thin blanket of snow had draped itself over the frozen earth. Lady Elgin felt her stomach churning as the carriage master Andrew Davidson helped her into the post chaise. Her father accompanied her, his demeanor grave. Mrs. Nisbet was ill and had been ordered to remain at home by her physician.

*Auld Reekie** seemed to be choking under heavy layers of black smoke. Lady Elgin remembered when her father first pronounced the name to her he rolled the *R* until he ran out of breath . . . days of peace and happiness . . . her entire world overflowing with love, and not one evil thought in the universe . . . .

A mob of people had already assembled on Princess Street. Off to the east rose Calton Hill, its grotesque gravestones jabbing the sky, the ancient dead lying deep within its bowels, cold, and forgotten. The snow was falling harder now and as the carriage approached the General Register House William Nisbet leaned forward and comforted his daughter. Within moments the post chaise pulled up in front of Parliament House.

More crowds had gathered on the steps and along both sides of the street. The snow did not deter them. Vendors darted everywhere with their carts of hot chestnuts while several men waved newspapers high in the air and yelled: "All the details of Lady Elgin's private life! Exclusive accounts of her Ladyship's affairs in France and England!"

Robert Fergusson was waiting for them outside the door of Parliament House. He first introduced them to his chief solicitor, Mr. Topping, a small balding man who suddenly became imposing after he put on his wig and robe, and then they were led across the great hall which was exactly as Lady Elgin had remembered it when the parish schoolmaster of Dirleton brought his class here on an annual visit to Edinburgh's ancient sites: the massive oak-timbered ceiling, the stained-glass windows, the solicitors in their solemn wigs and robes, the young pages scurrying back from room to room, the statues of each Lord President dating to the year 1685. As she entered the advocate's library behind Mr. Topping, Lady Elgin could hear the echo of the schoolmaster's voice: "This great library houses every book published in Scotland from the time of Charles III."

* The fond name for Edinburgh.

Topping only had a moment to tell them that Lord Elgin had retained a firm of expensive London solicitors and was bent on winning the case at any cost. He then led them to their chairs inside the main courtroom where a sea of inquisitive faces stared at them. The walls of the courtroom were deplorably old; an offensive odor seemed to leak out from their musty cracks. A few meters to Lady Elgin's right, a large coal stove belched out a sickening wave of heat.

There was a long silence.

Suddenly the main door of the courtroom opened and the Lord President walked in. He was followed by the four Lord Judges.

The
Trial
of

R. J. Fergusson
for

Adultery
with

The Countess of Elgin,
wife of

The Earl of Elgin

The defendant, Mr. Fergusson, having suffered a previous judgment to go by default, a jury was this day summoned for the purpose of assessing the quantum of damages:

A LIST OF THE JURY

William Weston, Esq.
Francis Dutton, Esq.
John Townshend, Esq.
James Rogers, Esq.
Thomas Bates, Esq.
John Johnson, Esq.
Joseph Oake, Esq.
Samuel Moody, Esq.
John Anderson, Esq.
Thomas Baylis, Esq.

William Page, Esq.
William Robertson, Esq.
John Sherrard, Esq.
John Sanderson, Esq.
David Dean, Esq.
Major Rhodes, Esq.
William North, Esq.
John Crawford, Esq.
George Brown, Esq.
Thomas Charles Gordon, Esq.

Samuel Gordon, Esq.

COUNSEL FOR THE PLAINTIFF:
Messrs. Garrow, Dampier, Stewart.

COUNSEL FOR THE DEFENDANT:
Messrs. Topping, Nolan, Adam, Horner.

Waiting until the Clerk seated himself, Mr. Garrow rose to his feet and addressed the Court: "My Lords and Gentlemen of the Jury, I have the honor of attending you on behalf of my noble plaintiff, the Seventh Earl of Elgin and Eleventh of Kincardine, for the purposes of ascertaining the damages to be allowed him for the misconduct of the defendant who permitted a previous judgment to go by default.

"Of the many melancholy cases with which my practice for twenty years in the Courts of Westminster has led me to become acquainted, this by far exceeds them all. I bring to your attention that the noble plaintiff is the representative of one of the most ancient and respected families in Scotland. He was solemnly joined in marriage to Lady Elgin, then

Mary Nisbet, who was also of a very respectable and opulent family. She was then at the age of twenty and possessed every accomplishment of mind and person which could make her the object of the warmest attachment. His Lordship was a dozen years her senior but there was no such disparity as could make the match in the slightest degree unequal. A short time before the marriage, Lord Elgin had been appointed Ambassador to the Sublime Porte at Constantinople, and such was the ardor of his attachment to his bride that he proposed to abandon all those splendid prospects which this appointment held out for him, and to retire to scenes of domestic happiness and endearment—if such a course should be more agreeable to her. However she agreed to accompany him in his embassy to Constantinople where they spent several years.

"My Lords and Gentlemen, it is my intention to prove that throughout this whole period Lord and Lady Elgin exhibited an example of the strongest mutual affection and regard, affording a true picture of perfect conjugal felicity. Their well-regulated family revealed a pattern of the best English manners and the most regular attention to domestic and religious duties. Lady Elgin resisted the batteries of ridicule and never gave card parties on a Sunday; nor did she indulge in the fashionable follies of dissipation. Quite to the contrary, she adhered strictly to the practice of those virtues in which she had been educated by her respectable parents. During this interval three children were born, a son and two daughters, and they found within themselves and in the endearments of their children all those means of pure and unmixed happiness which life can bring.

"The work of his embassy completed, Lord Elgin left Constantinople with his family and, after passing through Italy, arrived at France. We all recollect that breach of diplomatic courtesy which took place in France at that time, in consequence of which all the English then resident in that country were detained prisoners of war. Mr. Fergusson was also in Paris at this time. In Lord Elgin, he recognized a friend and a neighbor of his family, and thus their relationship was fixed upon terms of the greatest respect and honor.

"Shortly after this period, Lord Elgin was seized with an indisposition which made it necessary for him to seek the waters of Barèges for the recovery of his health. Here a fourth child was born, a male who was given the name of William. Several months later Lady Elgin travelled to Paris and was unceasing in her efforts to procure Lord Elgin's liberation from prison. But, my Lords and Gentlemen, was this her only purpose in visiting the infamous capital of France? And was her fourth child in fact the offspring of Lord Elgin?

"Upon the untimely death of her infant son, Lady Elgin was permitted to return to England while his Lordship remained confined in France. She resided for a short period with her parents in Portman Square, London, with whom her children then lived, but soon after her arrival there and while in a state of pregnancy, she left the house of her parents and took a house for herself at Number 60 Baker Street, near Portman Square . . . and here, my Lords and Gentlemen, she had an adulterous intercourse with the said Robert Fergusson, being carnally connected with him in London both before and after her delivery which happened in the month of January, and until she left London for Scotland on the following June.

"It is now my duty to submit proof of this criminal correspondence. I hope not to dwell long on this part of the subject because I do not mean to bring more pain upon the heart of that Lady whom Lord Elgin once revered; nor can I inflict any new wound on those most respectable parents who already have suffered so much from their daughter's indiscretion. My Lords and Gentlemen, before calling upon the noble plaintiff's witnesses, permit me to bring certain facts to your attention: in order to maintain an action for a case of adultery it is necessary to establish two points—that a valid marriage exists between two spouses, and that there is sexual intercourse between the defendant and the guilty spouse.

"Adultery, as a ground for divorce, may be proved by a preponderance of the evidence. However the proof must be sufficiently definite to show the appropriate time, the place of the offense, the circumstances under which it was committed, and the conclusion that the libellee was a party to the illicit act. Here I must remind you that it is a fundamental rule of English jurisprudence that it is not necessary to prove the direct act of adultery, since there could not be one case in a hundred in which such proof might be attainable. It is rare indeed that the parties are surprised in the direct act. In almost every case, the fact is inferred from circumstances that lead to it, otherwise no protection could be given to marital rights. Thus the two parties need not be caught in the very act of adultery; the crime may be sufficiently established by indirect or circumstantial evidence, or by evidence consisting in part of both.

"Secondly, my Lords and Gentlemen, I submit to you that in order to amount to adultery, a completion of sexual intercourse is not required; nor is the birth of a child essential. For the purpose of divorce, the most important element of adultery is a guilty intent. Intercourse must be voluntary. An act accomplished by force or fraud is not sufficient grounds for divorce.

"Therefore an adulterous disposition between two persons is usually of gradual development and even if it can be shown to exist with comparatively light proof or perhaps with negligible circumstantial evidence, nevertheless this shall be sufficient to justify an inference that adultery has taken place. I shall now proceed to furnish you with such proof. My Lords and Gentlemen, I submit that the defendant, Mr. Fergusson, in fact seduced by degrees and in such a way as to especially suit the innocent and naive character of Lady Elgin. The behavior, the views, and the objects of Lord Elgin were all to be misrepresented. His public and private conduct were to be attacked; he was to be brought down from being the object of her Ladyship's love and adoration, and be made a victim of scorn and disgust. Amidst all such exhortations, the defendant was considered to be a friend of the family. Demon is a more appropriate name! His one object was to prevail upon Lady Elgin to despise her husband and alienate him by the coolness of her conduct. For this reason did the defendant volunteer to convey the bier of her dead child to Scotland. Unhappy woman! How little did she foresee her fate that her own husband's friend should be the means of making her children orphans and entailing upon them such miserable consequences!"

Mr. Topping came slowly forward and in a calm voice objected: "My Lords, such theatrics as these may be appropriate in the Courts of Westminster—but surely not here in Edinburgh."

The Lord President agreed, then cast an impatient glance toward Garrow. "Is it not time that you called upon your first witness?"

Garrow wiped his brow with a silk handkerchief then tucked it into the cuff of his coat sleeve. "On behalf of my noble client, I call Mr. William Richard Hamilton to the witness chair."

Hamilton looked thin and older. Kneeling, and with his right hand on the Holy Evangil, he was sworn and purged of malice. He then hobbled to the witness chair.*

"Your name is William Richard Hamilton?"

"It is."

"What is your age?"

"I have just turned thirty."

"And your situation?"

"I am an Under Secretary in the Foreign Office."

"You held a situation under Lord Elgin?"

"I did."

"What exactly was this situation?"

"I acted as private secretary to his Lordship when he was at Constantinople."

"Did you sail with him on his embassy?"

---

* Hamilton had a deformity in his right foot.

"I did."

"At what time was that?"

"Upon the third day of September, shortly after his Lordship was appointed to the post."

"How long did you continue with him?"

"About two or three months at the Isle of Sicily, after which I remained with him for one year at Constantinople."

"Was Lady Elgin with him during all this time?"

"She was."

"Did you observe their demeanor as man and wife?"

"I did."

"During your residence at Constantinople, were you constantly at their table?"

"I was."

"And during the whole time of your being with them, did they conduct themselves toward one another as man and wife?"

"Indeed. His Lordship was an affectionate and tender husband."

"And Lady Elgin?"

"A most dutiful wife."

"Tender and affectionate also?"

"Yes."

"Mr. Hamilton, in what manner was the household conducted as to regularity in the offices of religion?"

"With great propriety. There was a chaplain attached to the embassy, Reverend Philip Hunt. His prayers were attended by the household on the Sunday, with the greatest regularity."

"And was the service of the Church of England?"

"Yes."

"Now then, had you the opportunity of observing whether Lady Elgin's affections remained to his Lordship with regard to his public as well as his private concerns?"

"Her Ladyship appeared to take a lively interest in everything that concerned Lord Elgin, either of a public or of a private nature."

"Were any children born to them while you were at Constantinople?"

"A son, the name of Bruce."

"Had you an opportunity of observing Lady Elgin's conduct toward the child?"

"She was quite patient at first."

"And later?"

"She became withdrawn. I suspect it was—"

Topping interrupted. "My Lords, must we subject ourselves to the suspicions of the witness?"

Garrow went on: "Mr. Hamilton, would you say that this withdrawal on the part of Lady Elgin was due to a definite reason?"

"Yes. While in Constantinople, Lord Elgin contracted a severe ague which consequently resulted in the loss of his nose."

The courtroom murmured.

"Mr. Hamilton, would you say that her Ladyship's interest in Lord Elgin began to wane at this point?"

"Yes."

"In your observations, did you see any outward manifestations of her Ladyship's waning love?"

"I did. It was first brought to my attention by Lord Elgin."

"What did his Lordship say to you?"

Hamilton hesitated.

"You must answer the question," warned the Lord President.

"His Lordship said that, because of her tender age, Lady Elgin often fell prey to adolescent behavior while in the presence of handsome men."

There was a second commotion in the courtroom. Garrow waited for silence then went on: "Were you able to substantiate this statement of Lord Elgin's?"

"Yes. While in her Ladyship's presence one day, I heard her remark of Signor Lusieri: 'and as for the painter . . . oh, mother!' "

The women in the courtroom giggled.

"Who is Signor Lusieri?"

"A painter, whom his Lordship assigned to supervise the work in Athens."

"Are you referring to the taking down of the Parthenon marbles?"

"Yes."

"And was Signor Lusieri in fact handsome?"

"I should believe so."

"Were there any other men to your knowledge, for whom Lady Elgin may have expressed a similar remark?"

"Count Sébastiani."

"Who is he?"

"The personal agent of Bonaparte. He visited with the household upon several occasions in Constantinople, and also at Pau."

"Would you say that he too was of handsome countenance?"

"I would."

"Were there any others, Mr. Hamilton?"

"Mr. Fergusson, of course."

"The defendant?"

"Yes."

"I ask you now to impress upon your memory, Mr. Hamilton, and tell this Court if you ever saw Mr. Fergusson in the company of Lady Elgin?"

"I did."

"Were they alone?"

"Yes."

"Do you remember where these meetings occurred?"

"In a house at Number 60 Baker Street in London."

"Did you come upon them by chance?"

"I was instructed to observe them."

"By whom?"

"Lord Elgin."

"For what reason?"

"His Lordship always nourished strong suspicions about Lady Elgin's demeanor where men were concerned. These suspicions were heightened when Lady Elgin and Mr. Fergusson were to leave France on the same ship."

"Do you recall the name of this ship?"

"I do not."

"You were not on board the vessel yourself?"

"I was residing in England at the time."

"Then how did you know that you were to keep them under surveillance?"

"Lord Elgin entrusted a letter to the Captain of the ship and, upon the ship's arrival in England, the Captain delivered it to my residence. Her Ladyship was residing at this time in a house at Number 60 Baker Street, near Portman Square."

"And you assumed the watch from this moment on?"

"Yes."

"Were you not detected?"

"I took every precaution."

Garrow moved to his bench and sipped from a glass of water. "Mr. Hamilton, will you tell the court how long Lady Elgin remained at Number 60 Baker Street?"

"Approximately six months."

"And was a child born to her there?"

"Yes. A female of the name of Lucy."

"Did you at any time observe Mr. Fergusson entering the house at Baker Street after the birth of this child?"

"Yes—both before and after the birth."

"Was he a frequent visitor?"

"Mr. Fergusson came almost daily."

"For how long a period would he remain?"

"Until the early hours of morning."

"After leaving London did Lady Elgin go directly to the home of her parents in Dirleton?"

"Yes, but subsequently she lodged herself at a hotel in Edinburgh."

"What is the name of that hotel?"

"Fortune and Blackwell's."

"Was your assignment now finished, Mr. Hamilton?"

"It was. Soon after I compiled this information I wrote immediately to his Lordship in France."

"And you swear again that your testimony is true?"

"Entirely true."

Garrow dismissed the witness and then took a batch of letters from his table. Holding them up high for the Lord Judges to see, he said: "My Lords and Gentlemen, I have here certain letters which fell into the hands of my noble plaintiff over a period of time, and with your kind permission I shall now read from them—but before doing so, let me say that when persons seal a letter with wax and seal also its envelope, this operation melts the wax of the inner one and causes it to open. Thus when Lord Elgin took off the outward cover of these letters he found them already open inside, discovering meanwhile that they had been written by Mr. Fergusson wrote, no allusion to the surviving children terms of affection that Lord Elgin could not doubt they were meant as an advance to criminal intercourse. While Lady Elgin was at Paris she bore a son who died soon thereafter. Its body being embalmed, the child was then committed to the care of Mr. Fergusson, who procured liberty to return to England and then personally attended its being deposited in the family vault at Dunfermline. In the various letters which Mr. Fergusson wrote, no allusion to the surviving children can be found. For an evident reason, he never hints even at their existence. But to this boy we find several allusions. At one time, Lady Elgin expresses the desire to visit her dear William's tomb but Mr. Fergusson begs her to 'resist this inclination.' 'I know,' says he, 'you will obey me and I entreat you to remember who placed that infant's head to rest.'

"Yet, prior to Mr. Fergusson's appearance on the scene, Lady Elgin's conduct was exemplary as proven from the following extracts of letters which she wrote to her husband while he was in confinement in France: 'Dearest Elgin: keep up your spirits. I will be with you. Willy is a darling infant. If I can be but with you even in confinement, I would not mind anything. I am well this morning though I was very ill last night. I have written to Mr. Talleyrand.' In another letter, she says: 'I have again written to Mr. Talleyrand and begged him to receive me. I have also written to the First Consul, which if he approves, I hope we are now in a fair way of procuring your exchange; may God bless my dearest Elgin. I am much more comfortable now that I am perfectly per-suaded that this is no ways personal against you. It is only a reprisal. Pray, write to me. Monsieur Talleyrand has been most polite to me. God bless you, my dear Elgin. I have written this morning to our First Consul and now to you. I have not lost time, have I? Pray, take the greatest care you can of yourself, my dear Elgin. For heaven's sake, we have not had much comfort in our marriage. But we have got over the worst. The good is to come. And it will come, my dearest Elgin. To be sure, it will!"

"My Lords and Gentlemen, if only this poor woman could see that she was soon to be separated from her devoted husband; that Mr. Fergusson would be answerable for break-ing this domestic happiness; and that one day he would de-prive her of a son and three daughters! If only she realized that this same Mr. Fergusson, by a very artful and subtle seduction, was to destroy her happiness forever! But for this, Mr. Fergusson today is to be accountable.

"I proposed to read to this Court extracts from his other letters to Lady Elgin which show that he was perfectly well-acquainted with the character of her Ladyship and that she had been educated in the best principles of morality. He knew that she was not a person to be taken by storm; that any rash attempt upon her virtue would only alarm her and put her upon guard; and that it was to be done solely by artifice. However I now feel considerable difficulty in having this task imposed upon me and therefore I shall burden you only with this last extract which Mr. Fergusson wrote to Lord Elgin while his Lordship was imprisoned in France: 'I have wrote a few lines to you, my Lord. Your letters to Lady Elgin acquainted her of your impression of mind. Let us hope the best that in this act of severity you will get away and see your Lady Elgin. I have to inform you that Mr. Talleyrand says he will permit that Lord Elgin should be exchanged for General Boyer. I am in hopes of your being liberated. Keep up your spirits; and endeavor to be as comfortable as you can.'

"This clearly marks the confidential situation in which Mr. Fergusson was placed. I could go on, my Lords and Gentlemen, but I wish to spare the feelings of others whose names are herein mentioned. Therefore I shall not trouble you further. Allow me instead to call upon my noble plaintiff's next witness, Mr. John Morier."

Morier, aged thirty, unmarried and residing in London, was solemnly sworn and examined. Garrow waited for him to be seated, then asked: "Did you also accompany Lord Elgin to Constantinople?"

"I did."

"In what capacity?"

"As his Lordship's second private secretary. I stayed at Constantinople until our expedition reached Egypt in the August following, and then I returned to Constantinople in May."

"How long did you continue at Constantinople?"

"Until January, two years following."

"Did you live in the same house with Lord and Lady Elgin?"

"I did."

"Then you had the same opportunity as Mr. Hamilton, the previous witness, of observing their conduct as man and wife?"

"Lord Elgin was a tender and considerate husband—"

"You must answer only the questions put to you," said the Lord President sternly.

Garrow rephrased his question. "Mr. Morier, what were your personal observations of Lord Elgin's conduct toward Lady Elgin?"

"He was a tender and considerate husband."

The courtroom erupted in laughter.

"And what were your personal observations of Lady Elgin's conduct toward Lord Elgin?"

"In the beginning, she was a most affectionate wife and mother."

"Do you mean to say that her Ladyship's conduct changed?"

"Yes."

"When exactly?"

"As Lord Elgin's affliction became more serious."

"You are referring to the loss of his Lordship's nose?"

"I am."

There was more commotion from the courtroom.

"Mr. Morier, were you able to discern any actual manifestations of her Ladyship's change of conduct at Constantinople?"

"Indeed. Lady Elgin became rather abrupt whenever she was in his Lordship's presence."

"Is this all?"

"Her Ladyship also left the house early each day."

"For what purpose?"

"I cannot truly say. However not a day passed without an afternoon tea or a stroll through the gardens at Pera."

"And what of the evenings?"

"Her Ladyship often chose to retire early, when not playing at cards."

"She had her own bed chamber?"

"Yes."

"Separate from his Lordship's?"

"Entirely."

"Mr. Morier, I want you to think carefully before answering this next question: did Lady Elgin in fact have a weakness for men?"

"Her Ladyship is a very beautiful woman. Men find her quite attractive . . . yes, I would say that she indeed had a weakness for men."

"Can you furnish us with any actual proof of such weakness?"

"Many times I observed a certain look in her Ladyship's eyes whenever a man, particularly a striking young man, would visit the household."

"Will you please describe this look more fully?"

"It was a look of admiration, I think."

"Nothing more?"

"Of attraction too."

"Sexual attraction?"

"My Lords!" protested Topping.

The Lord President nodded his head several times. "I must remind you, Mr. Garrow, that we are on direct examination. This Court will not permit you to lead your witnesses."

"I beg the Court's forgiveness, my Lord President."

"Proceed."

"Mr. Morier, will you give this Court a more lucid description of what you meant when you spoke of Lady Elgin's look?"

"It was a flirtatious look."

"You are quite certain?"

"Yes."

"I have no further questions to ask of this witness, my Lords," said Garrow, walking back to his bench. Topping did not choose to cross-examine. Mr. Richard Sterling was then called to the witness chair.

"Mr. Sterling, when did you first become acquainted with Lord and Lady Elgin?" asked Garrow, squinting.

"In Paris, during the time of our detention there."

"Was the defendant, Mr. Fergusson, also detained in Paris at this time?"

"He was."

"Did you have a friendly relationship with Lord and Lady Elgin?"

"I did."

"What was your impression of their attachment?"

"I found it rather strained."

"How so?"

"They were seldom together."

"Did you ever see Mr. Fergusson alone with Lady Elgin?"

"No. They were always in the company of the others."

"Others?"

"The Cockburns, Mrs. Fitzgerald, Colonel Crawford—"

"These were détunus also?"

"Yes."

"Where did these meetings occur?"

"At the Hotel de Richelieu in Paris; also at Barèges and Pau."

"Mr. Sterling, can you tell us anything further about the relationship between Mr. Fergusson and Lady Elgin?"

"It appeared to me that Lady Elgin was very interested in Mr. Fergusson from the outset. She was constantly inquiring of his whereabouts."

"Can you give a clearer description of this interest?"

"It went beyond mere friendship."

"Please be more explicit, Mr. Sterling."

"I would say that Lady Elgin was infatuated with Mr. Fergusson."

"Were you able to observe Mr. Fergusson's feelings toward Lady Elgin?"

"He too appeared to be enamored of her."

"Thank you, Mr. Sterling."

Again Topping did not cross-examine.

Charles Duff was next to be called to the witness chair. The sight of him set loose an avalanche of memories for Lady Elgin: it seemed only yesterday that he had gone ashore at Palermo to secure lodgings for them. So terrified he was of Captain Maling's wrath when he returned to *La Diane* with nothing to show for his efforts.

"I believe that you too were in the employ of Lord Elgin, Mr. Duff?"

"I was."

"Kindly state your age."

"Forty-five."

"You are married?"

"I am."

"And where do you reside?"

"At Number One Weymouth Street, Portland Place, London."

"Did you remain with Lord and Lady Elgin during their stay at Constantinople?"

"I did."

"Mr. Duff, what was the impression on your mind as to the manner in which Lord and Lady Elgin conducted themselves?"

"I never saw a happier couple in my life."

"Did you attend the funeral of their child who died in France?"

"I did."

"Who else was in attendance, Mr. Duff?"

"Mr. Fergusson, Lord Elgin's mother, the Rector of the church at Dunfermline, and a few relatives and friends."

"Where was the child interred?"

"In the family vault at Dunfermline."

"Now then, Mr. Duff, did you receive any instructions from Lady Elgin after she returned to England from France?"

"Her Ladyship asked me to hire a house for her, which I did accordingly."

"Why should she ask you to hire a house for her . . . was she not happy with her parents?"

"Mr. Nisbet came up to Town one day and visited me. He said both he and his wife were sorry to learn that Lady Elgin had decided to reside at Number 60 Baker Street. Mr. Nisbet expressed his disapprobation of her Ladyship's having left the Nisbet household in Portman Square."

"Mr. Duff, did you have any occasion to meet with Lady

Elgin's servants while she was residing at Number 60 Baker Street?"

"Yes. I had many conversations with Mrs. Sarah Gosling; also with Miss Nonweiler and Mr. Robert Draper."

"These were all servants in the family?"

"Yes."

"And what was the subject of your conversations?"

"Lady Elgin's conduct."

"In what regard?"

"Mr. Fergusson's frequent visits there."

"Can you elaborate, Mr. Duff?"

"Mr. Fergusson often came to the house as late as twelve and one in the morning, and went away at three or four in the morning. Sometimes even later. Mrs. Gosling disapproved of this very much but never expressed to me that there was any criminal connection between Lady Elgin and Mr. Fergusson—"

The Lord President interrupted: "You will answer only the questions put to you!"

"Mr. Duff, do you recall any conversations you may have had with Lady Elgin during this time?"

"I do."

"When exactly?"

"I was assisting her Ladyship in packing up, previous to her setting out for Scotland. She seemed to be much agitated and said to me: 'O! Duff, I am quite miserable! If they continue to plague me I shall go off with Fergusson!' "

"To whom was she referring?"

"Lord Elgin and her parents."

"And what was your response, Mr. Duff?"

"I said to her Ladyship: 'God forbid I should ever see that day, my Lady, as you would be looked upon as not better than a girl of the Town if you go off with Fergusson.' "

"Mr. Duff, were you aware of a correspondence by letters being carried on between Lady Elgin and Mr. Fergusson?"

"I was. Lady Elgin applied to Mrs. Duff by letter, to be

allowed to enclose a letter to Mr. Fergusson under cover to Mrs. Duff. Having opened my wife's letter, I disapproved of her being engaged in this and by my desire Mrs. Duff wrote immediately to Lady Elgin and informed her Ladyship that she refused to receive or deliver any such letter."

"What did your wife do with this letter, Mr. Duff?"

"She destroyed it."

"And was that the end of the matter?"

"No. Mr. Fergusson came to my house about a fortnight later and demanded her Ladyship's letter to my wife but I told him the letter had been destroyed."

"Did you verify for certain that this was a letter from Lady Elgin?"

"I am very familiar with her Ladyship's handwriting. It was indeed her letter."

"That is all, Mr. Duff."

In cross-examination, Topping asked: "Mr. Duff, is it correct to say that most of your testimony here does not arise from any personal observations regarding Lady Elgin's conduct in London but in truth results from hearsay information of servants and chambermaids?"

"I have known Mrs. Gosling for a long time; also Mr. Draper. They are respectable persons."

"Prior to your leaving for England, Mr. Duff, what were your actual observations of Lady Elgin's conduct at Constantinople?"

"Most commendable."

"What about her behavior toward Lord Elgin and her children?

"Equally so."

"Would you say that Lady Elgin was that type of mother who abandons the needs of her children for selfish pursuits?"

"No."

"Thank you, Mr. Duff. You may step down."

Here the Lord President announced a recess of one hour.

When court resumed, Garrow moved that the deposition of Mrs. Sarah Gosling (which formerly was made to "lye in retentis" until a proof was allowed) should now be opened and made a part of the proof in the nobel plaintiff's cause. (Mrs. Gosling died shortly after giving the deposition.) Topping brought up a vehement objection, but was overruled by the Lord Judges and the deposition was permitted to be read. Mrs. Gosling was a servant to Lady Elgin at Number 60 Baker Street, and Elgin's solicitors expected her to be the key witness until she fell ill. The Commissaries at Edinburgh agreed to grant a deposition commission to James Chalmer, confirming Mrs. Gosling's state of health and allowing Chalmer to examine her in the presence of a Clerk of the Court whose name was William Moncur:

Knightsbridge,*

APPEARED Sarah Gosling, now residing at Knightsbridge in the County of Middlesex, married, age thirty-three, and being solemnly sworn according to the form directed by the Commission, and the usual questions of a preliminary nature being put to her, hereby swears that she holds no malice or ill will toward either of the parties in this Cause; that she has neither received nor been promised any money or good deed for being a witness; that Mr. Bichnell† now present did apply to her and enquire what she knew concerning the conduct of the Countess of Elgin, to which the deponent answered, and Mr. Bichnell then told her that he was acting for Lord Elgin, asking her several questions with regard to an intercourse between Lady Elgin and Mr. Fergusson; that the deponent brought pen and ink to Mr. Bichnell and answered these questions to the best of her knowledge and conscience.

Mr. Spottiswood** acting on the part of Lady Elgin here objected to the examination proceeding, in respect

---

* A suburb of London.
† One of Lord Elgin's solicitors in London.
** Lady Elgin's solicitor.

that the witness, having furnished Mr. Bichnell with a statement of facts relative to this Cause, is thereby by the Law of Scotland disqualified from being a witness therein. The Commissioner repells the objection, and the witness, being then specially interrogated, DEPONES that she was one of the defender Lady Elgin's servants, lived with her in London in the year one thousand eight hundred and six, her Ladyship then residing at Number 60 Baker Street.

DEPONES that she knows Robert Fergusson Esquire of Raith, and that he used to visit Lady Elgin in her house at Baker Street during the time of Lord Elgin's imprisonment in France; that Mr. Fergusson called frequently in the daytime and often in the evenings; that Lady Elgin was in the habit of going out many nights; that her Ladyship returned home sometimes at ten, eleven, or twelve o'clock.

DEPONES that Mr. Fergusson at different times visited Lady Elgin after she had thus returned home from her evening engagements; that she observed Lady Elgin more than once after she came from her evening engagements take off her dress in which she had passed the evening and put on a loose gown; and that it was her general custom to do so.

DEPONES that she saw Lady Elgin admit the visits of Mr. Fergusson after her Ladyship had changed her dress; that at these visits there was no person with Lady Elgin except Mr. Fergusson; that she has known Mr. Fergusson to remain alone with Lady Elgin at these visits for an hour at a time and even longer; that when Mr. Fergusson retired from these visits the deponent has found Lady Elgin in bed; that she recollects Mrs. Nisbet calling on her daughter at Baker Street one night at twelve o'clock when Mr. Fergusson was then in the house.

DEPONES that Lady Elgin received Mrs. Nisbet on this occasion in the drawing room, but Mr. Fergusson was not in the drawing room while Mrs. Nisbet continued with Lady Elgin; that Mr. Fergusson was in Lady Elgin's bedroom during Mrs. Nisbet's visit and did not leave the house till after Mrs. Nisbet was gone; that Mr. Fergusson, when leaving the house after these evening visits, was sometimes let out by the deponent and sometimes by Lady Elgin's maid and not by any of the Footmen; and that at different times the men servants had gone to bed when Mr. Fergusson retired.

DEPONES that she has known Mr. Fergusson to continue with Lady Elgin till four and five o'clock in the morning; that there were no other persons in the house on these occasions except Mr. Fergusson and Lady Elgin; that it was Lady Elgin's general custom to direct the curtain of the Window which was behind the Sopha in the drawing room to be let down; that she generally gave this order in the morning when she came into the room, and it remained down all day; that she never made any observations on the state of the Sopha after Mr. Fergusson had been with Lady Elgin as to its being rumpled or otherwise, since this Sopha was of such a construction as a person sitting upon it could make no impression; and that, being interrogated by Mr. Bichnell as to what she means by a loose gown which she has said that Lady Elgin put on in the evenings, describes it as a loose wrapping gown which Ladies wear when they have their hair combed and which Lady Elgin used to put on every morning and evening.

All this is truth, as the deponent shall answer to God.

(Signed) Sarah Gosling.

James Chalmer, Commissioner
William Moncur, Clerk

What is written on the five preceding pages is the Report of the act and Commission mentioned in the first page, and returned to the Court sealed up as directed.

(Signed) James Chalmer, Commissioner
William Moncur, Clerk

At this point, Ann Crerar, now residing in Edinburgh, unmarried, aged twenty-two years, was sworn and examined by Garrow:

"What was your most recent occupation, Miss Crerar?"

"I was formerly Chambermaid in Fortune and Blackwell's Hotel."

"Here in Edinburgh?"

"Yes."

"Where exactly is the hotel located?"

"It is the Westmost house in the South side of Princes Street."

"Were you ever acquainted with the defendant, Mr. Fergusson, and Lady Elgin?"

"I was Chambermaid to Lady Elgin when she resided at the hotel during the month of August, eighteen hundred and six. Mr. Fergusson took residence there at the same time."

"Will you tell this Court everything you know regarding their residence at the hotel?"

"On the very day that Lady Elgin registered at the hotel, another woman came also. Her name was Lady Harvey. She remained only a short time and as soon as she left, Mr. Fergusson took her lodgings which consisted of a Parlor and bedroom, on the same floor with those occupied by Lady Elgin. The room numbers were Seven and Eight, and they had a communication with the rooms of Lady Elgin, being separated by a door between the two Parlors. I went into Mr. Fergusson's bedroom the morning after he came to the Hotel and I observed that his bed had not been slept in, and that it remained in the same state as when it had been made down by myself the preceding evening. I then went into Lady Elgin's bedroom and from the appearance of the bed I was satisfied that two people had slept in it, being convinced of this from the appearance both of the pillows and the sheets. The pillows had the mark of two people having lain on them, and the sheets were marked in the same manner. That same morning I saw Mr. Fergusson in Lady Elgin's Parlor. I went directly to John Fraser who is a waiter in the Hotel and told him that two people had slept in Lady Elgin's bed, and I wondered if Lord Elgin had come and slept there. Mr. Fraser said that he had not and warned me to hold my tongue as Lady Elgin might get into a scrape."

"That is all, Miss Crerar. Thank you."

Topping did not cross-examine.

John Fraser was called: waiter in Fortune and Blackwell's, married, aged thirty-eight, and now residing in Edinburgh. He confirmed the testimony of Miss Crerar and added that "Mr. Fergusson was personally known to me, having lodged at the Hotel many times previously. A few days after Lady Harvey left the Hotel, Mr. Fergusson came and was shewn into Lady Elgin's apartments where he continued with her Ladyship for about a quarter of an hour. Upon his coming out, he enquired whether he could be accommodated with lodgings on the same floor, and being told by myself that he could, he engaged those which had been occupied by Lady Harvey. Mr. Fergusson passed the next day entirely in Lady Elgin's company and even invited himself to tea, continuing with her Ladyship till about half past ten, at which time I lighted him to his own Parlour. He then desired the candles there to be lighted, as he had letters to write. Miss Crerar later came to me and said that Mr. Fergusson had not slept in his bed; and that from the appearance of Lady Elgin's bed, two people had slept in it. When Mr. Fergusson finally took his leave and had paid his bill, he requested that his arrival should not be put in the newspapers, mentioning that from his short stay in Town he would be plagued with his acquaintances calling on him. He had no servant or baggage with him; and I did not see him have a night cap."

Again there was no cross-examination.

Mary Ruper was summoned to the witness chair: servant at Broomhall, unmarried, aged twenty-five years, served Lady Elgin while she resided at Number 60 Baker Street, entering her service on the fifteenth of November and continuing with her Ladyship till the twenty-second of June following, or thereabouts . . . , concurring with the testimony of Sarah Gosling's deposition, and adding: "that when Mrs. Nisbet came to visit her daughter one night, Mr. Fergusson hid behind a screen which stood in the drawing room, and after Mrs. Nisbet left, Mr. Fergusson remained till a late hour in the morning. The next day I mentioned to Mrs. Gosling that the dog had dirtied a green silk cushion which was on the Sopha—but Mrs. Gosling shook her head and said it was not the dog who had dirtied the cushion but that rogue, Mr. Fergusson."

Garrow waited for the courtroom to be silent before continuing: "Miss Ruper, did you and the other servants of the house form any opinion of this situation?"

"Indeed we did. We all agreed that there was an improper connection between Mr. Fergusson and Lady Elgin!"

The evidence against Fergusson and Lady Elgin was overwhelming, and Topping decided to place their cause upon the Court's mercy. Meanwhile the last witness for the plaintiff was called to the chair: Thomas Willey, formerly Lady Elgin's footman who was discharged by Lord Elgin "for having got drunk . . . and now servant to his Royal Highness, the Duke of Kent, widower, aged thirty-three years, and bearing no malice or evil against either party, depones that he was in Lady Elgin's service while she resided at Number 60 Baker Street, Portman Square, London . . . coming to her service from Scotland about two or three months after her Ladyship took residence at Baker Street:"

> I was well-acquainted with Mr. Fergusson of Raith. He was frequently in the practice of calling for her Ladyship, both through the day and during the evening while she resided at Baker Street. Occasionally Mr. Fergusson called at twelve and till half past one in the morning according as her child, I went up to the drawing room and opened the Elgin was always at home to Mr. Fergusson, and I hardly recollect one night that Mr. Fergusson did not call sooner or later. Sometimes he staid till three or half past three in the morning, and I was told by Sarah Gosling that she has let him out of the house even after four o'clock in the morning.
>
> Mr. Fergusson was shewn more attention by Lady Elgin than any other person who came to visit there. She seemed happier when in Mr. Fergusson's company than when in the company of any other person. Everytime they met they shook hands and shewed great familiarity. I recollect one

day about noon, six weeks after Lady Elgin had delivered her child, I went up to the drawing room and opened the door without knocking. I saw Lady Elgin at full length on the Sopha, and upon my coming in, both Lady Elgin and Mr. Fergusson had hold of a shawl and in great confusion threw it over Lady Elgin's legs . . . .

"Were her Ladyship's petticoats up?" asked Garrow.

"I could not positively say."

"Why not?"

"A little writing table stood in front of the Sopha and I was prevented from seeing exactly whether her Ladyship's legs were uncovered or not before the shawl was thrown over them. However from the hurry and confused way in which the shawl was thrown over her legs I would say that indeed her petticoats were up."

"And what about Mr. Fergusson . . . what was he doing at this time?"

"Mr. Fergusson tried to calm her Ladyship. Her face was much flushed. He then walked towards the fire with his back toward me and, turning only his head, said: 'It is only Thomas.' "

"Were you able to observe whether Mr. Fergusson's breeches were buttoned or unbuttoned?"

"I could not see any part of him in front. He continued at the fire in the same position with his back to me during all this time."

"Mr. Willey, why did you enter the drawing room without knocking?"

"It was always my custom to knock before going in—but on this occasion I was in a hurry to deliver a message to her Ladyship."

"Thank you, Mr. Willey."

When Topping made no attempt to cross-examine, Garrow asked Mr. Hay Donaldson to step forward, and after being duly examined, Donaldson was asked to disclose his occupation.

"I am a writer to the signet."

"Do you practice in Edinburgh?"

"I do."

"Have you any information regarding the entailed estate of the defendant's father?"

"I have."

"Upon whom is the estate entailed?"

"Upon Mr. Robert Fergusson, Esquire."

"The defendant?"

"Yes. It is entailed upon him after the death of the father, without division."

"Is Mr. Robert Fergusson the only son?"

"To my knowledge."

"In your professional opinion, would you consider this estate to be substantial?"

"Quite so."

"Have you ascertained its real value?"

"No."

"But it is opulent?"

"Yes. Very much so."

Garrow had no further questions. There was a brief silence and then Mr. Topping came forward to cross-examine: "Mr. Donaldson, during your investigation of the estate did you find strict clauses prohibiting any alienation or encumbrance?"

"I did."

"Were there also some clauses burdening the estate with certain debts?"

"There were."

"Mr. Donaldson, when did you last see the defendant's father?"

"Only a few days ago."

"And what was the state of his health?"

"Mr. Fergusson's father is a hale and stout man; and very strong for his years."

"One last question: do you honestly believe that this estate can produce twenty thousand pounds per year?"*

---

* Lord Elgin was asking the Court for twenty thousad pounds in damages.

"I cannot rightfully say."

"That is all, Mr. Donaldson. You may step down."

After studying the stacks of papers on his table, Garrow finally straightened up and announced: "My Lords, the noble plaintiff's case is closed!"

Topping slowly came forward and addressed the Court: "My Lords and Gentlemen, I have the honor of attending before you as the counsel for the unfortunate defendant in this cause. I am well-warranted in using this epithet, after hearing the manner in which my learned friend from London presented his client's case to you. He would venture to have you believe that this indeed is one of those melancholy examples of human frailty where a man has been placed in the way of temptations that are impossible to resist. Perhaps this is true. I need only to remind you that the defendant was twenty-seven years old when the supposed criminal intercourse took place.

"Certainly I should not complain of my learned English friend. To the contrary, I commend him. Furthermore, I hope and trust that each man on this Jury shall give due consideration of the whole circumstances in this case when called upon to arrive at a verdict. I trust that in your judicious and discerning minds, my client's interests shall lose nothing by my own inexperience in advocating cases of this description; or suffer by that comparison which you might make between the greater and more extensive experience of my learned English opponent. My feeble efforts cannot be contrasted with his superior and towering eloquence, for he brings here an incomparable learning and noble breeding while I, like yourselves, am but a simple Scotsman residing in a humble abode beneath *Auld Reekie's* soiled skirts."

There was a raucous burst of laughter which the Lord President momentarily permitted.

"Nevertheless, my Lords and Gentlemen, I feel that I am required to make certain observations on my part which I hope to impress briefly but strongly upon your minds: much has been said of the defendant's crime and yet no real evidence was offered here today in respect to Lady Elgin's unfaithfulness to her matrimonial bed. We listened to the testimony of many witnesses, during which not a few deplorable charges were made against the honor and good name of Lady Elgin and the defendant, however not one of these witnesses could honestly admit that Mr. Fergusson was actually seen in criminal conversation with Lady Elgin.

"As for the letters that fell into Lord Elgin's hands, let me say that they furnish no conclusive proof that adultery was indeed committed. Bear in mind that Lady Elgin's health was seriously impaired at this time, both physically and emotionally. My learned English friend feels that it is your duty to scourge the defendant in punishing an offense of this nature. Thank God it is not within the province of this jury to scourge. If there is an injury here, it is of a civil nature and the compensation, if any, must be a requital by a civil remuneration. It pleases me to say that the laws of Scotland know of no vindictive return for an injury such as this. 'Vengeance is mine, saith the Lord!'

"When my learned English friend talks of twenty thousand pounds as a requital I feel great surprise. On the one hand he admits that no pecuniary reimbursement can repay his noble client's injury. Yet he seeks precisely this. And more, for he would convert this civil transgression, if such it is proven to be, into a criminal case. But it is my strong conviction that the Courts of Scotland will never permit such an innovation in the law.

"With respect to the financial condition of Mr. Fergusson, I am free to disclose that in fact he is not worth one shilling. He exists merely upon the bounty of his father. Quite to the contrary, he is not an only child but is the eldest son of a large family. His father may live many additional years and thus Mr. Fergusson cannot command a guinea. As we all know, the laws of Scotland almost universally entail the estates. At best, Mr. Fergusson can be but a life-tenant, without the power of raising twenty shillings, let alone twenty thousand pounds. He may also be burdened with provisions for relatives which would preclude the possibility of his ever paying heavy damages, should they be imposed upon him today. This is exactly his state and condition.

"I am persuaded that his cause is now in honourable and sympathetic hands. Furthermore, I entertain no doubt but that you will deal with him in mercy and consideration. My Lords and Gentlemen, I thank you."

Before retiring to their chamber, the jury was charged by the Lord President: "Gentlemen, I call your attention to the importance of this case which involves an injury, perhaps the greatest injury that one can inflict upon another. In all actions of this description, it is the task of the plaintiff to make out his title to a claim and to show that such claim is well-founded. It remains now for you to say if this claim should be granted. You must act with caution, deliberately considering if there is an offense here, and if so, its appropriate punishment. I am fully persuaded that your verdict will also afford public gratification. Retire then, into your chamber. This case is left entirely in your hands."

In less than five minutes, the jury returned "with a Verdict for the Plaintiff: damages of ten thousand pounds."

Chapter Eleven

Telos

IN THE CIVIL action held at London Fergusson claimed that no adultery had taken place in France, "especially in the voluptuous and fascinating capital of the French Empire where temptation is ever busily at work. But when Lady Elgin arrived in England, without the protection of her husband, and possessing sweetness that might rivet an anchorite, charms that could command and fascinate the coldest heart, he—all alive to such unequalled excellence and beauty—fell a devoted victim to such a shrine!"

This statement was quickly brought to the attention of the Commissaries when the divorce decree was heard shortly after the trial against Fergusson had ended:*

At Edinburgh, anent the action and cause for divorce, raised, intended, and pursued before the Commissary at the instance of the Right Honourable Thomas, Earl of Elgin and Kincardine, against Mary, Countess of Elgin and Kincardine, by virtue of the said Commissary, his libelled summons raised there anent which maketh mention that where the said Thomas, Earl of Elgin and Kincardine, pursuer; and where the said Mary, Countess of Elgin and Kincardine, defendant . . . were regularly married and

* Lord Elgin received the full payment for damages of ten thousand pounds from Fergusson, whose father was a wealthy man. Fergusson's claim of poverty was a courtroom maneuver which failed to sway the jury.

cohabited together as husband and wife, owned and ac-
knowledged each other as such and were holden, treated,
and reputed married persons by their friends and neigh-
bours, of which marriage five children were procreated, of
whom four are alive today.

And although Mary, Countess of Elgin and Kincardine,
stood bound and obliged to preserve the marriage bed in-
violate, yet true it is that she, regardless of her marriage
vows and of the whole attachment which ought to subsist
between married persons, and of her duty as wife and
mother, has for sometime past had carnal intercourse with
a man or with men known not to be the said Thomas, Earl
of Elgin and Kincardine, and has been guilty of an act or
acts of adultery.

Lady Elgin felt that she was suddenly back at Palermo
harbor on board the *Phaeton;* and she could see thin little
Masterman wringing her hands and crying: 'Her poor Ladyship! A fine honeymoon is this!' Even now the smell of that
horrible vinegar was saturating every pore of her soul with
the memory of that fitful voyage:

And more particularly, the said Mary, Countess of Elgin
and Kincardine, has had such carnal conversation and intercourse, and committed such act or acts of adultery with
Robert Fergusson Esquire of Raith, in all or one of the
nights or days during their journey together from France
to London, and also in the city of Edinburgh. And therefore concluding that in all law, equity and justice, the said
noble pursuer ought and should have the said Commissary, his sentence and decreet, finding and declaring that
the defender has been guilty of the crime of adultery.
And discovering and separating her from his society,
fellowship and company, in all time coming. And finding
and declaring that the pursuer is free of the marriage
contracted, solemnized and completed between him and
the said defender. And that the said pursuer may marry
when and whom he pleases in the same manner as if the

defender were naturally dead, or as he might have done
if he had never been married to her.

It ought finally to be found and declared that the said
Mary, Countess of Elgin and Kincardine, has forfeited and
lost all manner of right, interest, or benefit by the said
marriage—either legal or conventional. And that the noble
pursuer has a just right and title to the provisions made in
his favour which shall include the care and upbringing of
the surviving children. And thus the said Commissary gives
and pronounces his sentence and decreet in the aforesaid
manner; divorcing, separating, finding and declaring in
form at length before written.

In the years that followed, *The Times* and other English
publications steadily wrote of Lord Elgin's misfortunes, referring in great detail to his enormous debts and legion of
creditors. Foreseeing a life of abject poverty, Elgin wrote
again to the Prime Minister, Spencer Perceval, repeating his
long list of expenses and once more requesting "a mark of
Royal approbation as a Scotch Peer. I need hardly add that
such an arrangement would be in the highest degree gratify-
ing to my feelings; and if such a Peerage is conferred I shall
be prepared to accept payment by installments, or partly by
annuity, if this would be more convenient."

Perceval's reply came quickly and sharply: "I must candidly say that I should feel it quite impossible to recommend
any arrangement of that nature!"

Lord Elgin's income from his estates in Scotland totaled
only two thousand pounds a year. By the usual standards of
nobility, he was never a wealthy man nor "easy in his circumstances" as Dundas once suggested to King George III when
recommending Elgin for the embassy at Constantinople. Although Elgin's salary in Constantinople was almost seven
thousand pounds it was hardly enough when compared to
the domestic expense of more than eight thousand pounds
for maintaining the embassy his first year alone. This did not
include the salaries and expenses of his large staff, the
maintenance of his house at Pera, the cost of postage,

couriers, and other sizable expenses of an actively large embassy. But beyond all this, he spent close to twenty thousand pounds of his own money to buy tents, horses, medical supplies, gunboats and military equipment for the British Expeditionary Forces in Egypt. "Of this amount, the Government reimbursed him only with ten thousand pounds."

The Elgin Marbles were moved to the British Museum in August, 1816. Under the terms of the Act passed by Parliament which transferred their ownership to the English government, Lord Elgin and his heirs were to be made Trustees of the British Museum. From the purchase price of thirty-five thousand pounds, the government put a claim on eighteen thousand, in payment for a debt cunningly transferred to them by one of Elgin's creditors. The balance of the money was then dispersed among those creditors who were fortunate enough to get their share before it ran out. Elgin did not receive one penny.

But he refused to give up. Several months later he wrote again to Perceval's successor, Lord Liverpool,* and once more recounted his many disasters on his journey from Constantinople and the expectation to return to England, only to be seized in France and persecuted with the most vindictive animosity by Bonaparte:

> It was while suffering under these severities and separated from all but the most constrained communications from my family in England, that the foulest and most insidious intrigue was darkly at work here, preparing the ruin of my domestic peace, creating prepossessions in regard to my official conduct, which however I had subsequently the good fortune to remove at least from Mr. Perceval's mind; nor were the true motives of this undefined, unavowed, yet most injurious persecution brought home to its real source in disappointment and jealousy till Mr. Spencer Smith, finding a willing instrument in Mr.

* Perceval was assassinated on 11 May 1812, in the lobby of the House of Commons.

Robert Tweddell to distort one of the most ordinary incidents in foreign stations, could not refrain from standing prominently forward in the publications that then appeared against me. And presuming upon the ill will against my operations in Greece, in which some late travelers had indulged, he actually transmitted anonymous abuse against me to the newspapers at the moment when the House of Commons was entering upon the subject of my marbles.

The last line of Elgin's letter was an outright plea for mercy:

> All the money I had drawn upon public account, the whole proceeds of my patrimonial estate, my dowry, and every private fund at my disposal have been entirely absorbed!

Lord Liverpool sympathized with Elgin's plight, but the peerage was not granted. During these negotiations Elgin suffered still another setback: His son Bruce fell gravely ill and Elgin's physicians in Edinburgh were unable to diagnose the sickness or cure it. Fighting desperately to save his only son and heir, Lord Elgin brought the boy to London where he was examined by the finest physicians of the time. They all concurred that Bruce was a hopeless epileptic.

> First on the head of him who did this deed,
> My curse shall light, on him and all his seed;
> Without one spark of intellectual fire,
> Be all the sons as senseless as the sire!

Despite all these reversals, Lord Elgin was still hopeful "of bequeathing something to his children besides his debts." Doggedly, he made a final request for a British peerage, but it was denied. Whatever assets he possessed were now put immediately into trust. To add to his embarrassment, the disfigurement of his face brought on a deeper depression and he began avoiding people, even those who were closest to him. It was not long before his beloved Broomhall became the target of his many creditors, and although the title of the estate was protected by ancient English law, he could no longer maintain it properly. Most of its rooms remained unfurnished and the large force of servants had to be discharged.

"In 1820 Elgin returned to the House of Lords as one of the representative peers for Scotland. A year later he was, with the long-despised Byron,* one of the first to subscribe to the Philhellenic Committee to support the Revolutionary Forces in Greece."

It was no surprise to anyone in Edinburgh when Lord Elgin married again. His second wife was Elizabeth Oswald of Dunnikeir, daughter of a wealthy land-owner from Fife. Immediately after the marriage, Elgin departed for France with his wife, leaving the care of the children to his mother, the dowager Countess of Elgin. For the rest of his life, "he was obliged to live in France to escape his creditors."†

A few weeks after the trial Lady Elgin and Robert Fergusson were quietly married. For a time they lived at Raith, Fergusson's family home, and later they resided at Archerfield. When Fergusson entered political life, Lady Elgin accompanied him to London and they took residence in the Nisbet house at Portman Square until Fergusson's death.

Lady Elgin's last years were spent at Archerfield. While walking across the east meadow one morning, she came to the jagged cliffs that overlooked Aberlady Bay and stood

---

* Lord Byron died, after a series of feverish attacks, in the small Greek village of Missolonghi, where he had gone to train some peasant troops whom he himself had subsidized. For three and a half months Byron lived a Spartan existence at Missolonghi but the village had many unclean swamps and Byron soon succumbed to fever. He died at 6:15 p.m. on Monday, 19 April 1824. He regarded himself a complete failure at Missolonghi but history has proved otherwise: "Lord Byron accomplished nothing at Missolonghi except his own suicide; but by that single act of heroism he secured the liberation of Greece."

To this day, Bryon is revered as a national hero in Greece.

† Lord Elgin was in adject poverty when he died in Paris on 4 November 1841. His enormous debts were not fully paid off by his family until 1875.

entranced by the pounding sea below. The powerful tide was leaving a trail of sadness in its wake; and from the cavernous depths of her memory she beheld the raw sight of a mortally-wounded Parthenon with spidery scaffolds clutching its west pediment as sweating laborers worked on ropes and pulleys. She heard the deafening echo of chisels eating into the veins of the first marble frieze; the haunting sound of that exquisite cornice as it fell to the ground in a thousand pieces; Elgin's wild voice staining the Attic sky with eternal shame; and finally she felt the warmth of the Turkish Disdar's tears when he threw his arms upward and cried: "Telos!"

Yet this was not the end.

That same tide was pulling her heart to those wretched marbles lying on a cold floor. She heard them mocking her, avenging their ravaged divinity with a hatred that would never end. Almost instantly she was paralyzed by the pull of time, the fierce growth of grass under her feet, the thundering pulse of the Firth on Scotland's ribs. It was a terrible augury. Like those violated gods now imprisoned in a stifling room of the British Museum, she too was to be condemned to a life of utter loneliness and grief:

"What a desperate horrible idea that nothing but death can make me free!"*

* After her death in 1855, Lady Elgin was put "to rest in a tomb not only unkempt and forlorn but nameless too." Her name was finally inscribed on "the hideous stone" in 1916.

Bibliography

Principal Sources

"Decreet Divorce, Thomas, Earl of Elgin and Kincardine, against Mary Countess of Elgin and Kincardine." *Commissary Court Record*, Scottish Records Office, Edinburgh, 1808, pp. 1273–1473.

Elgin, *The Letters of Mary Nisbet, Countess of London*, John Murray (Publishers), Ltd., 1926.

Farington Diary, James Grieg, ed. London, British Museum, 1922.

Fergusson, The Trial of R. London, J. Day, 1807.

GENNADIOS, IOANNES, *Lord Elgin and the Previous Archeological Invasions of Greece, Especially Athens.* Athens, Privately printed, 1930. Published in Greek, this book is devoted entirely to the reaction of travelers to Lord Elgin's taking down of the Parthenon marbles.

HEROLD, J. CHRISTOPHER, *The Age of Napoleon.* New York, American Heritage Publishing Co., 1963.

SMITH, ARTHUR HAMILTON, "Lord Elgin and His Collection." *Journal of Hellenic Studies of 1916.* This long article, published on the hundredth anniversary of the acquisition of the Elgin Marbles by the British Museum, is the definitive source on Lord Elgin's endeavors in Athens. Smith was a relative of the Elgin family and had access to many important letters and documents.

ST. CLAIR, WILLIAM, *Lord Elgin and the Marbles.* London, Oxford University Press, 1967. A thorough, accurate work, this book strongly supports Lord Elgin's position.

General Sources

BARROW, JOHN, *Life and Correspondence of Admiral Sir William Sidney Smith GCB.* London, R. Bentley, 1848.

BLACKSTONE, SIR WILLIAM, *Commentaries on the Laws of England.* London, 1765.

BROWN, WILLIAM J., *Syphilis and other Venereal Diseases.* Cambridge, 1970.

BYRON, LORD, *English Bards and Scotch Reviewers,* 1809.

————, *The Curse of Minerva,* 1812,

————, *Childe Harold's Pilgrimage, Cantos I and II,* 1812.

Byron's Correspondence Chiefly with Lady Melbourne, Mr. Hobhouse, The Hon. Douglas Kinnaird and P. B. Shelley. John Murray, ed. London, John Murray (Publishers), Ltd., 1922.

Byron, A Self Portrait, Letters and Diaries 1798 to 1824, Peter Quennell, ed. London, John Murray (Publishers), Ltd., 1950.

CARLYLE, JOSEPH DACRE, *Poems.* London, T. Cadell and W. Davis, 1805.

CHOISEUL-GOUFFIER, Comte de, *Voyage Pittoresque de la Grèce,* 1782–1809, Paris, J. P. Aillaud, 1812.

CLARKE, EDWARD DANIEL, *Greek Marbles.* London, Cambridge University Press, 1809.

————, *The Tomb of Alexander.* London, R. Watts, 1805.

————, *Travels in Various Countries of Europe, Asia and Africa.* London, T. Cadell and W. Davies, 1823.

COCKERELL, C. R., *Travels in Southern Europe and the Levant, 1810–1817.* London, Longsman, Green, and Co., 1903.

CREASY, SIR E. S., *History of the Ottoman Turks.* London, Colonial Press, 1878.

CUST, LIONEL, and COLVIN, SIDNEY, *History of the Society of Dilettanti.* London, Macmillan and Co., 1898.

Description of the Collection of Ancient Marbles in the British Museum. London, 1812–1861.

DODWELL, EDWARD, *A Classical and Topographical Tour Through Greece.* London. Rodwell and Martin, 1819.

DOUGLAS, HON. F. S. N., *An Essay on Certain Points of Resemblance Between the Ancient and Modern Greeks.* London, John Murray (Publishers), Ltd., 1813.

ELGIN, LORD, *Memorandum on the Subject of the Earl of Elgin's Pursuits in Greece.* Edinburgh, 1811.

————, Letter to the editor of the Edinburgh *Review* on the subject of an article in No. L of that journal on "the remains of John Tweddell." Edinburgh, 1815.

————, Postscript to a letter to the editor of the Edinburgh *Review*.

Edinburgh, 1815.

FELLOWS, C., *Excursion in Asia Minor.* London, John Murray (Publishers), Ltd. 1839.

FURTWÄNGLER, A., *Masterpieces of Greek Sculpture,* London, W. Heinemann, 1895.

GALT, JOHN, *Autobiography.* Carey, Lea, Blanchard, 1833.

_____, *Letters From the Levant.* London T. Cadell and W. Davis, 1813.

_____, *Life and Studies of Benjamin West, Esq.,* London, 1816.

_____, *Life of Byron.* London, H. Colburn, R. Bentley, 1830.

GARDNER, E. A., *Ancient Athens.* London, Macmillan and Co., 1902.

_____, *Handbook of Greek Sculpture.* London, Macmillan and Co., 1915.

_____, *Six Greek Sculptors. London, Duchworth & Co., 1915.*

GELDART, WILLIAM H., *Elements of English Law.* London, Williams and Norgate, 1911.

GILLIES, JOHN, *History of Greece.* (dedicated to King George III) London, A. Strahan. 1786.

HAYDON, BENJAMIN ROBERT, *Autobiography and Memoirs.* London, Oxford University Press, 1926.

_____, *Correspondence and Table Talk.* London, Chatto and Windus 1876.

_____, *The Diary of Benjamin Robert Haydon.* Cambridge, Harvard University Press, 1960.

HERTSLET, SIR E., *Treaties Regulating the Trade Etc. Between Great Britain and Turkey.* London, Butterworth, 1875.

HISTORICAL MANUSCRIPTS COMMISSION, *Report on the Mss of J. B. Fortescue Esq. Preserved at Dropmore.* London, 1892–1927.

HOBHOUSE, JOHN CAM, *A Journey Through Albania and Other Provinces of Turkey in Europe and Asia, to Constantinople.* Philadelphia, M. Carey and Son, 1817.

HOLDSWORTH, W. S., *History of English Law.* London, Methuen, 1909.

HUGHES, REV. T. S., *Travels in Sicily, Greece and Albania.* London, J. Mawman, 1802.

HUNT, REV. PHILIP, *A Narrative of What Is Known Respecting the Literary Remains of the Late John Tweddell.* London, 1816.

HUNTER, JOHN, *Treatise on Venereal Disease.* Royal Society of London, 1786.

KATSAINOS, GEORGE M., *Syphilis.* (in Greek) Athens, private printing, 1939.

Keith Papers, The letters and papers of Admiral Viscount Keith, Navy Records Society. London, 1927–1955.

KNIGHT, RICHARD PAYNE, *Specimens of Antient Sculpture,* London, Dilettanti Society, 1809 and 1835.

LARRABEE, S. A., English Bards and Grecian Marbles. London, 1943.

LEAKE, W. M., *Journal of a Tour in Asia Minor.* London, John Murray (Publishers), Ltd., 1824.

LECHEVALIER, J. F., *Voyage de la Troade.* Paris, Dentu, 1802.

LEGRAND, PH.-E., *Biographie de Louis-Francois-Sébastien Fauvel,* in Revue Archéologique, Third Series XXX, Paris, 1897.

LEWIS, MICHAEL, *Napoleon and his British Captives.* London, Allen and Unwin 1962.

MAITLAND, F. W. and Pollock, Sir F., *History of English Law.* London, Cambridge University Press, 1898.

MAUROIS, ANDRÉ, *Byron.* New York, D. Appleton, 1929.

MENZIES, SUTHERLAND, *Turkey, Old and New.* London, W. H. Allen & Co., 1880.

MICHAELIS, A., *Ancient Marbles in Great Britain.* London, Cambridge University Press, 1882.

————, *Der Parthenon.* Leipzig, Breitkopf and Härtel, Leipzig.

MOORE, T., *Letters and Journals of Lord Byron with Notices of his Life.* London, Private Printing, 1830.

MORRITT OF ROKEBY, J. B. S., *Letters Descriptive of a Journey in Europe and Asia Minor in the Years 1794–1796.* London, John Murray (Publishers) Ltd., 1914.

MURRAY, A. S., *Sculptures of the Parthenon.* New York, E. P. Dutton, 1903.

NICOLSON, SIR HAROLD, *Byron, The Last Journey.* London, Constable, 1940.

OTTER, W., *The Life and Remains of the Rev. Edward Daniel Clarke.* London, G. Cowie, 1825.

PATON, A. A., *History of the Egyptian Revolution.* 2nd edition. London, Trubner, 1863.

PHILLIPS, O. HOOD, *The Principles of English Law.* London, Sweet and Maxwell, 1939.

PHILLIPS, W. ALISON, *The War of Greek Independence.* London, Smith, Elder, 1897.

PULLAN, R. P., *Principle Ruins of Asia Minor.* London, C. Texier and R. P. Pullan, 1865.

RUSSELL, JACK, *Nelson and the Hamiltons*. London, Blond, 1969.

SCHLIEMANN, H., *Troy*. London, John Murray (Publishers), Ltd., 1875.

Select Committee Report of the House of Commons on the Earl of Elgin's Collection of Sculptured Marbles. London, House of Commons, 1816.

SICILIANOS, D., *Old and New Athens*. Athens, private printing (in Greek), 1937.

SMITH, ARTHUR HAMILTON, *The Sculptures of the Parthenon*. London, British Museum, 1910.

————, *Catalogue of Sculpture in the Department of Greek and Roman Antiquities*. London, British Museum, 1892.

Specimens of Antient Sculpture. London, Dilettanti Society, 1809 and 1835.

STEVENS, G. P., *The Erechtheum*, Cambridge, Harvard University Press, 1927.

TODD, H.J., *Catalogue of the Archepiscopal Manuscripts in the Library at Lambeth Place*, London, Law and Gilbert, 1812.

An Account of the Greek Mss Chiefly Biblical which had been in the possession of the Late Professor Carlyle, the Greater part of which are now deposited in the Archepiscopal Library at Lambeth Palace, London, Law and Gilbert, 1820.

TWEDDELL, REV. ROBERT, *Remains of John Tweddell late fellow of Trinity College Cambridge, being a selection of his correspondence, a republication of his Prolusiones Juveniles, an appendix containing some account of the author's collections, Mss. Drawings etc., and of their extraordinary disappearance, preceded by a biographical memoir of the deceased, and illustrated with portraits, picturesque views and maps*, London, J. Mawman, 1816.

WALDSTEIN, C., *Essays on the Art of Pheidias*, London, Cambridge University Press, 1885.

WALPOLE, REV. ROBERT, *Memoirs Relating to European and Asiatic Turkey*, Londan, Longman, Hurst, Rees, Orme and Brown, 1817.

WALSH, REV. ROBERT, *A Residence at Constantinople*, London, F. Westley and A. H. Davies, 1836.

WILLIAMS, H. W., *Travels in Italy, Greece and the Ionian Islands*, Edinburgh, private printing, 1820.

WITTMAN, WILLIAM, *Travels in Turkey, Asia Minor and Syria*, London, R. Phillips, 1803.

Notes

"*Had not these lovely things . . .*", Sir Harold Nicolson, "The Byron Curse Echoes Again," As quoted in *The New York Times Magazine*, March 27, 1949, p. 12.

Prologue

"This year the Elgin Marbles were bought . . .", *The Diary of Benjamin Robert Haydon*, entry of 31 December 1816.

"Lord Elgin's robberies", A letter from Lord Byron to John Cam Hobhouse, 31 July 1811, as quoted in *Lord Byron's Correspondence*, I, p. 43.

"to consider returning the Elgin Marbles . . .", Hansard, (Commons) 9 May 1961.

"Mr. Macmillan is advised . . .", *The Times*, London, 10 May 1961.

"Elgin's aims . . .", William St. Clair, *Lord Elgin and the Marbles*, London, p. 274.

Chapter One: SICILY

"A fortnight in Lisbon. . .", *The Letters of Mary Nisbet*, p. 7.

"fair favourite, Madame Ferchenbeck. . .", Lord Grenville Leveson Gower, *Private Correspondence* (1781/1821) I, p. 262.

"impossible to get on shore. . .", *Letters of Mary Nisbet*, p. 20.

"My Lord and Lady. . .", A letter from Rev. Philip Hunt to his father, 17 July 1799. Hunt Papers.

"beleaguered everyone. . .", Rev. Robert Walpole, *Memoirs Relating to European and Asiatic Turkey*, pp. 82 ff. (Section XV).

"As the Turks have now made. . .", A letter from Hunt to his father, 2 April 1799. Hunt Papers.

"a great indifference. . .", A letter from Hunt to his sister, 22 September 1799. Hunt Papers.

"stood by and allowed. . .", *Ibid.*

"He has much good sense. . .", A letter from Colonel Anstruther to Lord Elgin, 19 March 1799. Elgin Papers.

"An esteemed medical authority. . .", *The Letters of Mary Nisbet,* p. 7.

"His Majesty's Government. . .", *Historical Manuscripts Commission, Report on the Mss. of J. B. Fortesque, Esq.,* V, p. 91.

"the young artist. . .", *The Farington Diary,* London, 22 April 1799.

"Seventy-six foot long. . .", *The Letters of Mary Nisbet,* p. 30.

"I was met at the door. . .", *Ibid.,* p. 20.

"While serving as Ambassador. . .", A. Michaelis, *Ancient Marbles in Great Britain,* (1882) p. 109.

"Now that is a fine woman. . .", *The Letters of Mary Nisbet,* p. 22.

"Nelson seemed. . .", *Ibid.,* p. 22.

"not only was he to keep. . .", Foreign Office Papers, London, 78/22.

"Europe is a molehill. . .", J. Christopher Herold, *The Age of Napoleon,* p. 68.

"The sea was choppy. . .", *Ibid.,* p. 69.

"The Battle of the Pyramids. . .", *Ibid.,* p. 73.

"Josiah Wedgwood. . .", A. Michaelis, *Ancient Marbles in Great Britain,* p. 111.

"I never saw. . .", *The Letters of Mary Nisbet,* p. 23.

"Many people were laying bets. . .", *Ibid.,* p. 25.

"The first painter. . .", A. H. Smith, *Lord Elgin and his Collection,* p. 169.

"They are upon. . .", H. W. Williams, *Travels in Italy and Greece,* 1820, Vol. II, p. 331.

"Her Majesty had spent. . .", *The Letters of Mary Nisbet,* p. 25.

"he accepted an invitation. . .", John Barrow, *Life and Correspondence of Admiral Sir William Sydney Smith,* 1848, Vol. I, p. 378.

"actually Greeted!. . .", *The Letters of Mary Nisbet,* p. 25.

"Lusieri was to supervise. . .", A. H. Smith, *Lord Elgin and His Collection,* p. 168.

"It is agreed. . .", *Ibid.,* p. 168.

"1. A man for casts. . .", *Ibid.,* p. 171.

"A Carro of Virtuosi. . .", *The Letters of Mary Nisbet,* p. 75.

"My dear Lord. . .", A letter from Hamilton to Lord Elgin, 4 February 1800, Elgin Papers.

"on an exploration. . .", *The Letters of Mary Nisbet,* p. 29.

"Provisions were also made. . .", A letter from Sir John Spencer Smith to Lord Grenville, 30 October 1799, Foreign Office Papers, 78/22.

"When Sir Sydney Smith. . .", John Barrow, *Life and Correspondence of Admiral Sir William Sydney Smith,* Vol. I, p. 381.

"Along the way. . .", *The Letters of Mary Nisbet,* p. 39.

"They were first discovered. . .", A. H. Smith, *Lord Elgin and His Collection,* p. 182.

"Permission was granted. . .", William Wittman, *Travels in Turkey, Asia Minor, and Syria,* p. 65.

Chapter Two: TURKEY

"As soon as they arrived. . .", A letter from Hunt to his sister, 22 September 1799, Hunt Papers.

"a good honest English bed. . .", *The Letters of Mary Nisbet,* p. 56.

"the dwellings of the Turks. . .", *Ibid.,* p. 44.

"My dear Lord. . .", A letter from Hamilton to Lord Elgin, 1 March 1800, Elgin Papers.

"General Officer Commanding. . .", *Historical Manuscripts Commission, Report on the Mss. of J. B. Fortesque, Esq.,* VI, p. 89.

"I have infinite satisfaction. . .", A letter from Lord Elgin to Lord Grenville, 16 February 1800, Foreign Office Papers, 78/28.

"Elgin then wrote to Nelson. . .", A letter from Lord Elgin to Lord Nelson, 18 February 1800, *Ibid.*

"In the eyes of Turkey. . .", A letter from Lord Elgin to Lord Grenville, 10 March 1800, *Ibid.*

"The British Government. . .", A letter from Lord Grenville to Lord Elgin, 28 March 1800, *Ibid.,* 78/29.

"Sir John Spencer. . .", A letter from Lord Grenville to Lord Elgin, 7 April 1800, *Ibid.*

"a very pleasant. . .", *The Letters of Mary Nisbet,* p. 147.

"he had hoped. . .", A letter from Hamilton to Lord Elgin, 9 May 1800, Elgin Papers.

"Seven leeches. . .", *The Letters of Mary Nisbet,* p. 59.

"Noseless himself. . .", *The Sloane Notebooks,* 13 August 1816, Sir John Sloane Museum, London.

"Bouyouk Deré. . .", A letter from Lady Elgin to her mother, 16 August 1801:

Preparations for a Tour, Hunt Papers.

"The library here. . .", Rev. Robert Walpole, *Memoirs Relating to European and Asiatic Turkey,* (1817) p. 162.

"Nicaea hail!. . .", J. D. Carlyle, *Poems,* (1805) p. 13.

"Bonaparte is not idle. . . ", *Ibid.,* pp. 14 ff.

"Indeed, the Turks. . .", *The Letters of Mary Nisbet,* p. 119.

"All British warships. . .", Foreign Office Papers, London, 78/33.

"she was carried. . .", *Ibid.*

"Wasting no time. . . ", *Ibid.*

"His Majesty is well pleased. . .", *Ibid.*

"*Memorial to the King.* . .", Navy Records Society, London, II, p. 406, The Keith Papers, 1927-1955.

"thus he remained. . .", A letter from Lord Elgin to Lusieri, 10 July 1801.

"My dear Lord. . . ", A letter from Lusieri to Lord Elgin, 20 September 1801, Elgin Papers.

"of visiting all the Pashas. . .", Hunt Papers.

"only seemed to want breath. . .", A. H. Smith, *Lord Elgin and His Collection*, p. 205.

"Congratulate me. . .", A letter from Lacy to Rev. Philip Hunt, 8 October 1801, Hunt Papers.

"made every effort. . .", A. H. Smith, *Lord Elgin and His Collection*, p. 230.

"Under the penalty of death. . .", *Ibid.*, p. 190.

"Travelling through this country. . .", *The Letters of Mary Nisbet*, p. 141.

"Hunt is in raptures. . .", *Ibid.*, p. 97.

Chapter Three: GREECE

"At the northernmost. . .", *The Letters of Mary Nisbet*, pp. 106 ff.

"and spy upon their women. . .", William St. Clair, *Lord Elgin and The Marbles*, p. 60.

"giving everything to Lusieri. . .", *Revue Archéologique*, 3rd Series, XXX and XXXI, 1897.

"I should wish to have. . .", A. H. Smith, *Lord Elgin and His Collection*, p. 207.

"to put about a rumor. . .", A letter from Lady Elgin to Lord Elgin, 19 May 1802, Elgin Papers.

"It was an easy task. . .", A. H. Smith, *Lord Elgin and his Collection*, p. 172.

"I must relate. . .", *Ibid.*, p. 172-173.

"his presence in Athens. . .", A. H. Smith, *Lord Elgin and his Collection*, pp. 191 ff.

"All the public buildings. . .", Plutarch, *The Lives of Noble Grecians and Romans*.

"to measure each temple. . .", *Report of the Select Committee*, p. 40.

"many such Venetian fortifications. . ." Patrick Leigh Fermor, Mani, *Travels in the Southern Peloponnese*, New York, Harper and Row, 1958, p. 27.

"a mingling of ancient Greek rite. . ." *Ibid.*, p. 214.

"Some workmen, employed. . .", Edward Daniel Clarke, *Travels in Various Countries of Europe, Asia and Africa*, 1811-1823 Section II, Part 2, p. 483.

"During my first tour to Greece. . .", Edward Dodwell, *A Classical and Topographical Tour Through Greece*, (1819) London, Section I, p. 322.

"judicious mixture of threats and bribes. . .", William St. Clair, *Lord Elgin and the Marbles*, p. 94.

"a coarsely-carved piece. . .", *Ibid.*, p. 104.

"this was the site. . .", R. Chandler, *Travels in Greece*, 1776, p. 191.

"the arm of any person. . .", Edward Daniel Clarke, *Greek Marbles*, p. 32.
"I found the goddess. . .", W. Otter, *The Life and Remains of Edward Daniel Clarke*, p. 505.
"I began by saying. . .", A letter from Lady Elgin to her husband, 24 May 1802, quoted in A. H. Smith, *Lord Elgin and His Collection*, p. 209.
"In hopes that I shall be. . .", A letter from Lady Elgin to her husband, 25 May 1802, quoted in A. H. Smith, *Lord Elgin and his Collection*, p. 218.
"If a large Man of War. . .", *Ibid.*, p. 196.
I have been at a monstrous expense. . ." Navy Records Society, The Keith Papers, II, p. 405.
"Having received the most pressing. . .", *The Letters of Mary Nisbet*, p. 184.
"melancholy abode. . .", *Ibid.*, p. 207.
"of nymphs and Bacchanalians. . .", A. H. Smith, *Lord Elgin and His Collection*, p. 176.
"After calling at Smyrna. . .", Foreign Office Papers, London, 78/36.

Chapter Four: CONSTANTINOPLE

"My very dear Mother. . .", A letter from Lady Elgin to her mother, 30 November 1802.
"that Elgin might be able. . .", A letter from Lusieri to Lord Elgin, 16 September 1802. Also quoted in A. H. Smith, *Lord Elgin and His Collection*, p. 232.
"The largest pieces. . .", A. H. Smith, *Lord Elgin and His Collection*, p. 233.
"The *Mentor* sailed. . .", *Ibid.*, p. 237.
"Huge holes had to be cut. . .", *Ibid.*, 238.
"He daily boasted. . .", A letter from Philip Hunt to his father, 31 July 1801, Hunt Papers.
"The plague still continues. . .", *The Letters of Mary Nisbet*, p. 217.
"For hundreds of years. . .", Rev. Robert Walpole, *Memoirs Relating to European and Asiatic Turkey*, p. 98.
"to dispel the rumor. . .", *The Letters of Mary Nisbet*, p. 228.
"For centuries the Knights of St. John. . .", William St. Clair, *Lord Elgin and the Marbles*, p. 85.
"The joy these slaves showed. . .", Foreign Office Papers, London, 78/33.
"If I had still three years. . .", A. H. Smith, *Lord Elgin and His Collection*, p. 234.
"danced out of their beds. . .", *The Letters of Mary Nisbet*, p. 176.

Chapter Five: ATHENS

"but as the *Braakel*. . .", A. H. Smith, *Lord Elgin and his Collection*, p. 240.
"to watch the spectacle. . .", William St. Clair, *Lord Elgin and the Marbles*. p. 119.

"How was the weather?. . .", A. H. Smith, *Lord Elgin and his Collection,* p. 239. (Also William Falconer, *The Shipwreck,* which contains Captain Clarke's personal account of the incident. London, (1811) p. 207.

"I am sure if you saw Athens. . .", A letter to Philip Hunt from Ioannes Benizelos, Hunt Papers.

"Ioannes Benizelos who was the master. . .", Ioannes Gennadios, (in Greek) *Lord Elgin and the Previous Archeological Invasions of Greece, Especially Athens:* 1440-1837, p. 2.

"I have said nothing. . .", John Cam Hobhouse, *A Journey Through Albania and Other Provinces of Turkey in Europe and Asia to Constantinople,* London, (1813) p. 347.

"In fact they had nothing. . .", Hon. F. S. N. Douglas, *An Essay On Certain Points of Resemblance Between the Ancient and Modern Greeks,* I, p. 85.

"As he observed to us. . .", Rev. T. S. Hughes, *Travels In Sicily, Greece and Albania,* London, (1820) p. 266, Section I.

"The last time I visited. . .", Peter Edmund Laurent, *Recollections of a Classical Tour,* London, (1821) p. 110. The destruction of the Caryatids at the Erechtheum is also mentioned by H. W. Williams, *Travels In Italy, Greece and the Ionian Islands,* London, (1820) p. 316.

"When Elgin's agents. . .", H. W. Williams (*op. cit.,* Sect. II, p. 307).

"even as far as the cold shores of England. . .", John Cam Hobhouse, *A Journey Through Albania and Other Privinces of Turkey in Europe and Asia to Constantinople,* p. 347.

"Please be advised. . .", A letter to Lord Elgin from his mother, Elgin Papers.

"Count Sébastiani had been sent to the Levant. . .", William St. Clair, *Lord Elgin and the Marbles,* p. 121.

"There is a smart French Beau. . .", *The Letters of Mary Nisbet,* p. 234.

"that only six thousand men would be needed. . .", An excerpt from the French newspaper, *Moniteur,* No. 130.

"the ancient sites near Palatine Hill. . .", Edward Gibbon, *The Decline and Fall of the Roman Empire,* Viking Press, New York, 1952, p. 686.

"A highland lad my love was born. . .", Robert Burns, an air from, *The Jolly Beggars.*

"the vestibule of the Pitti Palace. . .", H. W. Janson, *History of Art,* Prentice-Hall, Abrams, New York, 1962, p. 385.

"The galleria of Uffizi. . .", *Ibid.,* p. 384.

Chapter Six: PARIS

"All the English enrolled in the Militia. . .", A. H. Smith, *Lord Elgin and his Collection,* p. 347.

"We intended remaining. . .", *The Letters of Mary Nisbet,* p. 286.

"The Treaty of Amiens. . .", J. Christopher Herold, *Bonaparte in Egypt*, p. 133.

"From the first days of the Revolution. . .", Charles Maurice de Périgord-Talleyrand, *Mémoires*, Paris, 1891, Vol. I, pp. 33 ff.

"in the circles of philosophers. . .", Lady Blennerhasset, *Talleyrand*, Berlin, 1894, pp. 117 ff.

"As a sub-deacon Talleyrand witnessed. . .", Joseph McCabe, *Talleyrand, A Biographical Study*, London, 1906, p. 234.

"surely there would be at least one good whist player. . .", *The Letters of Mary Nisbet*, p. 239.

"that in every relationship between a man and woman. . .", Colonel Crawford was quoting a well-known remark of Lord Byron.

"And how is your father?. . .", *The Letters of Mary Nisbet*, p. 241.

"Talleyrand's reply to Elgin's letter. . .", *Ibid.*, 286.

"and wrote a lengthy dispatch to Lusieri. . .", A. H. Smith, *Lord Elgin and his Collection*, p. 360.

"But despite his repeated assurances. . .", *The Letters of Mary Nisbet*, p. 248.

"Furthermore a decree was about to be issued. . .", Michael Lewis, *Napoleon and his British Captives*, London, 1962, p. 183.

Through Sébastiani's persuasion, William St. Clair, *Lord Elgin and the Marbles*, p. 124.

"a summer resort high in the Pyrenees. . .", *Correspondance de Napoléon Premier Publiée par Ordre de l'Empéreur Napoléon III*, 8, p. 387.

Chapter Seven: BARÈGES

"Barèges is the most dreary place. . .", *The Letters of Mary Nisbet*, p. 263.

"were spent at dinner parties. . .", William St. Clair, *Lord Elgin and the Marbles*, p. 125.

"Le Comte de Choiseul-Gouffier. . .", A. H. Smith, *Lord Elgin and his Collection*, p. 360.

"but the loss of one piece particularly distressed him. . .", *Revue Archéologique, XXIV*, p. 92.

"on board the French frigate *l'Arabe*. . .", Edward Smith, *Life of Sir Joseph Banks*, London, 1911, p. 209.

"with the exception of the Parthenon frieze. . .", *Bulletin de la Société Nationale Des Antiquaires de la France, Sér. 6*, (1900) p. 245.

"still being held at the London Customs House. . .", *The Farington Diary*, London, (1922) 5 December 1806.

"he had delivered the children. . .", *The Letters of Mary Nisbet*, p. 242.

"Ah, c'est Milord Elgin. . .", *Ibid.*, p. 278.

"a French diplomat named Beauchamp. . .", *Moniteur*, No. 131.

"Elgin is to be confined. . .", *The Letters of Mary Nisbet*, p. 290.

"I am to go to Lourdes. . .", A letter from Lord Elgin to his wife, Elgin Papers.

"in retaliation. . .", *Correspondance de Napoléon Premier Publiée par Ordre de l'Empereur Napoléon III*, 8, p. 315.

"crowned by Chartres' ancient cathedral. . .", A. Plerval, *Chartres, Sa Cathédral, Ses Monuments*, Paris, 1896, p. 87.

"His rooms were inside the old Palace of Luxembourg. . .", G. Michaud, *Talleyrand, Histoire Politique et Vie Intime*, Paris, (1843) Vol. II, pp. 77 ff.

"by protesting her helplessness. . .", William St. Clair, *Lord Elgin and the Marbles*, p. 129.

"I have this moment dined. . .", A letter from Lady Elgin to Lord Elgin, 18 November 1803, Elgin Papers.

"I am in sad distress today. . .", *The Letters of Mary Nisbet*, p. 247.

"sent out streams of letters. . .", William St. Clair, *Lord Elgin and the Marbles*, p. 129.

"stir up political support. . .", Foreign Office Papers, London, 27/68.

Chapter Eight: PAU

"During his confinement at Lourdes. . .", *Correspondance de Napoléon Premier Publiée Par Ordre de l'Empereur Napoléon III* 8, p. 315.

"that he was to be sent. . .", *Ibid.*

"On the day of his arrest. . .", A letter from Lord Elgin to Sir Spencer Perceval, 6 May 1811, British Museum Additional Mss. 38246 f 119.

"J'aurais volontiers donné. . .", *The Letters of Mary Nisbet*, p. 296.

"which was the means. . .", *Report From the Select Committee of the House of Commons on the Earl of Elgin's Collection of Sculptured Marbles*, p. vii.

"Nor was there a bed. . .", *Ibid.*, p. 43.

"I was not removed to Prison. . .", *Memorandum on the Subject of the Earl of Elgin's Pursuits in Greece*, p. 93, 1815 edition.

"In point of fact. . .", *Ibid.*, p. 94.

"a fellow Prisoner. . .", *Ibid.*, pp. 95 ff.

"Throughout most of Lord Elgin's confinement. . .", *Report from the Select Committee of the House of Commons on the Earl of Elgin's Collection of Sculptured Marbles*, pp. 43 ff.

"no sooner was the messenger dismissed. . .", From the memorandum of Lord Elgin's imprisonment at Lourdes, signed by himself and found among Lady Elgin's papers.

"on the condition that Elgin cede his entire collection. . .", From a letter of Lord Elgin to Sir Spencer Perceval, 6 May 1811, (British Museum Additional Mss. 38246 f 119.)

"The situation (in Pau) is most delightful. . .", *The Letters of Mary Nisbet*, p. 321.

"Downing Street. . .", A letter from Lord Hawkesbury to Lady Elgin, 23 December 1803, found among Lady Elgin's papers.
"If, in the month of dark December. . .", Lord Byron, *Written after Swimming from Sestos to Abydos.*
"I am so changeable. . .", A letter from Lord Byron to Lady Blessington.
"Hymettus looming before it. . .", André Maurois, *Byron,* p. 139.
"a contest between East and West. . .", *Ibid.,* p. 140.
"Hail, Byzantium!. . .", *Ibid.,* pp. 140 ff.
"And when we left Falmouth. . .", *Lord Byron's Correspondence Chiefly with Lady Melbourne, Mr. Hobhouse, the Hon. Douglas Kinnaird, and P. B. Shelley,* London, 1922.
"Comfort must not be expected. . .", André Maurois, *Byron,* p. 125.
"Adieu, you pretty fellow. . .", *Ibid.,* p. 126.
"We then boarded the Malta packet. . .", *Lord Byron's Correspondence Chiefly with Lady Melbourne, Mr. Hobhouse, the Hon. Douglas Kinnaird, and P. B. Shelley,* London, 1922.
"also in platonic love. . .", André Maurois, *Byron,* p. 128.
"Maid of Athens. . .", Lord Byron, *Maid of Athens, Ere We Part.*
"In one fleeting moment. . .", A letter from Lord Byron to John Cam Hobhouse, 31 July 1811.
"At the front entrance. . .", André Maurois, *Byron,* p. 119.
"I lived, I loved. . .", Lord Byron, *I Lived, I Loved, I Quaff'd Like Thee.*
"If you could but look. . .", André Maurois, *Byron,* p. 143.
"What right had he. . .", William St. Clair, *Lord Elgin and the Marbles,* p. 189.
"But who of all the plunderers. . .", Lord Byron, from the Second Canto of *Childe Harold's Pilgrimage.*
"*Lord Elgin has been teazing. . .*", A letter from Lord Byron to John Cam Hobhouse, 31 July 1811. *Lord Byron's Correspondence,* Section I, p. 43.
"I do not consider him", (Byron) A. H. Smith, *Lord Elgin and His Collection,* p. 313.
"want of taste and utter barbarism. . .", Edward Daniel Clarke, *Travels in Various Countries of Europe, Asia and Africa,* Part II, Section 2, p. 484.
"It appears to me a very flagrant piece. . .", F. S. N. Douglas, *An Essay On Certain Points of Resemblance Between the Ancient and Modern Greeks,* p. 89.
"insensate barbarism and devastating outrage. . .", Edward Dodwell, *A Classical and Topographical Tour Through Greece,* Section I, p. 324.
"wanton devastation and avidity for plunder. . .", Rev. T. S. Hughes, *Travels in Sicily, Greece and Albania,* Section I, p. 261.
"without even having been to Athens. . .", J. C. Eustace, *A Classical Tour Through Italy,* London, 1813, Section II, p. 20.
"even though he too had a piece of the Parthenon. . .", Chateaubriand, *Travels to Jerusalem,* London, 1835, Section I, p. 187.

"and even the ugly disfigurement of his nose. . .", Sir John Soane, *Notebooks,* 13 August 1816; also Ioannes Gennadios, (in Greek) *Lord Elgin and the Previous Archeological Invasions of Greece, Especially Athens,* p. 77.

"Noseless Himself. . .", in *Medwin's Conversations of Lord Byron,* edited by Ernest J. Lovell Jr. London, 1966, p. 211.

"whether his poem which he speaks of. . .", Ms. Journal of Edward Everett, in the Library of the Massachusetts Historical Society.

"A pirated copy found its way. . .", *New Monthly Magazine,* April 1815, "The Malediction of Minerva."

"Mortal!", "twas thus he spoke. . .", Lord Byron, *The Curse of Minerva.*

"Yet still the gods are just. . .", *Ibid.*

"Her tyrant empire will be shaken. . .", *Ibid.*

"First on the head of him. . .", *Ibid.*

"The Scottish novelist John Galt. . .", John Galt, *Letters from the Levant,* London, 1813, 1 March 1810.

"Galt was also an eye-witness. . .", Edward Daniel Clarke, *Travels in Various Countries of Europe, Asia and Africa,* Part II, Section 2, p. 484.

"Two circumstances occasioned. . .", John Galt, *The Life and Studies of Benjamin West, Esquire,* London, 1816, Section II, p. 75.

"Covering up all my past woes. . .", Foreign Office Papers, London 78/68.

"John Galt took passage. . .", A. H. Smith, *Lord Elgin and His Collection,* p. 280.

"Galt anticipated that Lord Elgin's bankers. . .", John Galt, *Autobiography,* Section I, p. 159.

"Here was a chance. . .", *Ibid.,* pp. 159 ff.

"an amateurish piece. . .", William St. Clair, *Lord Elgin and the Marbles,* p. 198.

"the bold youth that fired. . .", John Galt, *Atheniad,* The Monthly Magazine, 1820, Vol. 49.

"certain standards of excellence. . .", Richard Payne Knight, *An Analytic Inquiry Into the Principles of Taste,* London, 1805, p. 4.

"I have found in this collection. . .", West's remarks were published as an Appendix to the *Memorandum on the Subject of the Earl of Elgin's Pursuits in Greece.*

"the highest quality of Art. . .", *The Farington Diary,* entry for 27 February 1808.

"All of them now admitted. . .", *Ibid.,* entry for 30 March 1808.

"as was Nollekens. . .", *Ibid.,* entry for 8 June 1807.

"to pay my homage to your Lordship's exertions. . .", A letter from J. M. W. Turner to Lord Elgin, 7 August 1806, Elgin Papers.

"To Park Lane then we went. . .", B. R. Haydon, *Autobiography and Memoirs,* London, (1926) edited by Aldous Huxley, p. 66.

"spent every spare moment of his life. . .", William St. Clair, *Lord Elgin and the Marbles*, p. 171.

"Then often have I gone home. . .", B. R. Haydon, *Autobiography and Memoirs*, p. 69.

"8 September. . .", *The Diary of Benjamin Robert Haydon*, London, (1960) edited by W. B. Pope.

"Drew at Lord Elgin's. . .", *Ibid.*, entry for 5 November 1808.

"of meeting once a month. . .", William St. Clair, *Lord Elgin and the Marbles*, p. 176.

"Of Phidias' general style. . .", *Specimens of Antient Sculpture*, by Richard Payne Knight, London, 1809, Vol. I, p. xxxix.

"which all this time. . .", A. H. Smith, *Lord Elgin and his Collection*, p. 295.

"William has cut his first tooth. . .", *The Letters of Mary Nisbet*, p. 324.

"Lyons truly amazed them. . .", S. Charlety, *Histoire de Lyon*, Paris, 1903, pp. 24 ff.

Pray for me, dearest mother. . .", *The Letters of Mary Nisbet*, p. 351.

"Robert Fergusson would also be sailing. . .", Michael Lewis, *Napoleon and His British Captives*, p. 183.

"Elgin's family vault at Dunfermline. . .", E. d'Hauterive, *La Police Secrète Du Premier Empire, Bulletins Quotidiens, Adresseés par Fouché à l'Empereur*, Vol. I, p. 387.

"When I was a prisoner in Paris. . .", *Report from the Select Committee of the House of Commons on the Earl of Elgin's Collection of Sculptured Marbles*, p. 43.

"to transfer his services. . .", Rev. Philip Hunt, *A Narrative of What Is Known Respecting the Literary Remains of the Late John Tweddell*, London, 1816, p. 4. Also in the National Library of Scotland: 5645 F 210.

"A considerable number of English gentlemen. . .", *The Farington Diary*, entry for 20 June 1808.

"A month or so later. . .", *Ibid.*, entry for 29 July 1808.

"Throughout her stay in London. . .", *The Trial of R. Fergusson*, London, 1807, p. 6.

"I have suffered so much from this event. . .", *Ibid.*, pp. 5 ff.

"even after the last guest had left. . .", *Ibid.*, p. 7.

"A man-servant named Robert Draper. . .", *Ibid.*, p. 39.

"One of Bonaparte's confidential ministers. . .", *The Times*, London, 16 December 1805.

To the Fellows of the French Institute, National Library of Scotland, 1709 F 202.

"In addition to Archerfield. . .", *The Trial of R. Fergusson*, p. 41.

Chapter Nine: SCOTLAND

"My dear Lord. . .", A letter from Lusieri to Lord Elgin, 20 June 1804, Elgin Papers.

"It is to be lamented. . .", Lord Byron, *Childe Harold's Pilgrimage*, Canto II, Note 2.

"had yet to receive. . .", A letter from Lusieri to Lord Elgin, 20 June 1804, Elgin Papers.

"His Lordship's release. . .", British Museum, Additional Mss., 38266 F 5.

"I can boast of loving you. . .", A letter from Robert Fergusson to Lady Elgin, 10 December 1806, as quoted in *The Trial of R. Fergusson*, London, 1807, p. 10.

"You must prove and act. . .", *Ibid.*, p. 11.

"If ever love reigned. . .", *Ibid.*, pp. 11 ff.

"Elgin was very much agitated. . .", As quoted in the Commissary Court Record, Scottish Records Office, Edinburgh, 1808.

"Lord Elgin's operations in Athens. . .", *The Times*, London, 16 December 1805.

"Tweddell was determined to surpass. . .", The chief source on the Tweddell case is a quarto volume published in 1815 by Tweddell's brother, Robert Tweddell. Its full title was *Remains of John Tweddell Late Fellow of Trinity College Cambridge, being a Selection of his Correspondence, A Republication of his Prolusiones Juveniles, an Appendix Containing some Account of the Author's Collections, Mss., Drawings etc., and of their Extraordinary Disappearance, preceded by aBiographical Memoir of The Deceased, and Illustrated with Portraits, Picturesque Views and Maps*. The volume was priced at three guineas and 225 pages of its appendix were devoted entirely to vicious accusations against Lord Elgin.

"that he had copied some notes. . .", Rev. Philip Hunt, *A Narrative of What is Known Respecting the Literary Remains of the Late John Tweddell*, as quoted from an article in the *Christian Observer*, August 1815.

"That the literary property. . .", Edward Daniel Clarke, *Travels in Various Countries of Europe, Asia and Africa*, Part II, Section 2, p. 533.

"promise to return them to the Patriarch. . .", A letter from Philip Hunt to Robert Liston, 20 June 1817, Hunt Papers.

"These ancient manuscripts. . .", Rev. Robert Walpole, *Memoirs Relating to European and Asiatic Turkey*, pp. 163 ff.

"amounted to near a tenth part. . .", H. J. Todd, *An Account of the Greek Mss., Chiefly Biblical which had been in the Possession of the Late Professor Carlyle, the Greater Part of which are now in the Archepiscopal Library at Lambeth Palace*, c. 1820 p. V.

Hints and Observations, *Ibid.*, p. IV.

"As to the manuscripts. . .", *Ibid.*, p. 38.

"that the National character suffers. . .", National Library of Scotland, 5645 F 210.

"Neither Stuart's drawings. . .", *Memorandum on the Subject of the Earl of Elgin's Pursuits in Greece*, p. 78.

"In their new situation. . .", Quoted from, *Two Memoirs Read to the Royal*

Institute of France on the Sculptures in the Collection of the Earl of Elgin, by the Chevalier E. Q. Visconti, Select Committee Report, 1816.

"You have lost your labour, my Lord Elgin. . .", B. R. Haydon, *Autobiography and Memoirs,* p. 207.

"the Elgin Marbles are the finest things. . .", Select Committee Report, p. 67.

"The finest works of art. . .", *Ibid.,* p. 70.

"There is in them. . .", *Ibid.,* p. 90.

"stood patiently by. . .", B. R. Haydon, *Autobiography and Memoirs,* p. 232.

"In no other profession. . .", *Ibid.,* p. 233.

"It was widely published. . .", A. Michaelis, *Ancient Marbles in Great Britain,* p. 148.

"Are you acquainted with the Elgin Collection. . .", B. R. Haydon, *Autobiography and Memoirs,* p. 233; also quoted in the Select Committee Report, p. 92.

"The amount is far more. . .", Select Committee Report, p. XVII.

"I beg once more to repeat. . .", *Ibid.,* pp. XVII ff.

"Giovanni Battista Lusieri fell victim. . .", Rev. Robert Walsh, *A Residence at Constantinople,* London, 1836, Section I, p. 122.

"Benjamin Haydon was always in attendance. . .", *The Diary of Benjamin Robert Haydon, I,* p. 15.

"If we cannot give them bread. . .", As quoted in the *Edinburgh Review,* 1816.

On Seeing the Elgin Marbles, John Keats, *Poetical Works,* edited by H. W. Garrod, London, 1958.

To B. R. Haydon, Ibid.

"Although these are not Keats' best poems. . .", M. A. Goldberg, *John Keats and the Elgin Marbles,* in Apollo, November 1965; also S. A. Larrabee, *English Bards and Grecian Marbles,* London, 1943.

"For the young poet. . .", William St. Clair, *Lord Elgin and the Marbles,* p. 267.

"again and again. . .", William Sharp, *Life and Letters of Joseph Severn,* p. 32.

"I was not an uncommon sight. . .", *The Farington Diary,* entry for 10 April 1816.

"This same frieze. . .", J. T. Smith, *Nollekens and his Times,* I, p. 289.

"No one knows more intimately than you. . .", *Historical Notices of the Society of Dilettanti,* London, 1855, p. 101.

"We are those whom Christmas overthrew. . .", Thomas Hardy, *Winter Words,* "Christmas in the Elgin Room." London, Macmillan and Co. Ltd.

"a court order had been issued. . .", Commissary Court Record, Scottish Records Office, Edinburgh, 1808.

"Auld Reekie. . .", James Grant, *Old and New Edinburgh,* London, 1880.

"the General Register House. . .", Robert Miller, *The Municipal Buildings of Edinburgh,* printed by order of the town council of Edinburgh, 1895.

"O Willie was a witty wight. . .", Robert Burns, *Epistle to William Creech,* in the Thistle Library of *Burns' Poems,* Edinburgh, pp. 238 ff.

"When she entered the Advocates' Library. . .", Robert Miller, *The Municipal Buildings of Edinburgh.*

Chapter Ten: The Trial of R. J. Fergusson, Esquire, for Adultery with the Countess of Elgin, Wife of the Earl of Elgin.

The chief sources for this chapter:

A. *The Trial of R. Fergusson, Esq.,* London, 1807, published by T. Marshall and kept in the National Library of Scotland at Edinburgh.

B. A subsequent edition was put out in 1808, *The Trial of R. J. Fergusson, Esquire.* This was published by J. Day and is also kept in the National Library of Scotland.

C. The complete record of the divorce proceedings before the Commissary Court of Edinburgh, 11 March 1808, pp. 1243–1473, as preserved in the Scottish Records office in Edinburgh.

"Mr. Fergusson was also in Paris. . .", Michael Lewis, *Napoleon and His British Captives,* p. 183.

"that breach of diplomatic courtesy. . .", E. d'Hauterive, *La Police Secrète du Premier Empire, Bulletins Quotidiens Adressés par Fouché à l'Empereur,* II, p. 101.

"Adultery, as a ground for divorce. . .", William Blackstone, *Commentaries,* London, 1765.

"a fundamental rule of English jurisprudence. . .", F. W. Maitland, *History of English Law,* London, 1898.

"and as for the painter. . .", *The Letters of Mary Nisbet,* p. 76.

"I know", says he. . .", A letter from Robert Fergusson to Lady Elgin, 4 March 1808, Elgin Papers.

"Dearest Elgin. . .", A letter from Lady Elgin to Lord Elgin, 12 December 1803, Elgin Papers.

"I have wrote a few lines to you. . .", A letter from Robert Fergusson to Lord Elgin, 2 December 1803, Elgin Papers.

"At Number One Weymouth Street. . .", Commissary Court Records, Scottish Records Office, Edinburgh, p. 1622.

"O! Duff, I am quite miserable. . .", *Ibid.,* p. 1624.

"God forbid. . .", *Ibid.,* pp. 1624 ff.

"Knightsbridge. . .", Mrs. Gosling's deposition was written and signed on 14 July 1807.

"with a Verdict for the Plaintiff. . .", *The Trial of R. Fergusson, Esq.,* p. 33.

Chapter Eleven: TELOS

"especially in the voluptuous and fascinating capital. . .", *The Trial of R. Fergusson, Esq.,* p. 19.

"At Edinburgh, anent the action. . .", Commissary Court Record, Scottish Records Office, pp. 1273-1280.

"Her poor Ladyship. . .", *The Letters of Mary Nisbet,* p. 9.

"And more particularly. . .", Commissary Court Record, Scottish Records Office, p. 1275.

"a mark of Royal approbation. . .", British Museum, Additional Mss., 38246 F 119.

"I must candidly say. . .", *Ibid.,* 38191 F 197.

"easy in his circumstances. . .", *Historical Manuscripts Commission Report on the Mss. of J. B. Fortesque. Esq., II,* p. 184.

"for the British Expeditionary Forces in Egypt. . .", A. H. Smith, *Lord Elgin and his Collection,* p. 312.

"Of this amount. . .", *Ibid.,* pp. 312 ff.

"From the purchase price. . .", *Ibid.,* p. 332.

"It was while suffering. . .", A letter from Lord Elgin to Lord Liverpool, British Museum, Additional Mss. 38266 F 5.

"All the money I had drawn. . .", *Ibid.*

"First on the head of him. . .", Lord Byron, *The Curse of Minerva.*

"of bequeathing something to his children. . .". *National Library of Scotland,* 1055 F 118.

"In 1820 Elgin returned. . .", William St. Clair, *Lord Elgin and the Marbles,* p. 270.

"Lord Byron accomplished nothing at Missolonghi. . .", Sir Harold Nicolson, *Byron, The Last Journey, April 1823–April 1824,* Preface.

"he was obliged to spend. . .", William St. Clair, *Lord Elgin and the Marbles,* p. 270.

"Telos! . . .", Edward Daniel Clarke, *Travels in Various Countries of Europe, Asia and Africa,* Section II, Part 2, p. 483.

"What a desperate horrible idea. . .", A letter by Lady Elgin to Robert Fergusson, 18 December 1806, Commissary Court Record, Scottish Records Office, Edinburgh, p. 1634.

"to rest in a tomb. . .", *The Letters of Mary Nisbet, Countess of Elgin,* p. 352.

"the hideous stone. . .", *Ibid.*

Index

245